THE FIRST EPISTLE OF PETER

THE
FIRST EPISTLE
OF PETER

*The Greek Text
with Introduction and Notes*

Edited by

FRANCIS WRIGHT BEARE

B.A. (Toronto), Ph.D. (Chicago)

*Professor Emeritus of New Testament in Trinity College,
Toronto*

Third Edition, revised and enlarged

BASIL BLACKWELL · OXFORD
MCMLXX

ISBN 0 631 12080 7

Library of Congress Catalogue
Card No. 70-95551

Printed by offset in Great Britain
by Alden & Mowbray Ltd
at the Alden Press, Oxford

CONTENTS

38175

PREFACE

MORE than twenty years ago, when I was still an undergraduate, a copy of Hort's fragment on First Peter came into my hands and left with me an ineffaceable impression of the masterly workmanship of the scholar and of the power and attractiveness of the Epistle. It is most regrettable that the demands of the primary task of constituting the text of the New Testament made it impossible for Hort to complete his commentary, let alone to make a start upon the Synoptic Gospels, which were also assigned to him in the division of work among the great Cambridge trio. The little that has found publication marks him as one of the greatest of exegetes — penetrating, independent, and thorough. In my own treatment of this book, I have found his work of inestimable value for the portion which it covers, and have felt the lack of any equally sure guide from the point at which his commentary leaves off.

I have not found it possible, however, to follow him in accepting the authenticity of the Epistle. The English reader is here offered for the first time a commentary based upon the thesis, now widely accepted, that First Peter is a pseudonymous work of the post-Apostolic age. This view has been adopted by several of the best German commentators, notably by Gunkel, Knopf, and Windisch, all of whom I have found particularly helpful; and has been put forward in the majority of recent writings on Church History and New Testament Introduction; but it happens that all previous commentaries in English have maintained the traditional view that St. Peter himself was the author and that it was written before the death of Nero. The critical questions involved are discussed in the Introduction (Parts IV and VI); but the justification of the thesis must depend upon the commentary.

Though I have offered a Greek text of the Epistle, and have made it the basis of the commentary, I have had constantly in mind the needs of the reader who knows little or no Greek, especially the parish minister who has found himself unable to keep up the acquaintance with the language which he acquired during his College days. The almost universal neglect of Greek in the seminaries makes it necessary to provide theological students also with materials for study which do not take for granted a greater competence in the language than they actually possess. Almost every Greek phrase, therefore, is accompanied by a translation, so that those who know only a little Greek, and those who have forgotten much of what they once knew, will be able to follow the argument without being unduly hampered by the barrier of language; while at the same time the actual comment does not remain at the elementary level, but seeks to bring out all the riches of thought which the Epistle has to offer.

The greater part of this commentary was written at the Union Theological Seminary of New York, while I was in residence as Visiting Lecturer in the Department of New Testament during the session of 1944-1945. It was completed at the Divinity School of the University of Chicago in the summer of 1945. I beg to express my thanks to both institutions for the facilities placed at my disposal. My gratitude is especially due to Professor F. C. Grant, Professor John Knox, and Emeritus Professor E. F. Scott of Union Seminary, and to President E. C. Colwell and Professor A. N. Wilder of Chicago, all of whom read much of the work in manuscript and offered helpful suggestions. I am also indebted to Dr. R. M. Grant of the University of the South for some general criticisms and especially for drawing my attention to some monographs which had escaped my notice.

F. W. BEARE

Toronto, Canada
December 1945

FOREWORD TO THE THIRD EDITION

WHEN the second edition of this work appeared in 1958, no general revision of the first edition seemed necessary or even desirable. Occasion was taken to make corrections in the few places where they were needed; a few notes were added within the body of the commentary, where space could be found for them without disturbing the existing pagination; the account of the ancient versions was largely rewritten; and a supplement of twenty pages offered a bibliography of the more important publications which had appeared during the intervening twelve years, along with a review of the course of criticism in the period.

During the last ten years, there has not been anything like the flow of important critical articles which appeared between 1946 and 1957. By way of compensation, there have been some remarkable developments in the study of the text. The place of first importance belongs to the publication of a 3rd-century Greek papyrus of the epistle, by which the history of the text is carried back a hundred years beyond our earliest vellum uncial (Codex B). We have also been provided with remnants of two other codices on papyrus, which are unfortunately too meagre in content to contribute much to our study. Scarcely less in significance is the Beuron publication of the Old Latin, which has provided a wealth of evidence for this group of versions far more copious than was ever at the disposal of scholars before; and this has been accompanied by a most careful and thorough study of the Latin versions made by W. Thiele, the editor of the Beuron *Vetus Latina* of this epistle. We still await the publication of the Crosby codex of the Sahidic, which will give us our earliest and our only complete manuscript of the epistle in this important version.

Accordingly, the principal changes in this third edition lie in the realm of textual criticism. As it was not practicable to break down and reset the whole apparatus criticus, the new materials could only be handled by a comparatively full treatment in the Introduction, where the new evidence is assessed and made available to the student. I have also offered a collation of the great Athos uncial, Codex ψ, which has now become available in a microfilm prepared in collaboration with the Library of Congress for the International

Project to Establish a Critical Apparatus of the Greek New Testament. When I first wrote this book, I had none of the evidence of this codex available to me except for the half-dozen readings which were cited in the Nestle text (sixteenth edition; now, under the editorship of Kurt Aland, in its twenty-fifth edition). I have also had at my disposal a microfilm of Codex S (049), but as it offers a Byzantine text with only a sprinkling of superior readings, I have not troubled to discuss it in particular.

I have to thank Professor Aland for supplying me with accurate information on the Greek manuscripts, and can only express regret that I have not yet been able to accept his invitation to visit his Institut für neutestamentliche Textforschung in Münster and to make use of its matchless resources for my work on the text.

Grateful acknowledgment must also be made to His Holiness, Pope Paul VI, who graciously provided for me a copy of the facsimile edition of the Bodmer Papyrus VIII of I and II Peter (*Petri Epistolae ex Papyro Bodmeriana*), which is not available through the usual channels, in response to a request made on my behalf by His Grace the Archbishop of Canterbury.

Toronto, Canada   F. W. BEARE.
  February 1969

INTRODUCTION

I. THE TEXT

1. *Manuscript Authorities for the Greek Text*

THE Greek text of the Epistle is contained in three papyri (two of them meagre fragments), in sixteen uncials of the 4th to the 10th centuries, and in more than 550 minuscules of the 9th to the 16th centuries, besides a certain number of passages in lectionaries (more in the menologion than in the synaxarion).

(*a*) Papyri:

𝔓⁷², Papyrus Bodmeriana VIII, 3rd century (now in the Vatican Library, the gift of M. Bodmer).

𝔓⁷⁴, Papyrus Bodmeriana XVII, 6th or 7th century. Parts of 62 lines of writing distributed over 10 pages of a codex; no single verse is complete, and in many lines only two or three letters are preserved.

𝔓⁸¹, Fragmentum Barcinonense, 4th century. Contains elements of I Peter 2:20-3:12, on one incomplete leaf of a codex.

(*b*) Uncials:

א, (01), Codex Sinaiticus, 4th century.
A, (02), Codex Alexandrinus, 5th century.
B, (03), Codex Vaticanus, 4th century.
C, (04), Codex Ephraemi Syri Rescriptus, 5th century.
K, (018), Codex Mosquensis, 9th century.
L, (020), Codex Angelicus, 9th century.
P, (025), Codex Porphyrianus Rescriptus, 9th century.
S, (049), Codex Athous Laurensis A88, 8th or 9th century.
Ψ, (044), Codex Athous Laurensis B52, 8th or 9th century.
048, Codex Patirensis Rescriptus, 5th century.
056, Codex Coislin. Gr. 26 (B.N., Paris) 10th century.
093, Codex Cantabrigiensis Rescriptus (Taylor-Schechter 12), 6th century.
0142, Codex Gr. 375 (Bayer. Staatsbibliothek, Munich), 10th century.

0203, Codex Londonensis (B.M. Or. 3579B [59]), 6th century.

0206, Codex Daytonensis (P. Oxy. 1353), 4th century.

0247, Codex Mamuciensis Rescriptus, 6th century.

(c) Cursives:

Out of the mass of cursives, the following are of exceptional interest:

33, Codex Colbertinus, 11th century. The readings of this codex are most readily available in the apparatus of Tregelles. Formerly designated 13 in Acts and the Catholic epistles.

69, Codex Leicestrensis, 15th century. Collated by Scrivener in the appendix to his edition of Codex Augiensis; the more significant readings are also to be found in Tregelles. I have also had at my disposal a microfilm of the manuscript. Formerly designated 31 in Acts and the Catholic Epistles.

1739, Codex Athous Laurae 184 (now B64), 'written about the middle of the tenth century by a monk, Ephraim, from whose pen three other manuscripts survive' (G. Zuntz, *The Text of the Epistles* [London, 1953], p. 71). In the opinion of Zuntz, it was copied from a 4th century manuscript, which in the Pauline epistles at least offered a text closely akin to that used by Origen, and was made in all its parts by a scribe who 'was not a copyist, but a scholar commanding a refined critical method and animated by a truly philological interest' (*ibid.*, p. 73). Collated by M. S. Enslin in *Six Collations of New Testament Manuscripts*, edited by K. Lake and S. New (Cambridge: Harvard University Press, 1932). Now available on microfilm, made for the Library of Congress in co-operation with the International Greek New Testament Project.

2412, Ira Maurice Price Praxapostolos, 12th century. Collated by D. W. Riddle in *Eight American Praxapostoloi*, edited by K. W. Clark (Chicago: University of Chicago Press, 1941). Written by the same scribe as the Milan codex 614, it offers virtually an identical text; the two appear to have been copied from the same archetype.

(d) Lectionaries:

The lectionary text of the Catholic epistles has not been

systematically examined. A number of lectionaries (perhaps as many as 88?) were used in the preparation of the apparatus of the text prepared for the associated Bible Societies (*The Greek New Testament*, ed. K. Aland *et al.* [1966]), but the methods of this edition provide for the citation (in great fullness) of a very small number of variants (28 for the whole of I Peter). Lectionary readings, mainly from the menologion, are cited for only 23 passages; in almost every instance, they are identical with the reading of the standard Byzantine text. The one exception that I noted occurs in 4:14, where it is indicated that 88 lectionaries read αναπεπαυται, followed by the gloss κατα ... δοξαζεται, for the αναπαυεται which appears to be the best attested reading (אB 1739 and much of the versional evidence) and is also that of the Byzantine text.

It is still true, as I wrote in my first edition, that 'Codex B maintains its general superiority to all other witnesses'. This superiority is confirmed by the new evidence of 𝔓72, which is now the earliest extant manuscript of this epistle (a century older than B) and represents a good Egyptian text of around A.D. 200. This papyrus has a great many errors, for its scribe was far from competent, and it would appear that Greek was not his mother tongue—the indications are that he was a Copt from the neighbourhood of Thebes.[1] But when due allowance is made for his manifest errors, it may fairly be said that the underlying text is of exceptionally high quality, and that it stands in a particularly close relationship to the underlying text of B. A recent investigator, Dr. S. Kubo, has gone so far as to claim that 'exclusive of singular variants, 𝔓72 has as a whole a text superior to that of B'.[2] This conclusion is based upon an examination of 95 variants in the three epistles which are included under the siglum 𝔓72. In all these instances, B and 𝔓72 differ in the reading which they offer; and Kubo's analysis has led him to conclude that in 60 passages the reading of 𝔓72 is to be preferred, as against 34 in which he would give the preference to B (in one instance, he

---

[1] *Papyrus Bodmer VII–IX*, ed. M. Testuz (Geneva, 1959), p. 32. Professor G. D. Kilpatrick has suggested that the whole collection of which this papyrus forms a part came from 'a locality between Panopolis and Thebes' ('The Bodmer and Mississippi Collection of Biblical and Christian Texts', in *Greek Roman and Byzantine Studies*, Vol. 4, No. 1, Winter, 1963, p. 34).

[2] 𝔓72 *and the Codex Vaticanus* (Studies and Documents, ed. J. Geerlings, No. XXVII; Salt Lake City, 1965), p. 152.

thinks that they are both inferior to variants which are found in other witnesses). There is room for differences of opinion in the assessment of particular readings, but it cannot be doubted that the papyrus is of the first importance for the establishment of the text of the epistle.[1]

As the published texts of the Bodmer papyrus are not readily available, I am presenting its evidence in some fullness. I have not felt it necessary to note the peculiarities of spelling into which the scribe is betrayed by his Coptic ear, nor his very numerous itacisms (he can even write ε for the αι of the feminine nominative plural of the article), nor the outright errors which reveal his imperfect knowledge of Greek. These weaknesses are sufficiently manifested in his marginal notes (a primitive system of lectionary indications?), which are:

at 1:15   περι αγειοσυνη

at 2:5   περι ιερατευμα αγιον

at 2:9   περι γενος εγλεκτον βασιλιον ιερατευμα εθνος αγιον λαον
           περι ποιησιν

at 3:19   περι θανατου εν σαρκι και ζωοποιου και ακεκλεισμενοιν

[The last word is probably an error for κατακεκλησμενοις, which is read by C and a few minuscules, and is widely represented in the Old Latin: *his qui in carcere conclusi erant spiritibus*.]

at 4:1   περι χρυ παθος εν σαρκι

---

[1] Its importance is comparable to that of the Chester Beatty papyrus (𝔓46) for the Pauline corpus. Cf. the remarks of G. Zuntz (*The Text of the Epistles: a Disquisition upon the Corpus Paulinum*, London, 1953). Here again we have a papyrus that 'is by no means a good manuscript. The scribe committed very many blunders . . .' (p. 18). Yet it 'affords a valuable criterion by which to assess the quality of the Vaticanus. It demonstrates the early currency of some readings for which previously B had been the only witness; it confirms, in a general way, the antiquity of its text, yet leaves it in sole possession of some readings of more than doubtful authenticity. Thus it warns us against the assumption that this manuscript, however prominent (pre-eminent?) could be infallible' (p. 41). Yet its overall effect is to confirm the excellence of B. 'Codex B is indeed an outstanding witness. Within the wider affinities of the "Alexandrian" tradition, the Vaticanus is seen to stand out as a member of a group (in our epistle, with 𝔓72). The early date of the text-form which this group preserves is fixed by its oldest member and its high quality is borne out by many outstanding instances. B is in fact a witness for a text, not of *c*. A.D. 360 but of *c*. A.D. 200. However, in saying this we are very far from describing its text as "neutral" ' (p. 83). The Bodmer papyrus of Luke (𝔓75) establishes the same conclusion with respect to the text of the Gospels.

at 4:6   περι σαρκος
at 4:8   περι αγαπη
at 4:19   περι Θ̅υ̅ κτειστη

(*a*) Singular readings of the papyrus:

1:5   om θεου
1:8   εν ω αγαλλιασθε⟩ αγαλλειασαντες
       ποικιλοις⟩ πολλοις
1:12   υμας⟩ υμειν
1:17   επικαλεισθε⟩ καλειτε

[There is some Old Latin evidence for *vocatis*]

2:3   εγευσασθε⟩+επιστευσατε
2:9   om αυτου
2:15   αγνωσιαν⟩ αγνοιαν
2:17   θεον⟩ pr δε
3:7   ζωης⟩+εωνιου (αιων-)
3:10   παυσατω⟩ παυσασθαι
       λαλησαι⟩ λαλειν
3:13   γενησθε⟩ γενεσθε (cf. ℵ* γενεσθαι)
3:15   καταισχυνθωσιν⟩ εσχυν—
3:18   πνευματι⟩ pr εν
3:20   om οκτω
4:2   βιωσαι⟩ σωσαι
4:15   add ως *ante* κλεπτης, κακοποιος
4:16   om ως *ante* χριστιανος
5:1   χριστου⟩ θεου (Patripassianism?)
5:5   αλληλοις⟩ pr εν
5:9   om ω
       στερεοι⟩ εδρεοι (εδραιοι) (ex Col. 1:23?)
       ειδοτες⟩+οτι
       επιτελεισθαι⟩ επει τελειται

[επιτελειται?—but see the article of J. D. Quinn,
'Notes on the Text of 𝔓⁷² I Pt 2,3; 5,14; and 5,9' in
Catholic Biblical Quarterly, Vol. 27, No. 3, July,
1965, 247ff.]

5:10   om σθενωσει
5:11   om το
5:12   δι ολιγων⟩ δια βραχεων (ex Heb. 13:22?)
5:14   om ειρηνη . . . χριστω

Colophon: ειρηνη τω γραψαντι
                και τω αναγινωσκοντι

(b) Significant readings with other support:

1:3   ελεος αυτου
1:6   εστιν (post δεον) cum ACΨ 69.   (om Bℵ*)
       λυπηθεντες cum BACΨς (-τας ℵ* 69.)
1:7   δοκιμον cum minusc. pc. (δοκιμιον cett)
1:8   [ε]ιδοντες cum BℵCΨ 1739. vg sah syrr (ειδοτες A 33.
       69. 2412. ς)
       αγαλλιασθε (BΨ αγαλλιατε)
1:11   χριστου (om B)
       προμαρτυρουμενον cum APS minusc. pc.;—ομενον
       BℵCΨς

       [Our earliest testimony to the reading of A]

1:12   πνευματι cum BAΨ 33. (pr. εν cett)
1:16   εσεσθε cum BℵACΨ 33. 614; (γενεσθε 1739. ς vet lat
       sap boh syrᵖ; γινεσθε L 69; Soden)
       ειμι cum CΨPSς (om BℵA*KL)
1:20   εσχατων χρονων (εσχατων των χρονων ς; εσχατου των
       χρονων BAC 1739; εσχατου του χρονου ℵ*Ψ)

       [This could be regarded as a singular reading of the
       papyrus; but probably it represents an underlying
       agreement with B etc., with a careless omission of
       του]

1:21   πιστευοντας cum ℵCΨς (πιστους BA vg)
1:22   δια πνευματος non habet
       καθαρας καρδιας cum ℵ*C 33. 69. ς vet lat sah boh
       syrr (om καθαρας BA vg)
1:23   εις τον αιωνα non habet
2:1   υποκρισεις (-σιν Bℵᶜ syrᵖ)
2:2   εις σωτηριαν (om ς)

2:3 ει cum Bℵ*A (ειπερ ℵᶜCΨS 69. 1739. ϛ)

χριστος cum KLS 33. 69. 2412. (χρηστος cett)

2:5 οικοδομεισθε cum BA*ΨSϛ (εποικ- ℵAᶜC 1739. vg)

2:5 θεω⟩ pr. τω cum ϛ

2:6 ακρογωνιαιον εκλεκτον (transp., cum ℵAΨ 33. ϛ)

2:8 πετραν cum ℵ*

2:12 εποπτευοντες cum ℵBC (-τευσαντες AΨϛ)

2:19 συνειδησιν⟩+αγαθην cum C (θεου αγαθην A*Ψ 33.)

2:20 και κολαφιзομενοι⟩ κολαзομενοι

υπομενειτε⟩–μενετε (bis) cum 69.

2:21 om και cum A

2:21 επαθεν cum Bϛ et test. fere omnibus; απεθανεν ℵΨ syrᵖ

υπερ⟩ περι cum A

υμων υμιν cum BℵACΨ etc. (ημων ημιν ϛ)

2:24 ημων⟩ υμων cum B (vid W-H marg.)

2:25 πλανωμενοι⟩–μενα cum CΨϛ

3:1 γυναικες⟩ pr ε (αι)

habet και

3:2 εποπτευσαντες⟩–τευοντες cum ℵ*

3:3 om τριχων cum CΨ

3:7 εκκοπτεσθε(θαι) cum C²Ψ 33. 69. ϛ

3:14 om μηδε ταραχθητε cum BL

3:16 καταλαλεισθε cum B 1739. 2412.

3:18 επαθεν⟩ υπερ υμων απεθανεν cum Bϛ

> [Modern critical editions all but unanimously read
> απεθανεν *without* υπερ υμων. But *no* extant manu-
> script reads απεθανεν without the *two* prepositional
> phrases. See my note in 'The Text of I Peter in
> Papyrus 72' (*JBL* 80, Pt. 3 [Sept. 1961], p. 258),
> where all the variants are discussed.]

3:21 om ω cum ℵ*

3:22 habet του

4:8 καλυψει cum ℵ 69. ϛ

4:11 om των αιωνων cum 69.

4:14 αναπαυεται⟩ επαναπεπαυται

4:19 αγαθοποιειαις⟩ (–ποιιαις) cum A 33 vg

5:2 θεου⟩+επισκοπουντες [See additional note, p. 202.]

ERRATUM

On p. 7, line 24 (referring to I Peter 3:18) 'cum Bϛ' should read
'cum A (ℵ)'.

[Strongly confirms my preference for this reading as indicated in my Additional Note, p. 202]

habet κατα θεον *contra* Bς

5:8   ζητων⟩+τινα *contra* B 0206 (W-H)
καταπιειν⟩—πειη(πιη) cum Aς

5:10   χριστω⟩+Ιησου cum Aς vg

5:11   om των αιωνων cum B
non habet η δοξα και cum B A vg

The closeness of the relationship of 𝔓⁷² to the major Alexandrian witnesses, and the wideness of its disparity with the Byzantine text will appear from the following table. This is taken from my article in *Journal of Biblical Literature* (September, 1961), and is based upon a more complete list of variants.

Agreements and Disagreements of 𝔓⁷²

	B	ℵ	A	C	Ψ	ς	sah
With	90	83	109	74	104	78	45
Against	54	66	43	33	44	73	19

This table does not take account of the singular readings of the papyrus, most of which are obvious scribal errors. If the singular readings of the uncials were likewise omitted from consideration, it would substantially increase the proportion of agreements with ℵ (which has a surprisingly large number of singular readings) and to a less degree also with B.

The proportion of agreements with A and Ψ is striking. The high proportion of agreements with the Sahidic would seem to indicate that a near ancestor of 𝔓⁷² was closely related to the Greek text which underlies that version—not unnaturally, if the scribe of the papyrus was in fact a native of the Theban region. (The Sahidic version was probably made before A.D. 200—that is, a generation or more earlier than the writing of the papyrus). There is nothing like the same proportion of agreements with any of the other versions. It is surprising to notice that there does not seem to be a single Byzantine reading which is supported by the papyrus against the united testimony of the non-Byzantine witnesses.

The papyrus reminds us forcibly that the Catholic epistles did not circulate as a group until a later period. In 𝔓⁷², only three of them are found (I Peter, II Peter, and Jude). They were not written as a group, even to this limited extent.[1] The epistle of Jude follows the eleventh Ode of Solomon, beginning on the same page as the conclusion of the latter text, and separated from it only by a band of arabesques. Its pages are numbered X B to X H (62 to 68), and I Peter begins on page A(1) of a new series of numbers, and on the second folio of a quaternion, of which the first folio has disappeared.[2] I and II Peter then follow in sequence, but there must have been a time when each of these circulated by itself, seeing that apart from the difference of authorship the second epistle was not anything like so generally recognized as the first, or at such an early date. This is quite different from the history of the text of the Pauline epistles and of the gospels. There is no doubt that all our extant manuscripts of the Pauline epistles are descended from an early collection (which did not always include Hebrews, and may not have included the Pastoral epistles), and all our extant manuscripts of the gospels are descended from an early collection of the four. In a way that is not true of any other book of the New Testament except the Apocalypse, each of the Catholic epistles has had a separate history of transmission for a not inconsiderable period. In most Greek manuscripts, the Catholic epistles follow the book of Acts, forming an established group with it; but this is not the earliest arrangement. In the Chester Beatty papyrus 𝔓⁴⁵ (3rd century), Acts is grouped with the four gospels; and initially it was almost certainly published as part of a two-volume work (Luke-Acts) in separation from the other gospels. What concerns us particularly is that the manuscripts which contain the Catholic epistles (usually Acts and the Catholic epistles) cannot be treated as if the several documents constituted a group with a common textual history. The character of the text must be determined individually for each epistle.[3] An illustration of this principle is afforded by the manuscript P, which in the other

---

[1] Jude is not even written by the same scribe as I and II Peter, contrary to the statement of M. Testuz. The single page of Jude which is given in photographic facsimile shows quite clearly a different hand from that of the other two epistles.
[2] This information is taken from the *editio princeps* of the papyrus, by M. Testuz, pp. 15, 29.
[3] Cf. the remarks of the Abbé Jean Duplacy, in *Recherches de Science Réligieuse* (Tome L, No. 2, April-June, 1962), p. 255.

Catholic epistles has an Alexandrian text, but in I Peter has an undistinguished Byzantine text, as it has also in Acts.[1]

The fragmentary remnants of $\mathfrak{P}^{74}$ and $\mathfrak{P}^{81}$ are too meagre to make any significant contribution to the study of the text.

Of the vellum uncials, the general superiority of B is manifest. There are not more than twelve scribal errors, nearly all being the omission of necessary phrases (1:1; 2:12, 25; 3:14, 18; and (much the most considerable) the omission of the entire verse 3 of chapter 5). It entirely lacks the glosses of the Byzantine text, some of which appear in every other witness except $\mathfrak{P}^{72}$. It has the uniform support of $\mathfrak{P}^{72}$, of the uncials א AΨ, and of the ancient versions, especially the Coptic.

Codex א has a large number of errors, some of them glaring (1:18, 23; 2:12; 3:7; 4:5); an unusually large number of singular readings, none of which commend themselves as original (1:1, 4, 17; 2:1, 5, 15, 21; 3:7, 20); and an exceptionally large number of transpositions.

The singular readings of C are of no interest, and the text shows a relatively strong contamination from the Byzantine text. The manuscript is deficient from 4:6 to the end of the book.

Codex A stands second only to B in the quality of the text which it offers in this Epistle; it has far fewer errors and false readings than א. It can no longer be maintained, however, with Harnack,[2] that it stands in a particularly close relationship with the excellent Greek text that underlies the Latin Vulgate of I Peter (though this is the case in I John). The quality of this manuscript is confirmed by observation of the remarkable degree of agreement with $\mathfrak{P}^{72}$ (109 agreements against 43 disagreements).

Codex Ψ is almost equally good, though it has a tendency to use compound forms of verbs and to omit words and even phrases;

[1] Cf. the remarks of J. H. Ropes (*The Beginnings of Christianity*, Part I, Vol. III [London, 1926], 'The Text of Acts', p. cclxxviii, note 2). 'Closer inquiry . . . needs to be made into the question whether P in Acts shows a mixed text retaining traces of its Old Uncial base in the midst of all the Antiochian improvements. Hort, "Introduction", pp. 153f., describes it as "all but purely Syrian (i.e., Byzantine) in the Acts and I Peter". In James, P contains a large ancient element, which bears a closer resemblance to B than to any other extant uncial.'

[2] *Zur Revision der Prinzipien der neutestamentlichen Textkritik: Die Bedeutung der Vulgata und der Anteil des Hieronymus an den Übersetzungswerk* (Beiträge zur Einleitung in das Neue Testament, VII). Leipzig, 1916. Cf. W. Thiele, *Die Lateinische Texte*, p. 114: 'Eine so spezielle Beziehung der Vulgata zu einem griechischen Einzelzeugen lässt sich für I Pt nicht feststellen'.

and it is the only good uncial to give the long gloss κατα μεν . . .
δοξαζεται in 4:14. The antiquity of this gloss is, however, shown
by its presence in the African Old Latin (Cyprian); it is not a
Byzantine gloss. Like A, it shows a remarkably high proportion of
agreements with 𝔓[72] (104/44).

As the readings of this very important manuscript are very
sparsely cited in the apparatus of all the printed editions, and no
collation has yet been published, I am venturing to offer here a
collation with my own printed text, which differs in only a few
details from that of Nestle-Aland (25th edition). Even von Soden
offers no more than six readings of Ψ, and it was not known to
Tischendorf.

Collation of Ψ (044) against the printed text of this edition.

[In this manuscript the Catholic epistles follow Acts in the
unusual order: I and II Peter, James, I, II and III John, Jude.]

Superscriptio: επιστολη πετρου πρωτη

1:4	ουρανοις〉 pr. τοις
1:6	δεον〉 +εστιν
1:8	ιδοντες〉 ειδοτες
1:10	εξηραυνησαν〉 ηρευνησαν
1:11	εραυνωντες〉 ερευνωντες
1:12	εν〉 om
1:13	χαριν〉 χαραν
	εν〉 om
1:16	αγιοι〉 pr. οτι
	αγιος〉 +ειμι
1:17	απροσωπολημπτως〉–ληπτως
1:18	αναστροφης πατροπαραδοτου〉—transp.
1:20	των χρονων〉 του χρονου
1:21	πιστους〉 πιστευοντας
1:22	καρδιας〉 pr. καθαρας
1:23	ζωντος θεου〉 transp.
1:24	διοτι〉 οτι
1:25	ως[1º]〉 om
	αυτης〉 ανθρωπου
2:1	υποκρισιν〉 υποκρισεις

2:3   ει) ειπερ
2:6   εκλεκτον ακρογωνιαιον) transp.
2:7   λιθος) λιθον
2:12   κακοποιων) pr. των
        εποπτευοντες) εποπτευσαντες
2:18   εν παντι φοβω) *ante* υποτασσομενοι pos.
2:19   χαρις) +τω θεω
2:20   συνειδησιν) +αγαθην
        θεου) om
        κολαφιζομενοι) κολαζομενοι
        υπομενειτε (*bis*))—μενετε
2:21   επαθεν) απεθανεν
2:25   πλανωμενοι)—μενα
3:1   γυναικες) pr. αι
3:3   τριχων) om
3:5   και) om
        αγιαι) om
3:6   υπηκουσεν)—κουεν
3:7   συγκληρονομοις)—μοι
        εγκοπτεσθαι) εκκοπ—
3:11   δε) om
3:13   γενησθε) εστε
3:14   πασχοιτε) πασχετε
3:15   ετοιμοι) +δε
3:15   αιτουντι) απαιτουντι
3:18   περι) + υμων υπερ
        δικαιος υπερ αδικων) om
        μεν) om
3:20   ολιγοι) ολιγαι
4:1   οπλισασθε) ενοπλ—
        αμαρτιας) αμαρτιαις
4:2   επιθυμιαις) αμαρτιαις
4:3   κατειργασθαι) κατεργασασθαι
        και αθεμιτοις) om
4:5   λογον) pr. τον
        εχοντι κριναι) κρινουντι
4:11   χορηγει) επιχορ—
        ο θεος[2°]) om

4:14 αναπαυεται⟩ επαναπαυεται
+κατα μεν αυτους βλασφημειται
κατα δε υμας δοξαζεται
4:15 αλλοτριεπισκοπος⟩ αλλοτριος επισκοπος
4:17 αφ⟩ απο
4:19 αγαθοποιια⟩—ιαις (wrongly cited in my apparatus)
5:1 ουν⟩ +τους
5:2 θεου⟩ +επισκοπουντες
5:5 ομοιως⟩ +δε
αλληλοις⟩ αλληλους +αγαπησατε
5:6 καιρω⟩ +επισκοπης υμων
5:8 ωρυομενος⟩ ορυωμενος
non habet τινα
5:9 στερεοι⟩ στερεα
τω⟩ om
5:10 χριστω⟩ +Ιησου
καταρτισει⟩—τιει
θεμελιωσει⟩ om
5:12 του⟩ om
οτητε⟩ . . τειτε
Subscriptio: πετρου επιστολη Ᾱ

A most interesting singular reading is that of 1:13—χαραν in place of χαριν. The omission of τριχων in 3:3 has the formidable support of 𝔓⁷², and the less significant support of C; it is also missing from the Armenian and Sahidic versions (Martini), and from a citation of Clement of Alexandria. The omission of θεμελιωσει in 5:10 is supported by BA 0206 and a number of cursives, and by the Vulgate (Clementine, Wordsworth-White, Beuron), though not by the Old Latin (*fundabit*). It was omitted by Hort, whose judgment is thus confirmed.

Codex C is deficient from 1:1-1:2 (πνευματος) and from 4:6 to the end of the book. Its singular readings are of little interest, and it has a greater admixture of Byzantine readings than any other manuscript of the Alexandrian group.

KLP are our oldest representatives of a relatively pure Byzantine text. K is accompanied by a catena, written in spaces between the verses. Its first page of I Peter is shown in a photographic facsimile in W. H. P. Hatch's *Principal Uncial Manuscripts of the New Testament* (Chicago, 1939).

Codex S gives in the main a predominantly Byzantine type of text, but has an unusually strong admixture of Alexandrian readings.

Codex Patirensis (048) is of interest because of its age (5th century). It originally contained Acts, the Catholic epistles, and the Epistles of St. Paul. Only twenty-one leaves remain, and only one of these contains any portion of I Peter, and that only the first ten verses. The codex was deciphered by Père Batiffol in 1899, so far as it could be done without further damaging the thin and brittle leaves. His transcription was examined by William Sanday, who published a collation limited to the more notable readings. None at all is given for the portion of I Peter which survives. See his 'Étude critique sur le Codex Patirensis du Nouveau Testament' in *Revue Biblique* Vol. IV, No. 2 (April, 1895), pp. 207-213. Evidently some progress has been made in the interval, for the *Greek New Testament* of the Bible Societies is able to cite two readings of this codex, viz., δοκιμιον (1:7) and ιδοντες (1:8, marked as doubtful).

Codex Daytonensis (0206) is a single leaf of a vellum codex of the 4th century containing part of chapter 5 (vv. 5-13 δωσι χαριν ... ασπαζεται υμας). It has the singular reading επιριψατε (for επιριψαντες) in v. 7; and agrees with B in the omission of τινα (v. 8), of θεμελιωσει (v. 10; with AΨ and vg); and of η δοξα και (v. 11; with 𝔓72 BAΨ and vg); in one case—the reading χριστω in v. 10—it agrees with ℵ 614. 2412. against B (τω χρ) and also against nearly all the other witnesses, including 𝔓72 AΨ 33. 1739. ς verss. (χρ. Ιησου).

There is little to say about the other six uncials. Codex Mamuciensis (0247), a single leaf of vellum, has nothing to offer but portions of three words in 5:13-14 (most of the leaf is given to II Peter). 093 is a fragment containing only 2:22-3:7. 0203 is a Greek-Coptic bilingual. The Greek portion contains only nine verses—2:7f., 9-15. 056, 0142, and 0157 appear to give the complete text of the epistle in the standard Byzantine text, but I have not been able to check them. For 056 and 0142, consistent agreement with ς is shown in the limited number of readings for which evidence is given in *The Greek New Testament* of the Bible Societies, which does not cite 0157.

Among the cursives, only the four which are listed above are cited with any fullness. 1739 appears to be the most interesting and valuable of them all, consistently supporting Codex B and its allies. 33, 69, and 2412 exhibit more mixture, but they are more closely allied to the Alexandrian text type than to the Byzantine, and they occasionally offer an interesting variant that is not found in any of the great uncials.

Of the remaining hundreds, only a small proportion has been examined or collated; even for von Soden's edition, most of those which he attempted to classify were not fully collated but spot-checked, and such partial checking can not form a satisfactory basis for classification.[1] It is not exceptional for a manuscript to change its textual character as it goes along. Nearly all the cursives, in so far as they have been examined, offer with an almost monotonous faithfulness the standardized text which was in general use throughout the Byzantine church for many centuries, from the time of St. John Chrysostom, who brought it from Antioch, where it was formed, to Constantinople, towards the end of the 4th century. It 'is furthest from the originals, and must be considered the poorest of all text forms' (Wikenhauser, *Introduction*, p. 132). Unfortunately, it dominated European scholarship for more than 300 years, from the time of the first publication of a printed edition (by Erasmus, at Basel, in 1516) until the later years of the nineteenth century, when the great critical texts of Tischendorf (8th edition, 1869-72) and of Westcott and Hort (1881) gradually displaced it. In the editions of Stephanus (*editio regia*, 1550) and of Elzevir (7 editions, beginning in 1624), it became known (from an Elzevirian phrase) as the Textus Receptus, and it was reprinted again and again without serious change, even by scholars like John Mill (who printed over 100,000 variant readings in his edition of 1707), J. A. Bengel (1734), and J. J. Griesbach (1775-1827). Acquainted though they were with much better material, they never ventured to constitute a superior text.

This Byzantine (Syrian, or Antiochian) text is cited in this edition under the symbol ç. The readings thus cited are taken

---

[1] 'No text or document is homogeneous enough to justify judgment on the basis of a part of its readings for the rest of its readings' (E. C. Colwell, 'Text and Ancient Versions of the New Testament', in *Interpreter's Bible*, Vol. I [1952], p. 79).

from Lloyd's edition (Oxford, 1889) of Mill's text of the Stephanus folio of 1550.

No citations are made from the lectionaries.

2. *The Ancient Versions*

1. *Latin*

(*a*) Old Latin (vet lat)

Manuscripts containing the text of I Peter in an Old Latin version are few, and most of them are fragmentary; not one contains the entire epistle without a portion which gives the text of the Vulgate. In the following list, the small italics of the traditional system of notation are given in brackets after the Arabic numbers of the new system devised for the Beuron edition. This is *Vetus Latina: Die Reste der altlateinischen Bibel*, I, 'Verzeichnis der Sigel', Freiburg, 1949: 1/1 'Verzeichnis der Sigel für Kirchenschriftsteller', 2nd ed., 1963, followed by *Ergänzungslieferungen* 1 to 4 (to 1967); 26.I.2.3. *Epistula I Petri*. Freiburg, 1958, 1960. "Nachträge und Berichtigungen" in 26.I.6, pp. 448-468 give supplementary material on I Peter. Professor G. D. Kilpatrick informs me that an introduction with a discussion of the text is given in 26.I.7, published this summer (1969), but this has not yet reached me. The edition includes a newly constituted text of the Vulgate of the epistle, based upon a fresh assessment of the evidence of the manuscripts and the *testimonia*. It differs in 49 readings from the text of the Wordsworth-White-Sparks edition (see below). This Beuron text (with two departures) has now been adopted in the latest edition of the Vulgate: *Biblia Sacra Juxta Vulgatam Versionem*, herausgegeben von Robert Weber OSB zusammen mit Bonifatius Fischer OSB, Jean Gribomont OSB, H. F. D. Sparks, W. Thiele. Handausgabe in 2 Bänden. Württemberg Bible Society, Stuttgart, 1969.

32—Codex Weissenburgensis 76—lectionary, palimpsest, early 6th century, contains 2:18-25; 3:8-17; 4:7-9, 19. 'Das älteste Liturgiebuch der lateinischen Kirche', ed. A. Dold, *Texte und Arbeiten* hsg. von der Erzabtei Beuron, I. 26-28 [1936]. Rechecked against photographs for the Beuron edition, by B. Fischer.

53 (*s*)—Fragmenta Vindobonensia—palimpsest, 6th century, contains 1:1-18; 2:4-10. *Old Latin Biblical Texts* IV, ed. H. J.

White (Oxford, 1897). For the Beuron edition, rechecked against photographs, by B. Fischer.

54 (*p*)—Paris, B.N. fonds lat. 321, 12th century. 'An Old Latin Text of the Catholic Epistles', by E. S. Buchanan, in *Journal of Theological Studies* 12 (1911). This is not in fact an Old Latin, but a Vulgate manuscript with some Old Latin variants in the Catholic Epistles. Newly collated from photographs for the Beuron edition.

55 (*h*)—Fragmenta Floriacensia—palimpsest, 5th century, contains 4:17-5:14. *Old Latin Biblical Texts* V, ed. E. S. Buchanan (1907). Citations for the Beuron edition rechecked by B. Fischer from fluorescent photographs.

56 (*t*)—Liber comicus Toletanus—Lectionary, 11th century, partly Old Latin, partly Vulgate, contains 1:16-21; 1:25-2:10; 2:21-25; 3:5-9; 4:7-11, 13-19; 5:1-5, 6-11. 'As a rule, has Old Latin readings only where these are widespread in the Vulgate witnesses' (W. Thiele, *Die lateinische Texte*, p. 127).

64 (*r*)—Fragmenta Frisingensia—7th century (in Catholic Epistles), contains 1:8-19; 2:20-3:7; 4:10-5:14. *Les Fragments de Freising*, ed. D. de Bruyne (Rome, 1921). New collation for Beuron edition, made from photographs.

65 (*z*)—Codex Harleianus—8th century, contains the complete text of the epistle, but partly in the Vulgate. 2:9-4:14 is Old Latin, the remainder Vulgate. Buchanan's edition (*Sacred Latin Texts* I [London, 1912]) is severely criticized by Thiele; the Beuron edition has derived its readings from a fresh examination of the photographs of the Codex.

67—Remnants of a Vulgate Bible, but gives an Old Latin text in the Catholic Epistles; palimpsest, half-uncial, 7th century, contains 1:1-7; 1:22-2:9; 3:1-14. Now in Leon Cathedral. Deciphered for the first time by Bonifatius Fischer, 'Ein neuer Zeuge zum westlichen Text der Apostelgeschichte', in *Biblical and Patristic Studies in Memory of R. P. Casey* (Freiburg, 1963), pp. 33-63.

[The Pseudo-Augustinian *Speculum* (*m*) is not given a number by the Beuron editors, but is listed among the 'Kirchenschriftsteller' under the symbol PS-AU spe. This is a 5th-century work composed in Spain (possibly in Africa) in the 5th century. From I Peter, it cites 1:13-16, 22; 2:13-20; 3:1-9, 15f.; 4:8f.; 5:1-7.

D. de Bruyne, 'Étude sur le *Liber de divinis scripturis*', in *Revue Bénédictine* 43 (1933), pp. 119-141.]

These manuscripts provide only a minor part of the evidence for the Old Latin. Strange as it may seem, a much greater amount of material is supplied by the manuscripts of the Vulgate, which are numbered in the hundreds and are often of very high quality. For it seems to be impossible to find a Vulgate manuscript which does not contain a certain sprinkling of Old Latin readings, and there are many which are heavily contaminated by Old Latin elements. There is nothing comparable to this in the history of other versions. In the Syrian churches, for instance, the Peshitta quickly and completely displaced the Old Syriac versions (for I Peter, it is probable that there was no earlier version to displace). But in the Latin churches, the victory of the Vulgate was neither swift nor complete. For centuries, it was used along with the older versions without displacing them, and scribes found it impossible—probably they did not try very hard—to screen out the older readings with which they were familiar. When attempts were made to bring out purified editions of the Vulgate, the effect was only to add fresh complications.

The richest quarry of materials, however, is to be found in the Latin ecclesiastical writers of the early centuries—whether catholic, schismatic, or heretical—Cyprian, Augustine, Pelagius, the Donatists, Ambrose, Cassiodorus, Priscillian and others beyond number (the Beuron *Verzeichnis* runs to nearly 500 pages without the index) all make their contribution.

Employing all these resources, the Beuron edition makes it clearly evident that when we speak of the Old Latin, we speak not of a single version with some degree of homogeneity (as, for instance, with the English Bible from Tyndall to the Revised Standard Version), but of at least four versions or groups of versions which were in use before the making of the Vulgate (late in the 4th century); and besides these main strands, the citations of Tertullian, Hilary of Poitiers, Lucifer of Cagliari and others represent versions that have no clear relationship with the general history of the Latin Bible.[1] The Beuron editors print not one but

---

[1] Notice the important observations of Thiele (*Die lateinische Texte*, p. 12): 'Ohne Frage sind die Belege bei Hilarius, Lucifer, Chromatius von Bedeutung, aber die von diesen Zeugen gebotenen Zitate reichen für eine sichere Feststellung in der Textgeschichte von I Pt nicht aus.' On Tertullian, see pp. 34-37.

four Old Latin texts in parallel lines (with a newly constituted text of the Vulgate in a fifth line below them all). Not one of the four varieties of Old Latin texts contains the entire text of the epistle. They are distinguished as follows:

K is the Old African text, for which the principal witness is Cyprian.

CA is the text as generally cited by Augustine. When he is the only witness, the symbol **A** is used alone; when we find supporting evidence in other writers, the symbol **C** is used. We have here a North African text related to that of Cyprian, but in a form which had developed something more than a century later.

S is a slightly later Spanish text, heavily dependent on the North African. The chief witnesses are the MS. 67 and the Pseudo-Augustinian *Speculum(m)*, and most of the citations of Priscillian (executed for heresy in 385, after a stormy career as Bishop of Avila).

T is a European text for which the principal witnesses belong to the 5th and 6th centuries, but which was certainly formed as early as the 4th century. It is the most widely used and the most broadly represented of all forms of the Old Latin, and the Vulgate is more closely related to it than to any of the others. The principal witnesses are the MSS. 32, 55, 64, and (for 2:9–4:15) 65. Among the many ecclesiastical writers who provide evidence for it, Thiele gives particular mention to Fulgentius (*d.* 532), Facundus (*d.* after 571), and Epiphanius Scholasticus, an associate of Cassiodorus. Cassiodorus also uses it, but not so exclusively. A certain amount of evidence for its use can also be drawn from Hilary, Ambrose, Rufinus, Jerome and (occasionally) Augustine.

(b) The Vulgate (vg)

The Vulgate of the New Testament is not a new translation, but a revision of an Old Latin text of European origin (of the **T**-type) intended to bring it into conformity with the best available Greek manuscripts. In the view of Thiele and of most recent investigators, the revision of the Catholic epistles cannot be the work of St. Jerome himself; in any case, it is made on the same principles and at about the same time (late 4th century). The underlying Greek text cannot be identified with any existing Greek manuscript — perhaps the reviser used several — but it is certainly a good Alexandrian base, akin to that of Codex B and its allies. So faithfully is this work carried through that the Vulgate of these epistles—more precisely, the Greek text which underlies it—might almost be regarded as a charter member of the Alexandrian family.

The Vulgate removes a number of glosses which are found in various strands of the Old Latin, rejects the freedom that is shown in some of the older versions in accommodations of language to the genius of Latin, and even changes the word order to bring it into conformity with the Greek text which the reviser has before him. It is painfully literal—this makes it all the more valuable as an indication of the underlying Greek.

The manuscript witnesses are very numerous, and it must suffice to mention only a few. The notations given are first of all those of the Wordsworth and White edition of 1911; then (if any change has been made) those of the Beuron edition.

[The quality of manuscripts of the Vulgate is judged primarily in accordance with the degree of freedom from contamination by the Old Latin, and then freedom from scribal errors and singular readings (these are usually scribal errors which happen to give an intelligible text). According to Thiele, 'the character of the Vulgate is so unbrokenly uniform that the Old Latin materials in the several branches of the transmission stand out clearly as foreign bodies' (p. 115).]

A Codex Amiatinus. Written c. 700, for the Abbot Ceolfrid, in Northumberland, by an Italian scribe. In the Catholic epistles, the text represents an Irish branch of the transmission, akin to D (below), but almost wholly free from Old Latin elements (19 variants).

C Codex Cavensis. Written in Spain in the 9th century, contains the best example of the Spanish strain of transmission. Has almost no singular readings, but a relatively strong admixture of Old Latin readings (180).

D Codex Ardmachanus, or Dublinensis. (The Book of Armagh.) Written in 812. Represents the Irish branch of the transmission, has a number of doublets and a relatively high proportion of Old Latin readings (105).

F Codex Fuldensis. Written in 546 for Victor, Bishop of Capua. An excellent representative of the Italian branch; few singular readings, and very few Old Latin readings (19).

G Codex Sangermanensis. 9th century. The best representative of the South Gallic branch. Amost free of Old Latin contamination (16 variants).

H Θ^H Codex Hubertianus. 9th/10th century, lacks 4:4 to end. A good ancient text, generally in agreement with Amiatinus. Includes in the margin readings from the revision made by Theodulf, Bishop of Orleans (early 9th century). 45 Old Latin variants.

V Φ^V Codex Vallicellianus. 9th century. The best witness of the revision made by Alcuin for Charlemagne (c. 800). Thiele makes use of three other manuscripts of the Alcuin revision, and tells us that they indicate that Alcuin in I Peter took as his base a current Gallic text and made corrections in very few places.

I Codex Iuvenianus. Written in Rome or the vicinity, 9th century. Has very few Old Latin readings (12), but its value is diminished by numerous singular readings and outright errors.

R Codex Veronensis. Probably written in Verona, 7th/8th century. Not used for the Oxford edition. An excellent Vulgate text, with a few more Old Latin readings than F and I (24), and almost no singular readings.

100 Codex Lugdunensis. Not used for the Oxford edition. 7th century, Gaul. Contains an exceptionally pure Vulgate text for I Peter 1:25-2:15, 3:8f., 4:7-11, found as a lection in the margins of three folios. In this (small) amount of the epistle, it contains almost no Old Latin readings (one certain, three possible), and not more than four singular readings.

In the judgment of Thiele, the best Vulgate witnesses for I Peter are G, 100, F, I, and R. As the consequence of the greater respect given to G, the Beuron text differs in 49 readings from the White text; in 43 of these, the effect is to give a Latin text that is still more in accord with the Greek (see list of differences in Thiele, *Die lateinische Texte*, pp. 117 f.).

2. Egyptian

(a) Sahidic (sah)

Mr. Horner's text of this version was pieced together out of a number of fragments: 9 codices, 1 on papyrus and 8 on parchment; and 14 lectionaries, 1 on papyrus, 11 on parchment, and 2 on paper. Of these, the most valuable was a ninth-century codex of the

Bibliothèque Nationale, which lacks almost the whole of Chapter 1. His other witnesses range from the 6th to the 9th century. Since his work appeared, it has been discovered that a parchment fragment of the 5th century had already been published by W. E. Crum, in his *Catalogue of the Coptic Manuscripts in the British Museum* (London: British Museum, 1905), but without being properly identified; Crum described it as part of 'a Homily dealing here with the cleansing power of baptism and the example of Christ's Passion'. In 1964, however, it was published afresh by Professor William H. Willis, who identified the text as that of I Peter 3:20-4:1, lacking the last clause of v. 21, the first two words of v. 22, and the last word of v. 4. It offers no significant variants from Horner's text. Much more important is the Crosby codex, now at the University of Mississippi, which contains the whole epistle, written in a hand which Professor Willis assigns to the first half of the 3rd century, or even earlier. It is said to show traces of 'archaic Achmimic influence' (Willis). The text has not yet been published, but Professor Willis informs me that it too has no significant variants from Horner's text. Its great importance lies in the fact that it makes it certain that the Sahidic version was made before the end of the 2nd century.[1] The only other manuscript known to exist which contains the complete text of I Peter in Sahidic is a ninth-century parchment codex of the seven Catholic epistles, now in the Pierpont Morgan Library in New York. It was published in photographic facsimile, but not edited, by Henri Hyvernat (Rome, 1922).

The Sahidic is the oldest of the Egyptian versions. It represents a very early form of the Greek text, and its evidence is of the greatest value. The underlying Greek is closely related to the text of the 3rd-century Bodmer papyrus.

(b) Bohairic (boh)

This version is not so old as the Sahidic; it was probably made in the 3rd century and cannot be later than the 4th. The manuscript tradition is good, though the codices are late (12th to 18th cen-

[1] Professor G. D. Kilpatrick dates this MS. later in the 3rd century, and thinks it probable that the version was not made until after 200.

turies). It is free of the corruptions of the Byzantine text and is quite independent of the Sahidic.

3. Syriac

(a) Peshitta (syr^p)

Made early in the 5th century, this version is generally held to be the work of Rabbula, Bishop of Edessa, but this view (first advanced by F. C. Burkitt), is disputed by A. Vööbus and M. Black. The discussions are based almost exclusively on the text of the Gospels. For the Catholic epistles there is no trace of an Old Syriac text; probably I Peter was translated into Syriac for the first time for the Peshitta. The underlying Greek text is an early form of the Byzantine.

(b) Harkleian (syr^{hl})

Generally regarded as a revision of the Philoxenian (itself a revision of the Peshitta, made for Philoxenus, the Monophysite bishop of Hierapolis, in 508), made by Thomas of Harkel, a later bishop of the same see, after he had been driven into exile in the neighbourhood of Alexandria in Egypt, in 616-617. The text is of the Byzantine type, rendered with extreme literalness. The margin contains variant readings from two or three Greek manuscripts of superior quality which Thomas found at Alexandria (syr$^{hl\ mg}$).

On the character and value of the Syriac versions, see G. Zuntz, *The Ancestry of the Harklean New Testament* (British Academy Supplemental Papers, No. VII). London, N.D.

The Armenian and Ethiopic versions have not been studied. Their evidence is most readily available in the apparatus to Mr. Horner's edition of the Sahidic, upon which I have relied for citations from the Syriac versions also.

The text has been transmitted with great fidelity, and there are few passages in which the critic has serious difficulty in making his decision. All the modern critical texts with the exception of von Soden's, show a very wide measure of agreement in detail. Von Soden's text is vitiated by his untenable view that the Byzantine (K) text is not secondary to the Alexandrian and Western texts (H and I in his nomenclature), and can be used along with them to reconstruct an H-I-K text which would underlie them all.

So far as I Peter is concerned, I am unable to find evidence for a genuine 'Western' text type. For this epistle at least, I would agree with E. C. Colwell that 'the so-called Western text or Delta text-type is the uncontrolled popular text of the second century. It has no unity and should not be referred to as the "Western text" ' ('The Origin of Texttypes of New Testament Manuscripts', in *Early Christian Origins: Studies in Honor of H. R. Willoughby*, ed. Allen Wikgren [Chicago, 1961], p. 137).

II. THE TITLE

The title in all its forms is of course editorial. In the early uncials, it is given as Πέτρου Ā (so in B and in the subscription and page-headings of א), or Πέτρου ἐπιστολὴ Ā (so in A, C, and the superscription of א). Later MSS. nearly all add the epithet καθολική, and describe the writer further as τοῦ ἁγίου ⟨καὶ πανευφήμου⟩ ἀποστόλου Πέτρου.

The adjective καθολικός is used in the sense of encyclical (Oecumenius, in the Preface to his *Commentary on the Epistle of St. James* — καθολικαὶ λέγονται αὗται, οἱονεὶ ἐγκύκλιοι). Origen is the first to apply the term to this Epistle. Its first official use as designating the group now commonly so called is found in Canon 59 of the Council of Laodicea (A.D. 363).

In the later Latin MSS., καθολική is frequently represented by *canonica*. Westcott (*Epistles of St. John*, p. xxix) traces the origin of this 'singular error' to a phrase of Junilius which, he thinks, was misinterpreted by Cassiodorus. Junilius, in his own list of *libri canonici qui ad simplicem doctrinam pertinent*, included from this group only First Peter and First John, but went on to say that 'some add five others *quae Apostolorum canonicae nuncupantur'*. Cassiodorus, in referring to the Latin translation of Clement's commentary on four Catholic Epistles, remarked that 'in epistolis autem canonicis Clemens Alexandrinus ... quaedam attico sermone declaravit'. It is not altogether evident that Cassiodorus had the words of Junilius in mind when he used this phrase; but it may at least be said that he is the first who clearly applies the epithet *canonicus* peculiarly to the Catholic Epistles. In the context, his use of the word suggests that it was already established in this sense in the West. (Cassiodorus, *De Inst. Div. Litt.* 8; Junilius, *De Part. Div. Leg.* I. 2.)

III. CHARACTER, CONSTRUCTION AND PURPOSE

The character and purpose of the Epistle are indicated by the writer himself at the close, in the words: 'I have written to you briefly, exhorting you and confirming the testimony (ἐπιμαρτυρῶν) that this is the true grace of God; in it, stand steadfast' (5:12). It is a message sent to the churches of Asia Minor to help them meet the first demoralizing shock of a sudden and violent outburst of persecution, to reassure them of the truth of their faith, and to encourage them to remain firm in their allegiance to Jesus Christ, whatever the cost.

It must be observed, however, that while the ever-present possibility of being called to suffer for righteousness' sake comes into view in several different passages, it is only in the section from 4:12 to the end that the writer speaks in specific terms of a persecution which is actually raging. In the remainder of the book, the problem of suffering is not the central theme, but is raised and dealt with only in relation to a general exposition of the nature of the Christian life. The long section from 1:3 to 4:11 is not epistolary in form or in content; it contains not a single local or personal reference, and not a line to suggest that the people to whom it is addressed are undergoing persecution. This section is complete in itself, and has all the appearance of a separate composition. It has an easy and natural beginning in a comprehensive exordium (1:3-12), and it is rounded off with a concluding paragraph of succinct general exhortations (4:7-11), sealed by a doxology. If we examine it for itself, without allowing our interpretation to be determined by the epistolary setting in which we find it, we shall readily perceive that it is not a letter but a sermon, and that its theme is the nature and significance of the Christian life. It takes for granted a certain schooling in the elements of the Christian faith, such as would naturally be given to candidates for baptism;

and upon this basis it instructs them in the nature of the life which they have now embraced, exhorting them to follow faithfully in the footsteps of the unseen but beloved Master despite all the difficulties that belong to their situation in an environment of heathenism. ＼In short, it is a baptismal discourse, addressed to a group of recent converts. The references to trials (1:6), to suffering unjustly (2:19ff.), to 'suffering for righteousness' sake' (3:14ff.), are of the most general character; and in the last of these passages, the writer clearly assumes that if they are innocent of wrongdoing they can confidently expect to be vindicated before the Roman magistrate (3:15-16), and to put their accusers to shame. The profession of Christianity, the Christian life in itself, will not normally incur punishment at the hands of the authorities, though they must be prepared for occasional miscarriages of justice which will oblige them to 'suffer for doing good' (3:17). The sky is not entirely clear by any means, but no storm has yet broken over their heads. ＾Moreover, the section is written with deliberate care and slow elaboration. The long sentences, balanced and polished; the calm and measured tone; the pervading mood of tranquillity, all suggest that it was composed for a solemn occasion, while the peace of the churches was as yet undisturbed by the sudden outbreak of terror which occasioned the publication of the Epistle.

The passage which immediately follows (4:12ff.) breathes an entirely different atmosphere. The style is direct and simple. There are no carefully constructed periods or nicely balanced rhythms and antitheses, such as mark the preceding discourse. It has the quick and nervous language of a letter written in haste and under tension, without care for elaborations of style or loftiness of diction, to a flock that is undergoing the actual ravages of persecution. The situation envisaged is definite, and stands forth in vivid clarity. Suffering is no longer contemplated as a vague possibility for which Christians must always be prepared; it has become a stark actuality in the 'fiery ordeal' which is putting their faith to the test (ἐν τῇ πυρώσει πρὸς πειρασμὸν ὑμῖν γινομένη— not 'which is to try you', as in A.V., which suggests that it still lies in the future; but 'which is upon you for a testing', 4:11). They *are sharing* in the sufferings of Christ (v. 12); they are liable to be upbraided 'in the name of Christ', and to suffer at the hands of the governing authority 'as Christians' (vv. 14, 16). The terror of the time is such that it can only be regarded as the beginning of the Judgment of God (v. 17). The devil is abroad in the earth, like a lion seeking prey; and the Christian brotherhood throughout the world is facing the same ordeal of suffering for the faith (5:8-9). This is no general warning about the possibility of persecution, but an urgent message called forth by a crisis, an ordeal which is strange and incomprehensible to its victims (4:12) — clearly a situation for which the normal experience of pagan hostility afforded little preparation.

This later part of the book is truly epistolary in form and in content, and to this the address (1:1-2) and the closing greetings (5:12-14) properly belong. Into this framework, the baptismal discourse has been intruded, possibly by a later editor, but more probably by the writer himself. For in recognizing the composite structure of the book, there is no need to postulate two different authors; on the contrary, there is every indication that the writer of the letter to the persecuted also composed the discourse to the newly baptized. It would appear, then, that the Christian teacher who writes to rally his flock against their sore trial incorporates into his letter the words that many of them had heard from his lips on the occasion of their baptism. He would thus remind them that through the sacrament of regeneration they were brought into inward union with Christ in death and in the new life over which death has no power; and he would strengthen and console them with the thought that this union of heart and spirit was now being sealed by the unity of experience of suffering endured at the hands of wicked men. For them as for us, the whole teaching of the discourse would thereby be set in a new light, and they would be led into a more profound understanding of the faith into which they had been baptized. The Epistle will then have been sent forth by the writer in the form in which we now have it before us, even though the major portion was composed for a different purpose, and in more tranquil times; and the whole work receives a secondary unity from the circumstances of its publication.

The division of the Epistle along these lines was first demonstrated by R. Perdelwitz in his essay 'Die Mysterienreligion und das Problem des ersten Petrusbriefes' (Giessen, 1911, in the series *Religionsgeschichtliche Versuche und Vorarbeiten* [XI, 3]). It was supported also by Canon B. H. Streeter, in his remarks on First

Peter in *The Primitive Church* (New York, 1929), pp. 129 ff.; and
by H. Windisch, in 'Die katholischen Briefe' (*Handbuch zum Neuen
Testament*, ed. H. Lietzmann, XV; 2nd ed. revised; Tübingen, 1930).

The structure of the book may then be outlined as follows:

I.   The Salutation (1:1-2)

II.   The Baptismal Discourse (1:3-4:11)

III. The Letter Proper (4:12-5:11)

IV.   The Closing Greetings (5:12-14).

IV. THE DATE OF THE EPISTLE

The Epistle is not dated, and there is no early tradition either to
guide or to mislead us. We are therefore obliged to resort to
conjecture, based upon evidence of literary relationship to other
writings of the first and second centuries, and upon an attempt to
relate the historical situation presupposed by the Epistle to known
conditions within the Roman Empire during the period in question.

The literary relationships to be observed are twofold: we may
seek (1) evidences of the dependence of this book upon other New
Testament writings, and (2) evidences of the use of the Epistle
itself by later Christian writers.[1]

The facts of literary relationship between First Peter and several
of the Pauline Epistles including the deutero-Pauline Ephesians
are patent, and all critics are now agreed that the dependence is on
the side of First Peter.[*] (The attempts of earlier critics such as
B. Weiss and Kühl to argue that our Epistle is prior to the letters
of Paul must be regarded as a curious example of critical perver-
sity.) The Epistle must therefore be later even than Ephesians.
Most scholars now regard the latter as a work of the second Christian generation, and the studies of Professor E. J. Goodspeed[2]

[1] These relationships are examined in detail in the following works:—A. E.
Barnett, *Paul Becomes a Literary Influence* (Chicago, 1941); O. D. Foster, 'The
Literary Relations of "The First Epistle of Peter" with their Bearings on Date
and Place of Authorship', *Transactions of the Connecticut Academy of Arts and
Sciences*, Vol. XVII (New Haven, 1913); Oxford Society of Historical Theology,
The New Testament in the Apostolic Fathers (Oxford, 1905); and best of them all
—J. M. Usteri, *Wissenschaftliche und praktische Commentar über den ersten
Petrusbrief*, Pt. II, chap. ii, 'Die literarische Stellung und kirchliche Bezeugung
des Briefes' (Zürich, 1887).

[2] *The Meaning of Ephesians* (Chicago, 1933).

[*] This statement must be qualified. See the essay on 'First Peter in Recent
Criticism' (pp. 212ff.).

would appear to have established this conclusion beyond the reach of serious dispute. But as several modern scholars of the highest standing are still inclined to attribute it to Paul himself, we are perhaps not entitled to claim for it an assured dating of later than A.D. 64, the year of the Apostle's death. This, then, is a *terminus post quem* for the writing of First Peter.

The Epistle has unmistakable literary relationships with other New Testament writings also, especially with Hebrews and James; but they are not of a character to establish dependence definitely in one direction or the other. James and Hebrews themselves cannot be dated with certainty, and the question of their dependence upon or priority to First Peter must remain to be determined by the dates which may be assigned to them severally upon other grounds.

The first Christian writer to show unmistakable evidence of acquaintance with First Peter is Polycarp of Smyrna, in a letter which P. N. Harrison[1] has dated with good reason in the reign of the Emperor Hadrian, in A.D. 135. In the other Apostolic Fathers there is not a single passage that shows clear evidence of dependence upon our Epistle. Some degree of relationship has been claimed for First Clement, but the evidence to which appeal is made falls far short of a demonstration[2] and can in any case be employed in either direction; in the view of Harrison, for example, 'the literary relations between 1 Peter and other Christian writings seem to favour, for its origin, a date seventeen years or so after, rather than before, First Clement'.[3] Polycarp thus remains our earliest certain witness to the use of the Epistle. On the basis of literary relationships, accordingly, we can do no better than fix its date within the broad limits of A.D. 64-135.

Within this period there are three persecutions mentioned by ancient writers, Christian or pagan or both. At the very beginning, there is the persecution instituted by Nero immediately following the burning of Rome in A.D. 64. There is no good reason to challenge the trustworthiness of the tradition that Peter and Paul

---

[1] *Polycarp's Two Epistles to the Philippians* (Cambridge, 1936).

[2] Usteri, *op. cit.*, p. 324. 'Reminiscenzen aus I. Petri zwar möglich, aber keineswegs mit Sicherheit zu behaupten sind. Durchaus lässt sich das Zusammentreffen in einzelnen Citaten, Wendungen, und Ausdrücken auch ohne schriftstellerische Abhängigkeit wohl denken.'

[3] Harrison, *op. cit.*, p. 300.

both suffered martyrdom at Rome at this time. In none of our authorities, however, is there any suggestion that this persecution extended to the provinces. Tacitus and Suetonius look upon it as purely local in its origin and effects[1] — an outburst of savagery designed to turn away the anger of the Roman populace from the Emperor, whom they regarded as having been himself responsible for the setting of the fires in the City. But if the Epistle cannot be attributed to the time of Nero, it cannot have been written by the man whose name it bears, the Apostle Peter.

No one has presented the evidence against the possibility of a Neronian dating more cogently than Sir William Ramsay.[2] He develops his argument along three lines: first, that the legal and political aspects of the situation presupposed by First Peter are very different from those of the Neronian period;[3] second, that Christianity cannot reasonably be supposed to have reached Pontus before A.D. 65, and that a further ten years or so must be allowed for the development of organization and inter-communication which is presupposed by the Epistle;[4] and third, that the manner in which Romans and Ephesians are employed requires us to

---

[1] W. M. Ramsay, *The Church in the Roman Empire* (New York, 1893), p. 209f., holds on the contrary that the effects of a policy once adopted by an Emperor must have been felt almost at once in the provinces. 'The imperial policy ruled absolutely in the provinces, and the emperors, though not present, were consulted before even slight modifications of the general rules were made. The representatives who ruled provinces were not viceroys but merely deputies. This fact is very important to our subject: the policy throughout the Empire was moulded wholly by the wishes and views of the reigning Emperor.' This conclusion, however, rests wholly upon the evidence of the relations between Pliny and Trajan. Now Pliny was in the first place something of a sycophant; and in the second place, he was not in the typical position of a provincial governor: he had been sent out as 'legatus Augusti consulari potestate' to a province which had been until that time under the control of the Senate. Moreover, there was all the difference in the world between a Trajan and a Nero; between an administration headed by a vain and incompetent playboy and that headed by the strong and skilful Flavian Prince. It is very much to be doubted whether provincial governors paid the same deference to Nero, especially as his reign drew to its cloudy close, as Pliny showed to Trajan.

[2] *Ibid.*, pp. 196-295.

[3] *Ibid.*, p. 242. 'Pliny and Trajan both assume that Christianity is in itself a crime deserving of death. . . . But under Nero it is otherwise. The trial is held, and the condemnation is pronounced, in respect not of the Name, but of serious offences naturally connected with the Name (flagitia cohaerentia nomini).'

[4] *Ibid.*, p. 285. 'If we assume that this great further development had taken place in time for 1 Peter to be written about 75-80, we are straining historical probability as far as the evidence will reasonably permit. So far as an opinion is possible, they that make Peter write to the congregations of Pontus during Nero's reign remove the story of early Christianity from the sphere of history into that of the marvellous and supernatural.'

conclude not only that they had been written, but that since their publication sufficient time had elapsed to enable them to acquire a recognized authority.

Ramsay at first took it for granted that these historical conditions told decisively against the Petrine authorship, and in his lectures on the subject at Mansfield College he stated this conclusion. In the interval before their publication, however, he discussed the question with Hort, who firmly maintained the authenticity of the Epistle; and as a result of this conversation, he put forward another possibility. He still held that 'if it be proved that [Peter] died before A.D. 70, we should have to assign the composition (like 2 Peter) to another author'; but he then suggested the novel theory — which has, as far as I know, attracted not one lone supporter[1] — that the Apostle did not perish in the persecution under Nero, but lived on into the later years of Vespasian (died A.D. 79). For this conjecture, he offered as 'the strongest bit of evidence which we possess on the point', the reference of Tertullian (*De Praescr. Haeret.* 32) to a Roman tradition that Clement had been ordained by Peter! How he could regard this as historical 'evidence', in any sense, it is hard to see; there is in any case no way of calculating the date of Clement's ordination. The reference to *Scorpiace* 15, which Ramsay also gives, tells against his conjecture, for it couples the martyrdom of Peter with the Neronian persecution and lists it before the death of Paul. The most that can be said is that the date of Peter's death is by no means so well established as the fact of his residence at Rome. But if we are to be guided at all by tradition — and in respect of this problem we have no other guide — we have no reason to doubt that Peter was put to death not later than A.D. 66. The rejection of Ramsay's conjecture about the date of the Apostle's death, however, ought not to have blinded the defenders of the traditional authorship to his demonstration that no other hypothesis could save the day for them. If Peter died in the reign of Nero, he did not write the Epistle.

It should be said further that there is no evidence to show that the legal and political situation of Christians changed significantly for the worse in the reign of Vespasian, or that the Church in any part of the Empire was persecuted under his administration. Yet the Church was not apt to forget its conspicuous enemies, and if Vespasian had actually initiated a policy of persecuting 'for the

[1] It was in fact taken up in the article on I Peter in *Ency. Brit.* (14th ed.) by P. Gardner-Smith.

Name', not for the 'flagitia cohaerentia nomini', it is incredible that no Christian writer should have mentioned the fact. Moreover, if persecution 'for the Name' had been the settled policy of the Empire for over thirty years, it is not possible that Pliny, an experienced administrator, should have been in doubt about it.

A great many critics and commentators of recent times, perhaps the majority, have been inclined to date the Epistle in the reign of Domitian (A.D. 81-96). This theory appears to rest upon two considerations: first, that the Epistle is used by Clement of Rome (A.D. 96-97?); second, that some of the persons accused before Pliny confessed that they had once been Christians, but that they had renounced the new faith, some as many as twenty years earlier; and it is confidently assumed that they renounced under the pressure of persecution. But we have already remarked that Clement cannot be shown to have utilized First Peter; and there is nothing in the language of Pliny to suggest that the accused in question had recanted because of persecution; as the interpretation of the Parable of the Sower indicates, men forsook the Church for many other reasons also (Matt. 13:18ff.). But the chief objection to a dating under Domitian lies in the fact that there is little or no evidence for a persecution of Christians under this Emperor. Unless the book of Revelation can be indubitably ascribed to this period, there is nothing worth calling 'evidence' of persecution at all.[1] Moreover, even if we were to admit that this Emperor was a persecutor, and that his administrators persecuted the Church in Asia, there would still remain the problem of Pliny's ignorance, sixteen years after Domitian's death, of the principles of jurisprudence applicable to the trial of Christians. If Roman officials in Asia had for nearly twenty years been punishing Christians for the mere profession of allegiance to Christ, how could Pliny be in doubt whether the Name itself or the *flagitia* associated with it were to be punished?

We are therefore brought to a consideration of the one persecution for which we have clear evidence in the very region with which we are concerned. In the reign of Trajan (A.D. 98-117), persecution broke out in the province of Bithynia and Pontus

[1] See the discussions by E. T. Merrill, *Essays in Early Christian History* (London, 1924), chap. vi; R. L. P. Milburn, 'The Persecution of Domitian', *Church Quarterly Review*, CXXXIX, No. 287 (January, 1945); and J. Knudsen, 'The Lady and the Emperor', *Church History*, XIV, No. 1 (March, 1945), 17-32.

under the administration of Pliny the Younger, who became its
governor in the year A.D. 110-111. In a letter to the Emperor,[1]
dispatched a few months after his arrival in the province, Pliny
asserts (1) that he has never taken part in an examination of Christians and does not know whether the name itself or the offences
associated with the name are to be punished; (2) that many of all
ranks and of both sexes, including some Roman citizens, had been
accused before him as Christians (tamquam Christiani ... ὡς
Χριστιανός, 1 Peter 4:16); (3) that his inquiries, though pursued
with the use of torture, had brought out no evidence of wrongdoing, but that 'the sum of their fault was this — that they were
accustomed to meet on a fixed day, and to sing responsively a
hymn to Christ as to a god; and to bind themselves with an oath,
not for any criminal purpose, but not to commit thefts, robberies,
or adulteries, not to break their word, not to refuse to restore a
deposit when called upon to do so'; (4) that when they confessed
themselves Christians, he had at first threatened them with punishment, and when they persevered in their confession had ordered
their execution, on the ground that 'stubbornness and unbending
obstinacy certainly deserve to be punished'; and (5) that when it was
found that he took these cases seriously, the accusations multiplied.

Pliny's description of his experience and methods could not
conceivably correspond more closely to the words of 1 Peter
4:12-16;[2] and there is certainly nothing resembling it to be found
elsewhere in ancient literature or in official documents. It would
therefore seem unnecessary to look further for the persecution
which called forth our letter, and we may make the tentative conjecture that it was written at about the same time as Pliny's letter
to Trajan, i.e., A.D. 111-112.

It is clear, however, that Pliny is not creating new jurisprudence.
He does not know precisely what the practice of the Imperial
authority has been in dealing with Christians; but he takes it for
granted that the profession of this faith is illegal and liable to the
penalty of death, and the Emperor appears to confirm this. 'You

---

[1] Pliny, *Epist*. x. 96.
[2] J. W. C. Wand, *The General Epistles of St. Peter and St. Jude* (London,
1934), p. 15. 'There are phrases in Pliny's correspondence with Trajan which
might almost have been taken from First Peter.' This admission is all the more
remarkable in that Archbishop Wand is nevertheless able to persuade himself
that the Epistle belongs to the time of Nero.

have followed the proper course, my dear Secundus', he writes in reply, 'in dealing with the cases of those who are accused to you as Christians.'[1] It is therefore possible that the conditions described by Pliny may be read back into earlier times, and in fact we must suppose that the action of Nero had made the profession of Christianity illegal throughout the Empire. But it is one thing to have such a situation existing in law, and another to find the law actively applied against all offenders.[2] Pliny evidently found nothing in the judicial records of his own predecessors in Bithynia to guide him, and his own by no means limited experience had never brought him into contact with the trial of Christians in other parts of the Empire. Moreover, his own words suggest that in the earlier months of his governorship, Christians were brought before his tribunal only occasionally, but 'after a short while, as the offence was dealt with, the charge became common' (*mox ipso tractatu, ut fieri solet, diffundente se crimine*, etc.). When informers found that the charge was taken seriously by the new governor, they began to search for more victims, and the hunt was on in earnest. Previous governors may well have refused to entertain such accusations, and it is quite possible, and even probable, that the persecution of Christians became general in Asia Minor only when Pliny by his severe judgments whetted the zeal of informers, and satisfied them that their accusations would bring the desired results.

A further confirmation of this dating is found in the fact that the letters of Ignatius of Antioch, written during his journey to Rome to suffer martyrdom under the same Emperor, probably four or five years earlier than the coming of Pliny, show no trace of acquaintance with the Epistle, though they make much use of the letters of St. Paul. Now if such a letter had been in circulation in the provinces of Asia Minor for fifteen or twenty years, it seems unlikely that it would never have come to the attention of Ignatius, or that it would have left no traceable impression on the mind of one who was himself in the toils of the persecutor. But too much weight cannot be given to this consideration in the present state

[1] Pliny, *Epist.* x. 97.
[2] Ramsay, *op. cit.*, p. 193. The fact that Christianity was a *religio illicita* 'does not constitute a sufficient explanation of the persecution. The same prohibition applied to many other religions which practically were never interfered with'.

of our knowledge concerning the conditions under which Christian literature circulated at this early period.

All these considerations apply only to the letter proper, not to the Baptismal Discourse, which contains no specific indication of the conditions existing at the time of its composition, beyond the negative evidence that no persecution was actually raging, though the possibility of being called to suffer for the faith was ever present and had to be taken into account by the new converts. The language and ideas clearly reflect a time later than the Apostolic Age,[1] but is there any means of setting narrower limits for the production of such a work?

An attempt has been made by R. Perdelwitz, in the essay to which reference was made at the end of the preceding section. After putting forward the argument for the twofold division of the book he subjects several passages of the Discourse to a searching examination, in comparison with the texts of the mystery-cults, especially the cult of Cybele, and comes to the conclusion that this part of the Epistle also belongs to the world of the early years of the second century.

Perdelwitz himself recognizes the fragility of the evidence upon which he is obliged to rely. He is not primarily concerned with the question of dating, but with the problem of the extent to which the fundamental ideas behind the mysteries may be shown to have affected the language of our writer, and his presentation of the Christian religion. He does not take the position that the religious conceptions embodied in these cults have modified, much less that they have positively determined the character of the faith here exhibited, but rather that 'Peter' has pointed the essential *contrasts*, with a view to emphasizing the immeasurable superiority of what Christianity has to offer. He suggests that many of the expressions of the Epistle take on greater vividness when they are read against

---

[1] Wand (*op. cit.*, p. 24) observes that acceptance of the Neronic dating obliges us 'to draw conclusions with regard to the development of Christian thought which are somewhat unusual at the present time. We should have to recognize the *early* existence of a type of Christianity which can best be described as "central", and which bears a close similarity to that which was generally accepted in the fully organized church of the second century'. But if it be perceived that the general Christian attitude of the Epistle reveals such close affinities with that which we find in the literature of the second century, the most natural conclusion to be drawn is surely that the Epistle also belongs to that century, not that we must recast the entire history of the development of Christian thought in order to assign it to the seventh decade of the first century.

the background of the type of religion which was familiar both to the writer and to his readers, many of whom may have been devotees of Cybele or of Isis before their conversion to Christianity.

A single example of his exposition may be given, to illustrate how he approaches the problem, and the degree of success which attends his efforts. In an examination of 1 Peter 1:3-4, he begins with a study of the general ideas of regeneration, which appear in connection with all the mysteries. He finds that in them all, there is the basic thought that a new and divine life is offered to all the initiates, following upon the death of the old nature. This death to the old, and regeneration to a new life is accomplished by a cultic act; in the mysteries of Cybele, to which he devotes particular attention, it is the Taurobolium. For this fearful ceremony, the candidate was lowered into a pit with a grating over him; above this a bull was slaughtered, and the blood allowed to pour down over his whole body. On emerging, he was hailed as one 'reborn for eternity' (*renatus in aeternum*);[1] he was crowned with a wreath of laurel; and his bloody garment was stored away for him in the temple against the time when the ceremony would have to be repeated, twenty years later; for we meet the curious notion to which numerous inscriptions bear witness, that the 'eternity' thus acquired was secure for only twenty years. Against this background, Perdelwitz now sets the language of the Epistle. Here again we have the thought of a regeneration accomplished through a cultic act — in this case, baptism. But the life thus conferred is not limited to a span of twenty years; it is ἄφθαρτος (incorruptible, truly immortal). The Christian's inheritance is laid up for him in heaven, not in any earthly temple; and it is no garment stained with blood, but a treasure ἀμίαντος (undefiled). After the ceremony the mystes is given a crown of laurel, which must soon wither; but that which the Christian receives is ἀμάραντος (unfading). The three epithets are thus given an explanation which depends upon a single setting, and that in relation to a cultic act which is held to effect regeneration. The parallelism appears to him too complex to be merely accidental. It must at least be admitted that it adds great vividness and pertinence to the language, if we find it permissible to adopt such a line of approach at all.

---

[1] This phrase occurs only rarely; but there is no doubt that the rite always signified a rebirth.

A difficulty arises in the dating of the documents of the cults to which appeal is made. Many of those cited by Perdelwitz are much later than the Epistle, and others are of undetermined date. It is necessary also to reckon with the possibility of an influence of Christian ideas upon the theory and practice of the mysteries themselves. There is in fact no direct evidence for the rite of the Taurobolium in the cult of Cybele until after the middle of the second century, and none for its use in Mithraism until still later. Perdelwitz points out, however, that the oldest inscription to mention the rite belongs to Lyons, far up the Rhone valley, in A.D. 160. But this is in a region far removed from the home of Cybele, which was in Phrygia; and it is not unreasonable to suppose that it would be introduced in Phrygia and would spread through Asia Minor some years before it found its way to Rome, let alone to such a distant point as Lyons. We may be permitted to conjecture, then, that it had its beginnings in the East in the opening years of the second century. Perdelwitz is far from seeking to establish such a date for the Epistle on this basis; it is sufficient for his purposes to show that the early date of the Epistle does not render any such reference to the phenomena of the Taurobolium quite inconceivable. 'Die historische Situation also spricht jedenfalls nicht dagegen, dass der Verfasser mit den Worten 1, 4 den Taurobolienkult hat treffen wollen' (p. 50). It must further be conceded that if we find ourselves able to agree that he has sufficiently justified his claim that this writer shows evidence of some acquaintance with the Taurobolium, it would tell in favour of the dating under Trajan rather than anything earlier.

The evidence is really too fragile to permit us to feel that an acquaintance with this particular ceremony has been established. It is, however, impossible to escape from the fact that more general traces of the terminology of the cults or of the philosophy of religion associated with them are to be found in the Epistle. These would not of themselves require us to postulate a second-century date and we must recognize the possibility that the Baptismal Discourse was composed some years earlier than the persecution. At the same time, it will be felt that the presence of these indications brings us into a time long after the death of the great Apostles, when Christianity was wholly transplanted to Gentile soil, when relations with Judaism had ceased to be a matter of pressing importance, and when the real struggle was being waged against the powerful rivalry of the mystery-cults. To say the least, it is difficult to imagine such a situation existing much earlier than the end of the first century; and the more one examines the points of contact between the Epistle and the cults, the more one is inclined to feel that he is indeed in the religious atmosphere of the second century, to which the other evidence has already pointed us.

V. THE DESTINATION OF THE EPISTLE

The Epistle is addressed to the Christians of five districts of Asia Minor, which are listed as Pontus, Galatia, Cappadocia, Asia, and Bithynia — Pontus and Bithynia forming a single province. In a general way, it may be said that these provinces included the whole of the peninsula north of the great divide of the Taurus mountains. This area possesses a certain geographical unity, and was called by the Greeks τὰ ἐντὸς τοῦ Ταύρου. (Strabo, Geog. II, 5, 31; Dio Cass. LXXI, 23; cf. Livy XXXVII, 35, 10, etc. — *cis Taurum montem*). The narrow and rugged coastal strip south of the mountains (τὰ ἐκτὸς τοῦ Ταύρου), including Lycia, Pamphylia, and Cilicia, had poor communications with the north, and was connected much more closely in trade, culture, and administration with Syria and Cyprus.

Roman Pontus had been associated with Bithynia for administrative purposes from the time of Pompey. After the defeat of Mithridates (65 B.C.), his kingdom was divided, and only a narrow strip along the coast in its western parts, from the old frontier of Bithynia to the district around Amisus, was united with Bithynia, which had been bequeathed to the Roman people some ten years earlier by its last king, Nicomedes III. Most of the inland country was left under the rule of local chieftains, and was incorporated some sixty years later (6 B.C.) into the province of Galatia. In 2 B.C. a small region around the delta of the Iris River, just east of Amisus, was likewise added to Galatia under the name of Pontus Galaticus; and eight years afterwards the same province was enlarged to include the remaining sector of the ancient kingdom, the coastal lands east of the Iris, to which the name Pontus Polemoniacus was given.

The provinces of the Roman Empire, under the Augustan settlement, were divided between the Senate and the Princeps. In general, the Princeps reserved for himself the administration of the frontier provinces, where fighting had still to be done, and where the armed forces of the Empire were chiefly concentrated; while the Senate held authority over the interior provinces, where only a few cohorts were needed to maintain order internally. Bithynia and Pontus was a Senatorial province until the time of Marcus Aurelius (A.D. 161-180), except for brief periods under Claudius, Nero, and Trajan, when it was transferred temporarily to the direct care of the Emperor (or Princeps).

The province of Asia was one of the wealthiest and most populous parts of the Empire. It included the regions bordering on the western coast of the peninsula, to which the old names were still attached in popular usage — Mysia, Lydia, and Caria; together with the adjacent islands of the Aegean, and the Phrygian highlands in the interior. Here were the great seaports of Ephesus and Miletus, the rich islands of Rhodes and Lesbos, masters of seaborne commerce for centuries past, and many inland towns of considerable importance, such as Sardis, Pergamum, and Philadelphia. All this region had been evangelized by St. Paul and other missionaries of the first Christian generation, and there was perhaps no other part of the Roman world in which the Christian cause had taken such firm root and brought forth so many able leaders.

The province of Galatia included most of the great central plateau of Asia Minor from the foothills of the Taurus in the south to the wild and rugged Paphlagonian country in the north. The addition of the eastern Pontic regions gave it an outlet to the sea, with the important harbour of Trapezum (Trebizond). St. Paul had established a number of Christian groups in the province during his 'first missionary journey' (Acts 13-14), and others had followed him, partly to criticize him and undermine his authority, partly also to extend the mission in their own way. This province was under the Senate until the time of Vespasian (A.D. 70-79), who transferred its south-west corner to the province of Lycia and Pamphylia, and Pontus Polemoniacus to Cappadocia, and put the administration of the remainder under his legate for the latter province.

The territory of Cappadocia was a wild and inaccessible country of heavy forests and deep gorges, lying to the east of Galatia, between the mountains of Armenia and the headwaters of the Euphrates. In 72, Vespasian added to it the region known as Commagene, thus extending it to the Euphrates in the south-east; in the north, he attached to it a small sector of western Armenia. From his time, the means of communication were greatly improved, for he and his successors undertook a great programme of roadbuilding and repair throughout Asia Minor, opening the whole region for commerce as well as for military transport, in a development that was as important in its time as the building of the railroads through the American West in the nineteenth century. Rome's eastern frontiers were now the only ones where she confronted a foe able to match her legions in combat. In Armenia and along the middle Euphrates she faced the power of Parthia. In case serious trouble should break out, the legions permanently quartered in the East would not suffice to meet the danger, and it would be necessary to shift additional troops from the West, chiefly from the Danube lands. The Flavians were therefore bent upon providing better communications with the fortresses of the Eastern provinces by way of the road system of Asia Minor.

Along these lines of communication, the province of Bithynia and Pontus occupied a place of the greatest importance, for two great highways to the East, starting from the Bosporus and the Hellespont and providing the most direct route for the Danubian legions, ran through several of its principal cities. It was thus a necessity for Trajan, when he was making ready for his great Parthian war, to arrange with the Senate to have this province placed for a time under his direct authority. By virtue of this agreement Pliny was sent out to serve as 'Imperial legate with consular powers' (*legatus Augusti consulari potestate*) from A.D. 111 to 113.

For this was a troublesome province; social conditions were unhealthy and unstable. Although it was rich in natural resources and productive of great wealth, the masses of the population were kept on a level of bare subsistence. The Roman administrators tried to remedy or at least to check the worst abuses, but there was a property qualification for membership in the local councils, and the oppressed had no means of redressing their grievances. As a consequence, the peace was perpetually disturbed by local uprisings. The uneasiness of the urban proletariat is reflected in Pliny's letters to Trajan. After a bad fire in the capital city of Nicomedia, Pliny thought of forming a fire-brigade of 150 men, from which he apprehended no trouble; but Trajan declined to permit him to carry out this very modest plan, on the ground that in the existing state of the province, any such group was likely to prove a nucleus of disturbance. In a letter which reveals with startling clarity the dangerous mood of the populace, he bids Pliny remember that 'that province and especially those towns have been troubled by bodies of this kind. Whatever name we give to those who are brought into association, and whatever the purpose, they soon become gangs (hetaeriae brevi fiunt)'.[1] He advises him therefore to provide machines for firefighting, and to lay upon the property-owners themselves the chief responsibility for extinguishing fires.

In Bithynia, then, the capital city could not be permitted to organize a fire-brigade, even though the governor promised to take care in the selection of the personnel and judged that 'it would not be difficult to keep an eye on so small a group'. Trajan had learned from experience that all such formations were dangerous to the public peace. In such an atmosphere, it was inevitable that the congregations of the faithful should take on a sinister aspect in the eyes of authority; it helps to explain why the governor should have judged the Christians worthy of death for their obstinacy in refusing to give up their illegal association. Every small group, however innocuous or even laudable its aims, was looked upon as a possible source of intrigue and rebellion. A governor who had received his appointment primarily in order that he might assure undisturbed passage for Trajan's legions as they were being mobilized for a major campaign could not afford to take the chance of allowing such associations to continue. The unbending refusal to perform the usual rites before the statue of the Emperor could only serve to confirm the suspicion that the movement was essentially subversive.

These considerations may help us to approach the puzzling problem of the order in which the provinces are named, for which no convincing solution has yet been offered. The most peculiar

[1] Pliny, *Epist*. x. 34.

feature of the list is that it begins with Pontus and ends with Bithynia, though these are the two departments of a single province. If we may suppose, however, in the light of the peculiar circumstances of this province, that the persecution began there, and was there felt most severely, is it not possible that the letter was addressed primarily to the Christians of Pontus and Bithynia, and only secondarily to the rest of the area? The order in which the three other provinces are mentioned would then have no particular significance. Galatia and Cappadocia would naturally be coupled, as they had been for many years under a single administrator.

The suggestion was made by Ewald and strongly supported by Hort, that the order of the names reflects the route which the bearer of the letter (presumably Silvanus, on this theory) was to follow in delivering it to the churches. These critics suppose that he planned to come by sea from Rome through the Bosporus to a harbour of Pontus, probably Sinope; to proceed then through Galatia, perhaps taking the road which branched off the main highway from Amasis to Ancyra, the capital and chief city of that province. From Ancyra, he might go by way of Tavium and Melitene to Caesarea in Cappadocia, then returning westward along the southern trunk road through Arabissus and Caesarea Mazaca to Ephesus, on the Aegean, the capital of Asia. He would then make his way north to Bithynia through many towns and cities where Christian congregations had been long established, and take ship for Rome from one of the harbours of the Propontis.

The suggestion is ingenious and attractive, but it seems to take too little account of the conditions prevailing at the time, which were the immediate cause of the letter. When a fierce persecution was known to be raging, is it likely that people in Rome would be able to plan the itinerary of their messenger so carefully in advance? And is it right to assume, is it indeed remotely possible, that such an urgent message would depend for its circulation upon a single copy and be entrusted to a single messenger? It seems much more probable that numerous copies would be made, and that they would be transmitted as rapidly as possible, by many different channels, as opportunity offered or means could be devised.

We may conjecture, then, though without too much confidence, that the names of Pontus and of Bithynia are put at the beginning and the end of the list in order to give them prominence, since the writer's anxious concern is focused upon them as the storm centre; and the names of the other provinces are inserted between them to reflect his care for the whole region within the Taurus, since there was always the danger that the wave of terror would not stop at provincial boundaries but would extend its havoc into the neighbouring states.

VI. THE PROBLEM OF AUTHORSHIP AND THE PLACE OF WRITING

The salutation attributes the letter to 'Peter, Apostle of Jesus Christ', and the conclusion intimates that it was written at 'Babylon', and that Silvanus and Mark were with the Apostle when he wrote it.

There is nothing to indicate that the attribution of the letter to St. Peter was ever questioned in ancient times, although it happens that there is no evidence to show that it was known by his name earlier than the end of the second century. No writer before Irenaeus (*post* 190 A.D.) mentions the Apostle as the author, and it is not listed in the Muratorian fragment on the Canon. On the strength of this silence, Harnack[1] has ventured to conjecture that it circulated during most of the second century without either salutation or conclusion, not as a letter but as an anonymous Christian treatise; and that the name of Peter, with appropriate epistolary furnishings, was added to it by ecclesiastical authorities sometime after the middle of the century, to justify its inclusion in the canon of New Testament writings, then in process of formation. This hypothesis has found favour with some distinguished scholars, but it has no positive evidence to support it, and very little to commend it. In view of the frequent resort to pseudonyms in both Jewish and Christian literature of the period, there is no reason to suppose that it was not published with the salutation as we have it. The composition of pseudonymous letters is a fairly common device in purely Greek circles also, in Hellenistic and Roman times.

---

[1] A. von Harnack, *Die Chronologie der altchristlichen Literatur bis Eusebius*, I, pp. 451-65. Criticized by W. Wrede, 'Miscellen 3: Harnacks Hypothese über die Addresse des I Petrusbriefes', *ZNTW*, I (1900), pp. 75-85.

There can be no possible doubt that 'Peter' is a pseudonym. It has been shown above (Introduction, Section IV) that there are strong reasons for dating the Epistle in the reign of Trajan, and that in any case it must be later than the persecution under Nero, in which the Apostle met his death. This conclusion was based upon a study of the external conditions which called it forth. Equally weighty arguments against the Petrine authorship are to be found in the language and style of the writer himself. It is certainly true that if the name 'Peter' did not stand at the head of the Epistle, it would never have occurred to anyone to suggest him as the author.

In the first instance, it seems incredible that Peter should show such clear dependence upon the Epistles of St. Paul, with whom he had never had any close relations, while he makes little use of the language of Jesus, with whom he had been intimately associated during the whole period of his public ministry; and that he should rely wholly upon the words of Deutero-Isaiah, not upon his own reminiscences, in holding forth the example of Jesus' demeanour under suffering (2:21ff.). It is true that he does not expound the distinctive Pauline doctrines of freedom from the law, justification by faith and the mystical union of the Christian with Christ; but this is in part at least a matter of emphasis, and due in large degree to the character of the writing and of the people addressed. Much of what is generally regarded as most distinctive in the theology of St. Paul is worked out in opposition to a peculiarly Jewish religious legalism, which was of no concern to the Gentiles for whom First Peter is written. Even so, the book is strongly marked by the impress of Pauline theological ideas, and in language the dependence upon St. Paul is undeniably great. All through the Epistle, we have the impression that we are reading the work of a man who is steeped in the Pauline letters, who is so imbued with them that he uses St. Paul's words and phrases without conscious search, as his own thoroughly-assimilated vocabulary of religion. Entire passages are little more than an expansion or restatement of Pauline texts, and whole verses are a kind of mosaic of Pauline words and forms of expression. As a theologian, the writer has a mind of his own and is no mere echo of Paul, but it is abundantly evident that he has formed himself on Paul's writings. And as we have remarked above (Section IV) he makes use also of the Epistle to the

Ephesians, which is almost certainly the work of a later Paulinist, not of Paul himself. The conclusion to which we are led is that his Epistle is not only later than the time of Paul, but sufficiently late to permit of at least a partial collection of the Pauline letters being made and circulated. For most of the Apostle's letters were addressed to particular congregations in relation to local difficulties and problems; they would not be likely to be brought to the attention of a wider circle until some years after his death, when his name had become revered in the memory of the entire Church. In his own lifetime, and indeed for most of the next generation, the several letters would have only a local circulation, and a Christian teacher would have no opportunity to become acquainted with any but those that had been directed to the churches of his own region. But quite apart from the question of dates, it is hard to conceive that Peter himself, who for a time at least was not in entire sympathy with his fellow-Apostle (cf. Gal. 2:11-14), should finally have become his admiring disciple to the extent displayed by the writer of this Epistle.

In the second place, the writer of this Epistle is thoroughly well acquainted with the Old Testament Scriptures; but he appears to know them only in the Greek version and there is not a word in his writing to suggest that this knowledge is anything other than literary. The ready familiarity with the language of the Septuagint which he displays all through the Epistle is scarcely imaginable in a man who would have no occasion to use the Greek Scriptures at all until late in life. It will be recalled that as late as the Jerusalem Council (Acts 15 and Galatians 2; probably in A.D. 44), it was agreed that Peter along with James and John should go 'unto the circumcision', while Paul and Barnabas went 'unto the heathen' (Gal. 2:9; cf. v. 7 — 'they saw that the Gospel of the uncircumcision was committed unto me, as the Gospel of the circumcision was to Peter'). At this time, clearly, Peter was not even contemplating a mission of his own among the Gentiles, and would have no motive for studying the Scriptures in the Greek version. It is probable that during his flight from Jerusalem in the persecution under Agrippa, only a few months later, Peter was led quite unexpectedly to follow the example of Paul and Barnabas in carrying the Gospel to Gentiles at Caesarea (see my article 'The Sequence of Events in Acts 9 to 15, and the Career of Peter' in the

Journal of Biblical Literature, Vol. LXII, Part IV, December 1943,
pp. 295-306). For this modest beginning, he would not need
Greek; he would address the centurion's household in Aramaic,
the language of the country. Only as he extended his missionary
labours to more distant lands would he find it necessary to preach
in Greek; and as he was by then some fifty years of age, it would be
a most unusual feat for him, 'unlearned and ignorant' as he was
(Acts 4:13), subsequently to become so versed in the Greek Old
Testament as the author of our Epistle.

Moreover, this knowledge of the Scriptures which he exhibits is
a literary knowledge, not that of one who has himself practised the
religion of the Old Testament before becoming a Christian. To
the Jew, the Torah was the heart of the religion in which he was
reared; but to this writer, the substance of the earlier revelation
lay in its testimony to 'the sufferings of Christ and the glory that
should follow', and there is never a suggestion that he is troubled
by the problem that so strongly occupied the mind of Paul, the
problem of showing how a faith which made constant appeal to the
Old Testament could at the same time reject the fundamental
principle which based the whole religious life upon obedience to
the divinely-given Law. If this man was a Jew, he had emancipated himself from his own religious inheritance to a degree that
was never possible to Paul. On the other hand, the numerous
points of contact with the religious conceptions of the mysteries —
and they remain abundant even if we are forced to reject the
hypothesis of an acquaintance with the Taurobolium — seem to be
of such a nature as to indicate that he has known them as a
devotee, and that his own religious past lies there, and not in
Judaism. (So Perdelwitz — 'ich glaube aber, dass alle Stellen
unseres Schreibens an Anschaulichkeit und Lebendigkeit nur
gewinnen, wenn man sie auf ganz bestimmte, sowohl dem Verfasser wie seinen Lesern durchaus bekannte Erscheinungen
beziehen kann . . . Wenn seine Leser aus den Kreisen stammten,
die mit den religiösen Anschauungen und Gebräuchen der
Mysterien und besonders des Kybelekults vertraut waren, dann
verstanden sie ihn sofort, was er ihnen damit sagen wollte', *op.
cit.*, pp. 92-93, and 103.)

In the third place, and most decisively, the Epistle is quite
obviously the work of a man of letters, skilled in all the devices of

rhetoric, and able to draw upon an extensive and even learned vocabulary. He is a stylist of no ordinary capacity, and he writes some of the best Greek in the whole New Testament, far smoother and more literary than that of the highly-trained Paul. This is a feat plainly far beyond the powers of a Galilean fisherman, who at the time of the Crucifixion could neither read nor write even his own native tongue (Aramaic). For the word ἀγράμματος in Acts 4:13 means exactly that — not merely 'unlearned', but actually 'illiterate'. It is quite probable that there was some bilingualism in Galilee, and that a fisherman would be able to manage enough of the Greek of the marketplace to bargain for a good price for his fish, but that he should ever become a master of Greek prose is simply unthinkable.

The force of these considerations is admitted even by those who are most determined to uphold the authenticity of the Epistle, but they think that the difficulty can be overcome by ascribing to Silvanus (5:12) a large degree of responsibility for the language and style of the letter. Inasmuch as we know very little about this man, apart from the fact that he accompanied Paul on some of his missionary journeys, it is impossible to deny that he may have been capable of writing good Greek prose; as far as our knowledge goes, he may have been highly educated or altogether uneducated; it may at least be said that he had been associated with the mission among the Gentiles from a very early period. We should then have to ask why a man of the standing of Silvanus should not write in his own name to a region in which he himself had laboured, or why he should not at least be associated with Peter in the salutation, as with Paul in the Thessalonian Epistles. The fatal objection to this hypothesis, however, lies in the character of the teaching, most conspicuously in the meagreness of the references to the doctrine of the Spirit. Unless we disregard all the evidence of Acts and the Pauline Epistles concerning the life and thought of the Apostolic Age, it is impossible to believe that any important leader of that early period could have written about the moral life of Christians without paying any attention at all to the transforming power of the Spirit. It may be noted in passing that some commentators (Usteri, von Soden, and others) have suggested that Silvanus, independently of Peter, is the author of the Epistle, and that he wrote it a number of years after the Apostle's death.

This form of the Silvanus-hypothesis is no more attractive than the other. It seems clear that the mention of Silvanus in the closing greeting is merely a part of the apparatus of pseudonymity (see the commentary on 5:12).

The case against the attribution to Peter is overwhelming. It has been shown that it could not possibly have been written during his lifetime, unless we reject the well-established tradition that he died in the Neronic persecution, and make him live on well into Flavian times. And such a letter could not have been written by him, the illiterate fisherman, if he had lived to be over a hundred. The attempt to get around these hard and stubborn facts is due only to the erroneous feeling that if we admit the Epistle to be pseudonymous, we somehow deprive it of its authority and deny it a right to a place in the Canon of New Testament writings. But spiritual authority cannot thus be tied to questions of authorship and date. The intrinsic qualities of our Epistle entitle it to an assured place among the Holy Scriptures of the Christian faith, whoever may have been the author or whenever he may have written.

The use of the pseudonym need not trouble us in the slightest; the feeling that it is somehow fraudulent is a purely modern prejudice. It was not intended to deceive anyone, or to confer an undeserved lustre on the writing, any more than the various pseudonyms used by Kierkegaard. The Christians of Asia Minor must have known that Peter was long since dead, for the fame of such a martyrdom would quickly be spread throughout the churches of all regions. They would recognize the pseudonym for what it was — an accepted and harmless literary device, employed by a teacher who is more concerned for the Christian content of his message than for the assertion of his own claims to authority. Where a writing conveys, not the views and reflections peculiar to an individual, but a presentation of the common teaching of the society, the question of authorship becomes unimportant. The writer is only a minister by whom they may be instructed; and his teachings are important, not as *his* teachings, but as the doctrine of the Church.

Under such circumstances, a writer may issue his work anonymously, as in the case of the four Gospels and the Epistle to the Hebrews; or he may send it forth under a pseudonym, as in the case of the Petrine literature, the Epistle to the Ephesians, and the Pastoral Epistles. The pseudonym introduces an element of dramatic creation, akin to that which we find in the monologues of Browning (Andrea del Sarto, etc.). It requires of the writer an effort of the creative imagination. He does not simply attach a great name, chosen at random from the honour roll of antiquity, to his own words; nor is he concerned to gain an artificial prestige for his work by giving it such an honourable attribution. Like the dramatist, he seeks to re-create the personality of the one whose name he has chosen, and to make him speak in his own personality and accents. In First Peter, the effort has been attended with marked success. The theology clearly belongs to a post-Apostolic stage of development, and the style and language are of course those of the writer; but his personality is veiled behind that of the martyred Apostle who is here made to speak his noble words of instruction and encouragement for the benefit of another generation in its time of trial.

An unreal difficulty has been alleged, in the use of the name of Peter to head a letter addressed to a region evangelized by St. Paul. In fact, it is not so clear that this is a Pauline 'Missionsgebiet'. St. Paul might indeed claim to have been the founder of the Church in Asia, and to have been the first to preach the Gospel in Galatia. But his own letters show that others, and indeed a Jerusalem group unfriendly to himself, had worked in both these regions with some success even in his own lifetime. In Asia, indeed, his memory seems to have been eclipsed at a fairly early date by that of a John, who was so revered that he came to be identified with the son of Zebedee; and it was certainly not St. Paul that evangelized Bithynia and Pontus, to which the Epistle is primarily addressed. That region owed its knowledge of the Gospel to many different preachers, most of them unknown; and indeed the salutation may reflect a tradition that St. Peter himself had laboured there at some period of his life. At any rate, the attribution to St. Peter of a writing so imbued with the language of St. Paul indicates that for this writer there was no longer any recollection of any disharmony between the two great leaders. He draws upon the letters of the one, and upon the name of the other, as upon two that were chief in the noble army of martyrs, and hallowed in the memory of the Church as co-workers with God in the building of the foundations on which all subsequent construction must rest.

The mention of Mark and Silvanus, and also of Babylon, has no significance except as part of the device of pseudonymity. Babylon, of course, can be intended to mean neither the ancient city on the Euphrates, nor the Roman garrison-town in Egypt. As in the Apocalypse, it means Rome. But Rome is mentioned as the place of writing, only because St. Peter is put forward as the writer, and the connection of St. Peter with Rome was already firmly established in the tradition of the Church. With the definitive abandonment of the Petrine authorship, all reason for connecting the letter with a Roman author vanishes. Moreover, on the theory of a Roman origin, it seems impossible to account for the fact that there is no trace of its use in the Latin churches until the time of Cyprian.[1] As mentioned before, it is not listed in the Muratorian Canon, which is a document of the Roman Church of the end of the second century. It seems probable, accordingly, that it was written in the area to which it is addressed, by a presbyter of the region, who knew at first hand the sufferings of his flock under the terror. But we have no means of penetrating behind the pseudonym, and the true author remains hidden from us by the veil which he has himself chosen to draw.

VII. THE THEOLOGY OF THE EPISTLE

The Epistle is in no sense a theological treatise. The central doctrines of Christianity are presupposed, but they are not expounded or discussed; except for the brief Christological passages in 2:21-24 and 3:18-22 they are not even stated. The writer is concerned to set forth the manner of life to be followed by the Christian in the Church and in the world, and he refers to the doctrines of the faith only as to principles held in common by him and his readers, to which he may therefore appeal with confidence in seeking to direct their conduct. The elements of doctrine which are thus introduced are few and simple, seldom

---

[1] The references in Tertullian occur in writings whose genuineness is suspected; if he knew the Epistle at all, it was not until late in life. Its use by Irenaeus, and also the traces in the Epistle of the Churches of Lyons and Vienne, reflects the connection of the Gallic church with Asia Minor.

going beyond the fundamental instruction about God and Christ that would be given in preparation for baptism. Accordingly, he does not present anything like a *system* of Christian thought, nor does he attempt to enter into the profounder implications of the doctrinal teaching. He is directly concerned not with thought but with conduct and character; and his ground of appeal lies not in doctrines as such, but in the living relationship which has been established between the Christian believer and God through the life, death, and resurrection of Christ and through entrance into the Christian community by baptism.

The Doctrine of God

Christians know God as the Father who has begotten them again into a new life, which is inspired and directed by the hope of immortality and of a part in the triumphant consummation of God's purpose for the universe, soon to be realized (1:3-5). As His children, dedicated to His obedience, their lives are no longer to be governed by the impulses of desire, but by the constant aspiration after His holiness (1:14-16). He whom they have learned to invoke as Father is the Judge to whom they must render account; therefore they may not presume upon the intimate relationship to which He has admitted them, but must live in awe of Him, remembering that He judges without partiality 'according to each man's work' (1:17). God is to them the beginning and the end of all things. It is He that 'called them out of darkness into His marvellous light' (2:9); His all-determining 'foreknowledge' predestined them to be His own (1:1-2); His grace endows them with the gifts that enable them to serve Him and their brethren (4:10-11); His glorious Spirit rests upon them in time of persecution (4:14). Even the sufferings which they bear come upon them in accordance with His will, for their present chastening and future glory (4:12-13). He is the 'faithful Creator' who takes into His keeping the souls which He has made (4:19); He cares for His people and invites them to cast upon Him the whole burden of their anxieties (5:7); and He will at the last manifest the fullness of His grace in restoring, confirming, and perfecting them (5:10). As He has so revealed Himself, their faith and hope are in Him (1:21); all their relations with others are determined by the desire to please

Him and to do His will (1:17, 2:15, 18, 20; 3:2, 4, 12; 4:2), to glorify Him (4:11) and to lead others to glorify Him also (2:12). Clearly, the thought of this writer is not Christocentric but theocentric; it begins from and returns constantly to the thought of God as Creator, Father, and Judge, as the One whose will determines all that comes to pass, who shapes the destiny and determines the actions of those whom He has chosen for His own, who sustains them through the sufferings which He sends to test them, and who at the last will vindicate them and reward them eternally.

The Doctrine of Christ

The thought of Christ in the Epistle revolves almost entirely around two poles, viz., His sufferings and death, and His subsequent exaltation. These are regarded by the writer as the twin themes of Old Testament prophecy — 'the sufferings destined for Christ, and the glories that should follow' (1:11), and they likewise form the substance of the Gospel proclamation — it is 'these things which were now proclaimed to you by those who brought you the Gospel' (1:12). The fullest statement of his Christology is given in 3:18-22. 'Christ once suffered for sins, a just man for unjust men, that He might bring you to God; put to death in the flesh, He was made alive in the spirit, wherein also He went and preached to the spirits in prison; . . . baptism now saves you through His resurrection; He is at the right hand of God, having ascended into heaven, with angels and authorities and powers made subject to Him.' Here we are given something like a pre-statement of the articles of the Creed — 'He suffered (under Pontius Pilate); was crucified, dead, and buried; He descended into hell; (the third day) He rose again from the dead; He ascended into heaven and sitteth at the right hand of God.' To this, there is elsewhere added the thought of His coming in power — 'the revelation of Jesus Christ' (1:7, 13) — to 'judge the quick and the dead' (4:5), to reward the faithful with 'glory and honour' (1:6; 5:4) and to punish their foes; in that great day His glory will be revealed and will be shared with His followers (4:13; 5:1, 6). No specific mention is made of His pre-existence (though this has sometimes been read into 1:11 and 1:20), of His birth, or of His earthly ministry (apart from the Passion).

The significance of the death of Christ is set forth in a number of passages, though it receives less attention than the thought of the pattern which He provides for Christian conduct in His sufferings as an innocent victim of man's injustice. The 'blood' of Christ, shed in sacrifice, is represented (in a figure drawn from the imagery of Exodus 24) as 'sprinkled' upon the faithful for the establishment of a covenant between them and God, sealing them for His service in obedience to Christ and binding them to Him in a living communion (1:2). Again, in 1:18-19, 'the precious blood of Christ as of a lamb without blemish and without spot' is brought to mind as the effective power which has liberated believers from the futile life of paganism which was their natural inheritance. The vicarious aspect of His sacrifice is brought forward in 2:24, where it is coupled with the thought of moral efficacy — 'He bare our sins in His body on the tree, that we might die to sins and live to righteousness'; and again in 3:18, where it is associated with His mediatorial office of bringing us into the presence of God — 'He suffered for sins once, a just man for unjust men, that He might bring you to God'. Yet again, the thought that 'He was put to death in the flesh' (3:18='suffered in the flesh', 4:1) is made the ground of an exhortation to Christians to 'arm themselves with the same mind'; that is, to count themselves dead to the old life that was governed by 'the desires of men', in obedience to 'the will of the Gentiles', and to 'pass the remainder of their time in the flesh in devotion to the will of God' (4:1-3; an elaboration of the thought already suggested in 2:24). If this brief Epistle may be taken as any index, the writer finds the chief significance of Christ's death in the motive power which it gives for the dedication of life to God; for this thought alone is developed. In keeping with the common doctrine of the Church, he also believes that Christ's death was sacrificial, vicarious, and redemptive; but none of these ideas is given more than passing notice, and they seem to belong rather to his inheritance than to the essential fabric of his own thought. It would be rash, however, to insist upon such a conclusion, for a single work may reflect a particular emphasis which would not always be given by the teacher.

But above all other thoughts, this writer sees in Christ, both in His sufferings and in His glory, the Pattern which is set before the Christian that it may be unfolded anew in his own life. Christ suffered as an innocent man, and He endured the suffering patiently, submissively, without retaliation. In both respects He set the example which we are to follow (2:21-23). The Christian must take care not to do any wrong to justify the infliction of punishment upon him; and if he is called to suffer in innocence, let him endure in the spirit manifested by Christ, without reviling or threatening, without returning evil for evil, but on the contrary blessing his persecutors and glorifying God in the Name for which he suffers (2:19ff.; 3:9; 4:14-16). In such trials, he is 'sharing the sufferings of Christ', and will at the appointed time have the joy of sharing the eternal glory to which Christ has already been exalted. Christians live in hope of the revelation of that glory; its gleams already brighten their inward being, as they look in faith to the unseen Lord and are joined with Him in the bond of love (1:8).

The life and example of Christ are mentioned only in this context of His demeanour in suffering, and it is noteworthy that much of the language is borrowed from the Old Testament Scripture (Isaiah 53). There is not a word to indicate that a disciple of Jesus, an eye-witness of His conduct, is speaking; there is nothing that lies outside the range of that which would be familiar to all who knew the story of the Passion, even in its most general outline. The life of holiness is not grounded in the imitation of Christ, but on the nature of God Himself (1:15-16) and on the 'immortal seed' from which the regenerate life springs (1:23).

The Doctrine of the Spirit

The Spirit of God is mentioned only four times in the Epistle. In 1:2 the writer speaks of the 'sanctifying action of the Spirit' which accompanies election 'according to the foreknowledge of God the Father'; but no other reference is made to the idea of the Spirit as exercising moral power in the life of the believer; nor, in speaking of the χαρίσματα, the 'gifts of grace' which are imparted to all Christians, does he associate them with the activity of the Spirit in the Church; it is God Himself who supplies the strength in which they do their various services. Here certainly our author is no follower of Paul; but more than that, he seems far removed from the general atmosphere of the Apostolic Age. For in the great place which he gives to the Spirit in the life of the believer and of the Church, Paul shows no indication that he is offering a doctrine peculiar to himself; indeed, it is just in this area that he appears to be moving most completely in the full stream of the common Christian life and thought of his time. The Apostolic Age was above all, in its own consciousness, the Age of the Spirit; if we may affirm anything with confidence about the primitive church, it is surely this; and a writing in which the sense of the active presence of the Spirit has fallen into eclipse as it has in First Peter betrays by that indication alone that it is the product of a later generation. It is utterly inconceivable that to Peter, or to Silvanus for that matter, the doctrine of the indwelling Spirit was wholly unknown, or was not of the first importance for the moral life of the Christian.

The writer speaks again of the Spirit in 1:11 and 12. The 'Spirit of Christ' was in the prophets, 'testifying beforehand to the sufferings destined for Christ and the glories that should follow'; and these things were proclaimed by men who 'preached the Gospel by the Holy Spirit sent down from heaven'. Here the thought is of the Spirit accompanying the message of the Gospel, formerly in the prophets, afterwards in the Apostles. There is still no thought of the Spirit as a constant Presence in the believer and within the community.

The fourth reference to the Spirit is in 4:14, where the persecuted Christians are assured that in the midst of their sufferings under persecution, 'the Spirit of glory and power, the Spirit of God rests upon them'. This is a new application of an O.T. passage (Isaiah 11:2). It suggests again the thought of a visitation which is given under particular circumstances — a power to sustain them and a glory to reward them when they are being most sorely tested. Even here, the thought is not that the Spirit dwells in their hearts, as in the teaching of Paul; it is more akin to the O.T. idea of the Spirit coming upon men of God at particular times, to equip them for the immediate task.

The doctrine, then, is singularly undeveloped in the Epistle. This is clear evidence of affinity with the trends of the second century, not with the first age of the Church.

Baptism, Regeneration, and the Christian Life

As we have previously observed (Introduction, Section III), the principal theme of the writer over the major portion of the Epistle is the nature of the Christian life; more particularly, the manner in which the Christian is to conduct himself among his pagan neighbours. References to suffering are incidental to the main theme, until in 4:12 there is a sudden shift of emphasis which reflects the outbreak of a violent persecution. The impression, once widely held, that the writer is pre-eminently the 'Apostle of Hope', as if Hope received a disproportionate attention in this Epistle as compared with the rest of the New Testament, is quite false. He is indeed animated by the hope of the future glory, the coming 'revelation of Jesus Christ', but not more conspicuously than other N.T. writers; in fact, there is an equal or even a greater emphasis on hope in some of the Pauline writings (e.g., Rom. 8:12-25; 2 Cor. 5:1-10). The hope that is set before us in the Gospel is in this Epistle not so much a theme of instruction as one of the presuppositions, one of the elements of the common faith of Christians on which the writer bases his exhortations to a life of holiness, humility, and love.

The Christian life begins with Baptism, the sacrament of regeneration, wherein the believer enters into a new relationship with God, as of child to Father, receives the gift of immortality, and becomes heir to all the glories that God has purposed and promised to His people. This note is struck in the opening words of the Discourse: 'Blessed be the God and Father of our Lord Jesus Christ, who has regenerated us to a living hope through the resurrection of Jesus Christ from the dead, to an inheritance incorruptible and undefiled and unfading, reserved in heaven for you' (1:3). Christians have 'purified their souls by obedience to the truth', and are 'begotten again, not of mortal ("corruptible") seed, but of immortal ("incorruptible"), through the living and abiding Word of God' (1:23). In keeping with the same thought, those who have been baptized are addressed as 'new-born babes', and bidden to 'desire the pure spiritual milk' that will foster their growth 'unto salvation' (2:2). Again, in 3:21-22, they are taught: 'Baptism — not a washing away of the filth of the flesh, but a petition to God for a good conscience — now saves you through the resurrection of Jesus Christ, who is at the right hand of God.'

Baptism is here regarded not as a merely formal rite of initiation into the Christian community, but as a sacrament which communicates to the believer the lifegiving power of the risen and glorified Christ. The outward act finds its true significance in the spiritual transformation which is accomplished — the 'regeneration' to a new life which is the gift of God, mediated through His Word, centred not in earth but in heaven, issuing not from mere amendment of the old life, but from an 'immortal seed' implanted within. It is to be observed that this manner of thinking is not derived from Judaism; the bewilderment of Nicodemus at the proclamation of the necessity of a new birth (John 3:4) reflects truly enough how alien to Jewish theology this idea really was; a man could be 'a master in Israel', and yet know nothing of these things. We are dealing here with a body of ideas that Christianity borrowed from the contemporary Hellenistic modes of religious thought.

If the doctrine of regeneration found a ready entrance into the Christian teaching, it was because nothing else was adequate to express the sense of newness which men experienced in Christ; the sense that the old life had ended and a new life begun — new, not merely in direction and intention, but in essence; the sense that the supernatural, the heavenly, the divine, had broken in and displaced the earthly, natural, mortal life. Over a wide area, the Hellenistic philosophy had marked out paths which were eminently congenial to the Christian experience: a salvation which meant deliverance from the tyranny of the passions, and regeneration to enlightenment, knowledge, and immortality through mystical participation in the death and resurrection of the Saviour-God. But in its borrowing, Christianity was not merely imitative. Resting upon a radically different conception of God, of man, and of human destiny, these words and ideas received in the hands of Christian teachers a new content and a significant transformation. In the pagan conception, the initiate became himself a god, awakening as from a drunken stupor to the sober realization of the divinity within him; to the Christians, on the contrary, the new life is still a 'creation' (2 Cor. 5:17 — καινὴ κτίσις), and God stands above it as Creator and as Lord. The regenerate life, in the

Christian conception, is not self-sufficient; it is 'guarded by God's power' (1:5), and subject to His will (4:2); it seeks to be conformed to His holiness (1:15-16), stands responsible to His impartial judgment (1:17), and devotes itself to making known His wonderful works (2:9) and to glorifying Him in all things (4:11). Moreover, it is lived in the community of God's people, and finds its necessary expression in the 'love of the brethren' (1:22) and in mutual service (4:8-10); in this, it differs profoundly from the individualism, the solitary mysticism which characterizes the Hellenistic conception. Again, the Christian regeneration is not wholly realized in the present experience, which is but an earnest of the glory that is yet to be revealed; its significance is not to be apprehended except in relation to the consummation of the divine purpose in the 'Last Time', in the 'revelation of Jesus Christ' (1:5, 7, 11; 5:1, 6, 10). In the general framework of Hellenistic religion, time and history have no reality,[1] but the Christian thinker sees even the highest life as set in the conditions of the historical process as it has been ordered by God; regeneration is made possible for man through the mighty acts of God in Christ, when 'He raised Him from the dead and gave Him glory' (1:21; cf. 3:21-22), and is an anticipation of the fulfilment of God's purpose in creation and in history. The Saviour who has died and risen again is not a mythical figure like the 'lords' of the mystery-cults, but One who has lived a true human life upon earth, as a man upon men; who has laid down His life in love and voluntary self-sacrifice,[2] in humble obedience to the will of God, leaving His followers an example, that they may follow in His footsteps (2:21ff.); and mystical union with Him in His death and resurrection is significant above all in the transformation which it effects in the moral life — it is a death to sin, and a life to righteousness (2:24; 4:1-3).[3]

[1] The theologians of the mysteries clearly realize that the myths are merely graphic representations of natural principles, not tales of the experiences of the saviour-god. 'All this did not happen at any one time: the mind sees the whole process at once, words tell of part first, part second.' (Re the Attis-cult, in *Sallustius' Concerning the Gods and the Universe*, IV, ed. A. D. Nock; Cambridge, 1926.)

[2] J. Weiss points out that the Christian conception of the moral and spiritual character of Christ owes nothing to Jewish Messianism or to the mystery-cults; it derives from the historical personality of Jesus. *The History of Primitive Christianity*, trans. by Four Friends, ed. by F. C. Grant (New York, 1937), II, 450.

[3] On the relationship of Christian ideas to the religious thought of the contemporary paganism, see especially P. S. Minear, *And Great shall be your Reward* ('Yale Studies in Religion' XII [New Haven, 1941]) c. 5; J. Dey, Παλιγγενεσία:

The life which is imparted to believers in their regeneration is radically different from the old in its outward expression, as in its essence. The old way of life was futile, a mere following of ancestral custom with no sense of aim or purpose (1:18); lived in ignorance of the truth of God, it had no better guide than the impulses of desire (1:14). It was, in consequence, enslaved to the mass will ('the will of the Gentiles'), and given over to the vilest debauchery (4:3). The new way of life is grounded in hope; it is lived in the light of the unseen, eternal realities which God has made known in Christ, of the divine purpose of salvation that is shortly to be revealed (1:3-5). In all its relationships, it is determined by the knowledge of God. Christians are to obey Him, as children obey a Father. They are to be holy as He is holy, knowing themselves to be responsible to Him for all their deeds (1:14-17). As Christ has liberated them from their old vain courses at the sacrifice of His life, they are now faithful to the God who raised their Redeemer from the dead and glorified Him (1:18ff.).

The new life is lived in the community of God's people. Purified in soul, and endowed with immortality, they are to love one another with all their hearts (1:22-23), and to put away all the selfishness and deceit that would be incompatible with the love of the brotherhood (2:1). In living union with Christ and with one another, they are being formed into a spiritual household, whose function is worship — 'to offer spiritual sacrifices', 'to tell forth the wonderful works' of the God who has called them into His service. They are enjoined to give the first place to the maintenance of a strong and steadfast love for their brethren, offering them ungrudging hospitality when they come as guests, and devoting to mutual service all the powers of speech and of action that God has given them (4:8-11).

Their conduct amid the pagan environment in which they are called to live, as temporary sojourners in an alien land, is to be a silent testimony to their faith, such a manifestation of the beauty of holiness as may open the eyes of the bitterest opponents and turn them at last to God (2:12; 3:1-2). They are to accept in submissive humility the inequalities and injustices of the society in which

Ein Beitrag zur religionsgeschichtliche Bedeutung von Tit. 3:5 (Münster, 1937); and P. Gennrich, *Die Lehre von der Wiedergeburt in dogmengeschichtlicher und religionsgeschichtlicher Beleuchtung* (Leipzig, 1907).

they live, for this is God's will. The new sense of spiritual freedom must not move them to break the bonds of authority. Again and again the writer insists on the virtues of humility and submission, as if he apprehended some danger that the Christian cause might be set in a false light by the rashness of some of its adherents in challenging the existing social order. All Christians are to be submissive to the Emperor and to the Governors whom he appoints (2:13ff.); slaves are to be submissive to their masters, even to the harsh ones who punish them for no fault (2:18ff.); wives are to be submissive to their husbands, adorning themselves with the 'immortal beauty of the meek and quiet spirit' (3:1ff.); Christians who are brought before the magistrates to give account of themselves for their action in embracing the new faith are to comport themselves 'with meekness and in the fear of God', that they may disarm their accusers by their manifest goodness (3:15-16). To suffer for doing good and to bear the suffering patiently, without retaliation or threatening, is the genuine mark of the Christian, wherein he follows the example set by Christ Himself (2:21ff.), and is true to his own calling (3:9ff.). God will call his accusers to account (4:5), and will vindicate his faithful followers (1:7); and as they now share the sufferings of Christ, they will in due time share His glory (4:13; 5:6).

BIBLIOGRAPHY

This bibliography combines that of the 1st edition with that given in the Supplement of the 2nd edition, and includes a selection of works published since 1958.

1. Texts and Studies of the Greek Texts and Early Versions

(a) Papyri

Papyrus Bodmer VII-IX, ed. M. Testuz. Geneva-Coligny, 1959. VII and VIII, containing Jude and I and II Peter, are listed together under the siglum 𝔓72.

Petri Epistulae ex Papyro Bodmeriana, 2 vols., Milan, 1968. (Privately printed by command of Pope Paul VI.) Vol. I. Facsimile; vol. II, Transcription, with Introduction and apparatus criticus by Carlo Martini, s.j. The text of the Clementine Vulgate, as edited for A. Merk's *Novum Testamentum Graece et Latine* (9th edition, Rome, 1964) is printed opposite the transcription.

Papyrus Bodmer XVII, ed. R. Kasser. Geneva-Coligny, 1961. Contains a much dilapidated text of Acts and the Catholic Epistles. Of I Peter, all that remains consists of bits and pieces of seventeen verses scattered over ten pages of the codex, from 1:1-3:5. Listed as 𝔓74.

Un nuovo frammento della prima lettera di Pietro, ed. S. Daris. Barcelona, 1967. Contains 2:20-3:12, incompletely, on a single broken leaf. Listed as 𝔓81.

(b) Manuscripts on vellum or (rarely, and of late date) on paper

The major uncials (Vaticanus, Alexandrinus, Sinaiticus) have long been available in photographic facsimile. Codex Ephraemi Syri is known through the transcription of C. Tischendorf, recently reviewed and corrected by R. W. Lyon . The great codex Ψ, from the Lavra of Mount Athos, and the much less important codex S from the same library, are now available on microfilm (made by the Library of Congress in collaboration with the

International Project to Establish a Critical Apparatus of the Greek New Testament. Codex Daytonensis (0206) is a leaf of vellum containing, with some lacunae, part of chapter 5 (5-13), but it was published, with a transcription, as Oxyrhynchus Papyrus 1353 (*The Oxyrhynchus Papyri*, Vol. XI, ed. B. P. Grenfell and A. S. Hunt [London, 1908]). Readings of the other uncials are taken from the apparatus criticus of printed editions, primarily those of C. Tischendorf (Editio Octava Critica Major, Leipzig, 1872), of S. Tregelles (London, 1872), and of H. von Soden (*Die Schriften des Neuen Testaments, Text mit Apparat*, Göttingen, 1913; with a completely different system of notation which has been found unacceptable and almost unusable). Occasional readings are more conveniently found in the Oxford text of A. Souter (2nd edition, 1947) and in the pocket edition ('Taschenausgabe') first brought out by Eberhard Nestle and now in its 25th edition, edited by Erwin Nestle and Kurt Aland (*Novum Testamentum Graece*, Stuttgart, 1963; a 26th edition is in preparation).

A very large number of minuscules is now available on microfilm. Of these I have had at my disposal the Leicester Codex (69), photographed by the Town Museum of Leicester; and the following from the many microfilmed for the Library of Congress in association with the International Project; viz., from Mount Athos, 959 (Dionysios 254), 1854 (Iviron 231), and 1739 (Lavra B64); from the Greek Orthodox Patriarchate in Jerusalem, 1315 (Pan. Taph. 37), 1319 (Pan. Taph. 47), 1888 (Pan. Taph. 38), and 1889 (Pan. Taph. 43); and from the monastery of St. Catherine on Mount Sinai, 1240 (Mt. Sinai 259), 1243 (Mt. Sinai 262), 1248 (Mt. Sinai 267), 1874 (Mt. Sinai 273), and 1876 (Mt. Sinai 279). 33 and 2412 I examined directly, the former in the Bibliothèque Nationale in Paris, the latter at the University of Chicago.

(*c*) Manuscript Studies

Beare, F. W.: 'The Text of I Peter in Papyrus 72', in *Journal of Biblical Literature* 30, Part II (September, 1961), pp. 253-260.

—— 'Some Remarks on the Text of I Peter in the Bodmer Papyrus ($\mathfrak{P}^{72}$)', in *Studia Evangelica* III, ed. F. L. Cross (Berlin, 1964), pp. 263-265.

Carder, Mariel M.: *An Enquiry into the Textual Transmission of the Catholic Epistles*. Unpublished dissertation, Toronto Graduate School of Theological Studies, 1968.

Duplacy, J.: 'Critique textuelle du Nouveau Testament', in *Recherches de Science Religieuse* 50, No. 2 (April-June, 1962), pp. 242-262. On I Peter, see pp. 252-255.

Kubo, S.: 𝔓⁷² *and the Codex Vaticanus* (Studies and Documents, No. XXVII, ed. J. Geerlings). Salt Lake City, 1965.

Massaux, É.: 'Le texte de la Iᵃ Petri du Papyrus Bodmer VIII', in *Mélanges G. Ryckmans* (Ephemerides Theologicae Lovanienses XXXIX). Louvain, 1963.

Quinn, J. D.: 'Notes on the Text of 𝔓⁷² I Pt 2,3; 5,14; and 5,9', in *Catholic Biblical Quarterly* 27, No. 3 (July, 1965), pp. 241-249.

(*d*) Versions

1. Latin

Bover, J. M. (ed.): *Novi Testamenti Biblia Graeca et Latina*, 2nd edition. Madrid, 1950. The Latin text is that of the Clementine Vulgate, scrupulously reproduced even to the orthography (sometimes peculiar), but with some freedom in the matter of punctuation. The Clementine edition (1592) is the standard text of the Vulgate in the Roman Catholic Church.

[Beuron]. *Vetus Latina: Die Reste der altlateinischen Bibel* nach Petrus Sabatier neu gesammelt und herausgegeben von der Erzabtei Beuron. 26/2, *Epistula Prima Petri*. Freiburg, 1957. Includes also a newly constituted text of the Vulgate of the epistle, based on a fresh assessment of the evidence of the manuscripts and the *testimonia*.

Thiele, W. *Die lateinische Texte des I. Petrusbriefes*. (Published in a series of studies ancillary to the *Vetus Latina*: *Aus der Geschichte der lateinischen Bibel*, 5.) Freiburg, 1965.

[Wordsworth, J.] and White, H. L. (ed.): *Nouum Testamentum Latine secundum editionem Sancti Hieronymi* (Editio Minor). Oxford, 1911. The major edition was completed after the death of White; the section containing the Catholic Epistles, edited by H. F. D. Sparks, appeared in 1949, with the same text but a much fuller apparatus. Until the appearance of the Beuron text, this was the only modern critical edition of the Vulgate.

ii. Coptic

Horner, G. W. (ed.) *The Coptic Version of the New Testament in the Northern Dialect, otherwise called Memphitic and Bohairic.* Vol. IV. Oxford, 1905.

―― *The Coptic Version of the New Testament in the Southern Dialect, otherwise called Sahidic and Thebaic.* Vol. VII. Oxford, 1924.

Hyvernat, H., 'The J. P. Morgan Collection of Coptic Manuscripts', *JBL* 31, Part 1 (January, 1912), pp. 54-62.

―― *Bibl. P. Morgan Codices Coptici* 10, pp. 1-11. Rome, 1922. Facsimile of a 9th-century manuscript of the Catholic Epistles. Not used by Horner.

Willis, W. H. 'An Unrecognized Fragment of *First Peter* in Coptic', in *Classical Mediaeval and Renaissance Studies in Honor of B. L. Ullman,* ed. C. Henderson, Jr. (Storia e Letteratura 93, Rome, 1964), pp. 265-271. The publication of the Crosby Codex of the University of Mississippi, to be prepared by the same scholar, is still awaited. It contains our earliest Sahidic manuscript of I Peter, dated by Professor Willis in the first half of the 3rd century.

2. COMMENTARIES

Bengel, J. A.: *Gnomon Novi Testamenti.* 3rd edition, curante E. Bengel. Tübingen, 1773.

Bigg, C. A.: *A Critical and Exegetical Commentary on the Epistles of St. Peter and St. Jude* (I.C.C.). New York, 1901.

Calvin, J.: *Commentarii in Epistolas Canonicas.* Geneva, 1551.

Clement of Alexandria: *Adumbrationes in Epistolas Canonicas.* Ed. O. Stählin, in *Die Griechische Christliche Schriftsteller der ersten drei Jahrhunderten,* Vol. XVII. Leipzig, 1909.

Cramer, J. A.: *Catena in Epistolas Catholicas.* Oxford, 1840 (Catenae in Novum Testamentum, Vol. VIII).

Cranfield, C. E. B.: *The First Epistle of Peter.* London, 1950 (Torch).

DeWette, W. M. L.: *Kürze Erklärung der Briefe des Petrus Judas und Jacobus.* Leipzig, 1847.

Didymus of Alexandria: *In Epistolam Primam S. Petri Enarratio.* Patrologia Graeca, ed. J.-P. Migne, Vol. XXXIII, coll. 1755-1772. Paris, 1858.

Ewald, H.: *Sieben Sendschreiben des Neuen Bundes übersetzt und erklärt.* Göttingen, 1870.

Gunkel, H.: 'Der erste Brief des Petrus'. In *Die Schriften des Neuen Testaments*, Vol. III, 3rd edition, ed. W. Bousset and W. Heitmüller. Göttingen, 1917.

Hauck, F.: *Die Briefe Jakobus, Petrus, Judas, und Johannes.* 8th edition. Göttingen, 1957 (Das Neue Testament Deutsch 10).

Holtzmann, O.: *Das Neue Testament nach dem Stuttgarter griechischen Text übersetzt und erklärt.* Vol. II. Giessen, 1926.

Hort, F. J. A.: *The First Epistle of St. Peter I.1—II.17. The Greek Text with Introductory Lecture, Commentary, and Additional Notes.* Published posthumously. London, 1898.

Hunter, A. M. and Homrighausen, E. G.: 'The First Epistle of Peter: Introduction and Exegesis' (Hunter), 'Exposition' (Homrighausen), in *The Interpreter's Dictionary of the Bible* Vol. XII. New York and Nashville, 1957, pp. 76-159.

Huther, J. F.: *1 Brief des Petrus, Brief des Judas, und 2 Brief des Petrus* (Meyer's Kritisch-Exegetisch Kommentar, 3rd edition, Part 12). Göttingen, 1867. 4th edition revised, translated by D. B. Croom and P. J. Gloag, Edinburgh, 1881.

Kelly, J. N. D.: *The Epistles of Peter and of Jude.* (Black's New Testament Commentaries.) London, 1969.

Knopf, R.: *Die Briefe Petri und Judae* (7th edition of Meyer's Kommentar). Göttingen, 1912.

Kühl, E.: *Die Briefe Petri und Judae* (6th edition of Meyer's Kommentar). Göttingen, 1897.

Meinertz, M. and Vrede, W.: *Die katholischen Briefe.* In 'Die Heilige Schrift des Neuen Testaments', ed. F. Tillman, Vol. IX. 4th edition revised. Bonn, 1932 (Roman Catholic).

Moffatt, J.: *The General Epistles of Peter and Judas.* New York, N.D.

Monnier, J.: *La Première Épître de l'Apôtre Pierre.* Macon, 1900.

Oecumenius: *Petri Apostoli Epistola Catholica.* Patrologica Graeca, ed. Migne, Vol. CXIX, coll. 513-578. This is not the work of the 10th-century bishop Oecumenius of Trikka, but a catena drawn up in the 9th or 10th century which incorporates notes of the Homilies of St. John Chrysostom on the Pauline epistles made by the philosopher Oecumenius (6th century). The commentary on the Catholic Epistles is all but identical with that of Theophylact (11th century), who appears to have copied it.

Reicke, Bo: *The Epistles of James, Peter, and Jude.* (Anchor Bible.) New York, 1964.

Schelkle, K. H.: *Die Petrusbriefe, der Judasbrief.* 2nd edition. (Herders Theologischer Kommentar zum Neuen Testament, Bd. XIII, 2.) Freiburg im Breisgau, 1964. A superb commentary in every respect.

Schneider, J. *Die Kirchenbriefe.* Göttingen, 1961. (Das Neue Testament Deutsch 10.) First edition of a new series, replacing Hauck's 8th edition of the original series, but scarcely matching it for quality.

Schweizer, E.: *Der erste Petrusbrief.* Zürich, 1942; 2nd edition revised, 1949.

Selwyn, E. G.: *The First Epistle of St. Peter: The Greek Text with Introduction, Notes, and Essays.* London, 1946; 4th edition, 1952. This commentary, especially in its hypothesis of a very large use of catechetical forms in the composition of I Peter, has had great influence on subsequent studies. See my criticism in the Supplement, pp. 212 ff., and my review in *JBL* 65, Part III (September, 1946), pp. 329-333).

Semler, J. S: *Paraphrasis in Epistolam I. Petri cum Latinae Translationis Varietate et Multis Notis.* Halle, 1783.

Soden, H. von: 'Briefe des Petrus'. In Holtzmann's *Handkommentar zum Neuen Testament,* Vol. III, Part 12. 2nd edition. Freiburg im Breisgau, 1892.

Spicq, C. *Les Épitres de saint Pierre.* Paris, 1966. (Sources Bibliques.) Most valuable for its remarkably full bibliographical references, and for good textual and lexicographical notes.

Theophylact: *Expositio in Epistolam Primam S. Petri.* Patrologia Graeca, ed. Migne, Vol. CXXV, coll. 1190-1252 (Copied verbatim in great part from Oecumenius).

Usteri, J. M.: *Wissenschaftlicher und praktischer Commentar über den ersten Petrusbrief.* Zürich, 1887.

Wand, J. W. C.: *The General Epistles of St. Peter and St. Jude.* Westminster Commentaries. London, 1934.

Weiss, B.: *Das Neue Testament nach D. Martin Luthers berichtiger Übersetzung mit fortlaufender Erläuterung versehen.* Part II. 2nd edition. Leipzig, 1907.

—— *Die katholischen Briefe. Textkritische Untersuchungen und Textherstellung* (Texte und Untersuchungen zur altchristlichen Literatur, VIII, 3). Leipzig, 1892.

Wiesinger, A.: *Der erste Brief des Apostels Petrus.* In Olshausen's 'Biblischer Commentar', VI. Königsberg, 1856.

Windisch, H. *Die katholischen Briefe* (Lietzmann's Handbuch zum Neuen Testament, 15). 2nd edition, Tübingen, 1930. 3rd edition revised. H. Preisker, 1951.

Wohlenberg, G.: *Der erste Petrusbrief und der Judasbrief.* In Zahn's 'Kommentar zum Neuen Testament', XV. 3rd edition revised. Leipzig, 1923.

Wordsworth, C.: *The New Testament of our Lord and Saviour Jesus Christ in the Original Greek; with Introductions and Notes.* 'The General Epistles, Book of Revelation, and Indices'. 3rd edition. London, 1864.

3. General Works of Reference

The older Introductions are obsolete, so far as I Peter is concerned. Good accounts of recent discussion will be found in W. G. Kümmel's (14th) edition of the Feine-Behm *Einleitung*, now in the English translation of A. J. Maddill, Jr.; and in the *New Testament Introduction* of A. Wikenhauser (E. T. by J. Cunningham, New York, 1958). The 2nd edition of A. H. McNeile's *Introduction to the Study of the New Testament*, revised by C. S. C. Williams (Oxford, 1953) is also useful, but much less thorough.

The great Blass-Debrunner *Grammatik des neutestamentliche Griechisch* (9th-10th German edition) is now available in the English translation by R. W. Funk, with some revision and supplementary notes by A. Debrunner, under the title *A Greek Grammar of the New Testament and Other Early Christian Literature* (Chicago, Cambridge, Toronto: 1961).

The *Grammar of New Testament Greek* begun by J. H. Moulton (Vol. I, *Prolegomena* [Edinburgh, 1906; 3rd edition, reprinted 1919]); and continued by W. F. Howard (Vol. II, *Accidence and Word-Formation* [Edinburgh, 1919]), has now been completed by N. Turner (Vol. III, *Syntax* [Edinburgh, 1963]).

The Kittel *Theologisches Wörterbuch zum Neuen Testament* (in process; Vol. I, Stuttgart, 1933) is being rendered into English by G. W. Bromiley (now published to Vol. VI, Grand Rapids, 1969), under the title *A Theological Wordbook of the New Testament*.

4. ESSAYS, ARTICLES AND MONOGRAPHS

Bieder, W.: *Grund und Kraft der Mission nach dem ersten Petrusbrief*. Theologische Studien 29. Zürich, 1950.

Blinzler, J. "Ἱεράτευμα: zur Exegese von I Petr. 2:5 und 9', in *Episcopus: Studien ... Kardinal von Faulhaber dargebracht*. Regensburg, 1949, pp. 49-65.

Boismard, M.-E.: *Quatres Hymnes baptismales dans la prèmiere Épître de Pierre*. Paris, 1961.

—— 'Une Liturgie baptismale dans la *Prima Petri*. I. Son influence sur Tit., I Jo. et Col.', in *Revue Biblique* 63, No. 2 (April, 1956), pp. 182-208. 'II. Son influence sur l'epitre de Jacques', *ibid*. 64, No. 2 (April, 1957), pp. 161-183. Note that the subheadings refer to the influence of the 'baptismal liturgy', not of I Peter, on the other epistles.

Brandt, W.: 'Wandel als Zeugnis nach dem ersten Petrusbrief', in *Verbum Dei Manet in Aeternum* (Festschrift for Dr. O. Schmitz), ed. W. Foerster. Wittenberg: Luther-Verlag, 1953.

Bultmann, R.: 'Bekenntniss- und Liedfragmente im ersten Petrusbrief', in *Coniectanea Neotestamentica* XI (in honorem A. Fridrichsen). Lund: Gleerup, 1947. Pp. 1-14.

Carrington, P.: 'Saint Peter's Epistle', in *The Joy of Study: Papers on New Testament and Related Subjects to Honor Frederick Clifton Grant*, ed. S. E. Johnson. New York: Macmillan, 1951. Pp. 57-61.

Coutts, J.: 'Ephesians i.3-14 and I Peter i.3-12', in *New Testament Studies* Vol. III, No. 2 (January, 1957), pp. 115-127.

Crehan, J.: *Early Christian Baptism and the Creed*. London, 1950.

Cross, F. L. *I Peter: A Paschal Liturgy*. London: Mowbray, 1954.

Dalton, W. J.: *Christ's Proclamation to the Spirits*. Analecta Biblica 23. Rome, 1965.

Dautzenberg, G.: 'Σωτηρία Ψυχῶν', in *Biblische Zeitschrift* N.F., VII.2 (July, 1964), pp. 262-276.

Foster, O. D.: *The Literary Relations of 'The First Epistle of*

Peter', with their Bearings on Date and Place of Authorship. Transactions of the Connecticut Academy of Arts and Sciences, Vol. XVII. New Haven, 1913.

Gennrich, P.: Die Lehre von der Wiedergeburt in dogmengeschichtlicher und religionsgeschichtlicher Beleuchtung. Leipzig, 1907.

Goguel, M.: 'La seconde génération chrétienne' (suite et fin) in Revue de l'Histoire des Religions CXXXVI, No. 2 (October-December, 1949), pp. 180-202; on I Peter, see especially pp. 200-202.

Goodspeed, E. J.: 'Some Greek Notes: IV Enoch in I Peter 3:19', in Journal of Biblical Literature 73, Part II (June, 1954), pp. 91ff.

Johnson, S. E.: 'Preaching to the Dead' [I Peter 3:18-23], in JBL 79, Part I (March, 1960), pp. 48-51.

Jeremias, J.: 'Zwischen Karfreitag und Ostern', in ZNTW XL (1949), pp. 194-201.

Kamlah, E.: Die Form der katalogischen Paränese im Neuen Testament. Tübingen, 1964.

Knox, J.: 'Pliny and I Peter: A Note on I Pet. 4:14-16 and 3:15', in JBL 72, Part III (September, 1953), pp. 197ff.

Krafft, E.: 'Christologie und Anthropologie im ersten Petrusbrief', in Evangelische Theologie (1950), pp. 120-126.

Leaney, A. R. C.: 'I Peter and the Passover', in NTS 10. No. 3 (April, 1964), pp. 238-261.

LeDéaut, R.: 'Le Targum de Gen. 28 et I Peter 1:20', in Recherches de Science Religieuse 49 (1961), pp. 103-106.

Lohse, E.: 'Paränese und Kerygma im I Petrusbrief', in ZNTW XLV (1954), pp. 68-89.

Meecham, H. G.: 'The Use of the Participle for the Imperative in the New Testament', in Expository Times LVIII, No. 8 (May, 1947), pp. 207f.

Mitton, C. L.: 'The Relationship between I Peter and Ephesians', in JTS, new series, Vol. I, Part 1 (April, 1950), pp. 67-73. Written later, though published earlier, than the following item, which took no account of Selwyn's commentary.

—— The Epistle to the Ephesians, c. XVII, 'The Relationship between Ephesians and I Peter'. Oxford: Clarendon Press, 1951.

Moule, C. F. D.: 'The Nature and Purpose of I Peter', in NTS 3, No. 1 (November, 1956), pp. 1-11.

Nauck, W.: 'Freude im Leiden: zum Problem einer urchrist-lichen Verfolgungstradition', in *ZNTW* XLVI (1955), pp. 68-80.

—— 'Probleme des frühchristlichen Amtsverstandnisses (I Ptr 5:2f.)', in *ZNTW* XLVIII (1957), pp. 200-220.

Perdelwitz, R.: *Die Mysterienreligion und das Problem des ersten Petrusbriefes* (Religionsgeschichtliche Versuche und Vorarbeiten XI.3). Giessen, 1911 (MR).

Reicke, Bo.: *The Disobedient Spirits and Christian Baptism: A Study of I Pet. iii. 19 and its Context.* (Acta Seminarii Neotestamentica Upsaliensis, ed. A. Fridrichsen, XIII). Copenhagen: Munksgaard, 1946.

—— 'Die Gnosis der Männer nach I Ptr. 3:7', in *Neutestamentliche Studien für Rudolf Bultmann*, ed. W. Eltester (Beiheft zur *ZNTW* 21). Berlin: Töpelmann, 1954.

Reitzenstein, R.: *Die hellenistichen Mysterienreligionen nach ihrer Grundgedanken und Wirkungen.* 3rd edition revised. Leipzig, 1927. (HMR³).

Selwyn, E. G.: 'Eschatology in I Peter', in *The Background of the New Testament and its Eschatology*, ed. W. D. Davies and D. Daube in honour of Charles Harold Dodd. Cambridge: C.U.P., 1956. Pp. 394-401.

—— 'Unsolved New Testament Problems: The Problem of the Authorship of I Peter', in *Expository Times*, Vol. LIX, No. 10 (July, 1948), pp. 256-259.

Spicq, C.: *Agapè dans le Nouveau Testament: Analyse des Textes.* Vol. II. Paris, 1959. Chapter V, 'Ἀγάπη, ἀγαπάω dans les Épitres de saint Pierre et de saint Jude' (On I Peter, see pp. 307-341. The Petrine letters are not treated in the article in the Kittel *Wörterbuch*).

Spitta, F.: *Christi Predigt an die Geister (I Petr. 3:19ff.): Ein Beitrag zur neutestamentliche Theologie.* Göttingen, 1890.

Staab, K.: 'Die griechischen Katenenkommentare zu den katholischen Briefen', in *Biblica* V (1924), pp. 296-353.

Thornton, T. C. G.: 'I Peter, a Paschal Liturgy?', in *JTS* n.s. 12 (1961), pp. 14-26.

Unnik, W. C. van: 'The Teaching of Good Works in I Peter', in *NTS* 1, No. 2 (November, 1954), pp. 92-110.

Weiss, B.: *Der petrinische Lehrbegriff.* Berlin, 1955.

Wibbing, S.: *Die Tugend- und Lasterkataloge im Neuen Testament.* Beiheft zur *ZNTW* 25. Berlin, 1959.

Windisch, H.: *Taufe und Sünde im ältesten Christentum bis auf Origenes: Ein Beitrag zur altchristlichen Dogmengeschichte.* Tübingen, 1908.

Zuntz, G.: *The Text of the Epistles: a Disquisition upon the Corpus Paulinum* (Schweich Lectures for 1946). London, 1953.

TEXT AND NOTES

I. THE SALUTATION

ΠΕΤΡΟΥ Α

I. ¹ Πέτρος ἀπόστολος Ἰησοῦ Χριστοῦ ἐκλεκτοῖς παρεπιδήμοις διασπορᾶς Πόντου, Γαλατίας, Καππαδοκίας, Ἀσίας καὶ Βιθυνίας, ² κατὰ πρόγνωσιν θεοῦ πατρός, ἐν ἁγιασμῷ πνεύματος, εἰς ὑπακοὴν καὶ ῥαντισμὸν αἵματος Ἰησοῦ Χριστοῦ· χάρις ὑμῖν καὶ εἰρήνη πληθυνθείη.

Peter, Apostle of Jesus Christ, to the chosen sojourners of the Dispersion in Pontus, Galatia, Cappadocia, Asia, and Bithynia; in accordance with the foreknowledge of God the Father, by the sanctifying action of the Spirit, unto the obedience and blood-sprinkling of Jesus Christ; — to you may grace and peace be multiplied.

I. ¹ εκλεκτοις)+και ℵ syrr Ασιας) om ℵ* και βιθυνιας) om B* ² υπακοην) +πιστεως sah Χριστου)+του κυριου ημων boh

(On the Authorship and Destination, see Introduction, Section v and vi.)

The salutation is a variation upon the form by which Greek letters of the period commonly opened — ὁ δεῖνα τῷ δεῖνα χαίρειν — 'A to B, greetings'. Each of the three elements receives elaboration, most significantly the last of them, where the colourless infinitive χαίρειν, conveying vague and formal 'greetings' is expanded into the distinctively Christian prayer for the divine gifts of grace and peace.

A similar conclusion to the salutation had been adopted by St. Paul and the language here is clearly influenced by his practice. 'Grace and peace from God the Father' is almost the hallmark of the Pauline correspondence. It must be noted that this phrasing did not establish itself in common Christian usage; wherever it is found, therefore, we are obliged to see direct and deliberate literary dependence upon St. Paul. Christian letters among the papyri use the formula ἐν κυρίῳ (πλεῖστα) χαίρειν, with minor variations.

The combination εἰρήνη πληθυνθείη, however, is not Pauline.

73

It is a borrowing from the Greek Old Testament, where it occurs in letters of Nebuchadnezzar and Darius in the Greek version of Daniel 3:98 and 4:34c (Lxx). It is used again in First Clement.

v. 1.   ἐκλεκτοῖς παρεπιδήμοις διασπορᾶς⟩ 'to the chosen sojourners of the Dispersion'. As the general form of the salutation reveals dependence upon the Pauline models, so this phrase is the first of a number in the Epistle which show a marked resemblance to the language of 'James', in the address to 'The Twelve Tribes which are in the Dispersion'. — (ταῖς δώδεκα φυλαῖς ταῖς ἐν τῇ διασπορᾷ). In neither case is the expression to be taken literally, as if the epistles were concerned primarily with Christian Jews resident beyond the bounds of Palestine. Whatever may be said of the Epistle of James, it is clear that First Peter is addressed to people who had been converted to Christianity from paganism (see 1:18, 2:10, 4:3 etc.); the Jewish Diaspora is here regarded as a symbol of the Christian Church.

In the form which the expression takes in our Epistle, it may quite possibly suggest initially that the Christians of these provinces were not yet organized in settled congregations; but that over most of the area there were individuals here and there, or occasional families isolated in the sea of paganism; or at most, scattered groups endeavouring to maintain a fellowship of faith without the stimulus of numbers or of strong, competent leadership. This would hardly be true of the province of Asia, for there the principal towns and cities had Christian congregations of some strength, and Ephesus was one of the main centres of evangelistic and theological work. But it is probable that in the rest of the Asian peninsula the Christian cause was as yet feeble and its adherents few and far between, so that they could be described with literal accuracy as 'sojourners of dispersion'. The words have, however, a deeper significance than any which derives from the temporary circumstances of the churches and people addressed; the symbol of the Diaspora, as we shall see, is full of meaning in relation to the life of the Church in the world at all times.

The word ἐκλεκτοῖς, which we render 'chosen', is not a passive participle as the translation would imply, but is a verbal adjective, a formation which had only a loose attachment to the verb system. It is indifferent to distinctions of tense and voice; it may be intransitive, active, or passive, and the verbal force itself frequently disappears. ἐκλεκτός in the papyri is used in the sense of our word 'select' or 'choice', much as we use 'picked' in the phrase 'picked troops'. This sense is conveyed here also. The 'sojourners of Dispersion' are choice souls, rare spirits, picked warriors, who can be counted on to maintain the faith of their Master amidst perils of torture and death. But like the word κλητός which St. Paul prefers in his own salutations (Romans, 1 Corinthians), it conveys also the sense of the divine election or calling which has made them what they are. The conviction that God had laid His mighty Hand upon them for good was a constant inspiration and strength to men who lived in daily jeopardy, facing trial by fire, and with no earthly refuge or support.

παρεπιδήμοις⟩ 'sojourners' — used of those who are temporary residents, not permanent settlers in the land; who have a deeper attachment and a higher allegiance in another sphere. It is the counterpart of the thought that everything in this life is transitory, and that Christians 'look not at the things which are seen, but at the things which are not seen: for the things which are seen are temporal, but the things which are not seen are eternal' (2 Cor. 4:18). He whose eyes are fixed upon the eternal can never feel himself anything but a sojourner among things temporal (Cf. Heb. 11:13-16.) It is in this sense that the writer imagines the Church as a new Diaspora. The Jewish communities which had established themselves in every port and commercial city of the Mediterranean world remained attached to the Holy Land and gave their primary allegiance to the spiritual authority of Jerusalem; they continued to regard themselves as sojourners in the various lands of their adoption, even when their families had been settled abroad for hundreds of years. The Christian communities likewise looked to another land as their true home. Not the earthly Jerusalem, but 'the Jerusalem which is above', was the centre of their life; their citizenship was in heaven (Phil. 3:20). Scattered over the whole earth, as alien residents of lands in which they could never be truly at home, they were united in the common bond of loyalty to the unseen State of which they sought to prove themselves worthy citizens.

The general thought is admirably expounded in an anonymous Christian writing composed some decades later. — 'Christians are not marked out from the rest of mankind by their country or their speech or their customs ... They dwell in cities, both Greek and barbarian, each as his lot is cast, following the customs of the region in clothing and in food and in the outward things of life generally; yet they manifest the wonderful and openly paradoxical character of their own (unseen) State. They inhabit the lands of their birth, but as temporary residents thereof; they take their share of all responsibilities as citizens, and endure all disabilities as aliens. Every foreign land is native to them and every native land, foreign territory ... They pass their days upon earth, but they hold citizenship in heaven' (*Epistle to Diognetus*, 5).

'Pontus, Galatia, Cappadocia, Asia, and Bithynia.' On the provinces to which the Epistle is addressed, see Introduction, Section v.

'In accordance with the foreknowledge of God the Father, through the sanctifying action of the Spirit, unto the obedience of Jesus Christ and the sprinkling of His Blood.' This threefold phrase cannot possibly be taken exclusively with ἐκλεκτοῖς 'chosen', from which it is separated by no less than eight words in the Greek text. It is related to the entire salutation, and has a measure of connection with each part of it — to the apostolate of Peter, to the election of the dispersed sojourners, and to the grace and peace which the writer prays may be theirs. The office of apostle, the call to discipleship, and the gifts of grace and peace come all alike 'according to the foreknowledge of God the Father, by the sanctifying action of the Spirit'; and issue in 'obedience to Jesus Christ and the sprinkling of His blood'.

'According to the foreknowledge of God the Father.' — The foreknowledge of God, in Biblical usage, always applies primarily to persons and includes the thought of the divine Providence and of the divine Will for human life. 'Before I formed thee in the belly, I knew thee; and before thou camest out of the womb I sanctified thee, and I ordained thee a prophet unto the nations' (Jeremiah 1:5). In this first 'word of the Lord' which came to Jeremiah, it is the man himself that is the object of the divine foreknowledge, and his sanctification and ordination to the prophetic calling are immediate developments and consequences thereof. The same connection of ideas is characteristic of Paul; see especially Romans 8:29-30; where God's foreknowledge leads through predestination, calling, and justification, to ultimate glory. Another Pauline phrase is perhaps more directly relevant to the thought here. In Romans 11:2, the Apostle writes 'God hath not cast away his People (i.e. Israel), which He foreknew'. By a further extension of the thought of the Church as the true Israel, this writer now affirms that God's foreknowledge, with all that it conveys of providential care, appointment to His service in the world, and glorious privilege, embraces also these feeble and scattered communities of Asian Christians and ensures the fulfilment of their high destiny.

v. 2. ἐν ἁγιασμῷ πνεύματος⟩ 'by the sanctifying action of the Spirit'. ἁγιασμός may mean either 'sanctifying action', or 'holiness'; and the phrase is thus susceptible of two interpretations. In the first sense it would refer to the hallowing power which the divine Spirit brings to bear upon the life of believers; in the second, it would mean the inward, spiritual sanctity of character — 'holiness of spirit' — which results from dedication to the service of God. The same phrase occurs, with something of the same ambiguity, in 2 Thessalonians 2:13 — 'God chose you unto salvation'. . . ἐν ἁγιασμῷ πνεύματος καὶ πίστει ἀληθείας — 'through sanctification of spirit (the Spirit?), and belief of the truth'. In that passage it seems best to take the two phrases as parallel, both expressing not the divine activity but the human response — 'holiness of spirit and belief in the truth'. In this salutation, however, it is natural to suppose that the writer has in mind the trinitarian baptismal formula 'In the Name of the Father, and of the Son, and of the Holy Spirit'; and for that reason the rendering 'by the hallowing activity of the Spirit' is to be preferred. In the words of Dr. Hort (cited below, p. 53), the Christian is 'daily breathed upon by an invisible Power of good'.

εἰς ὑπακοὴν καὶ ῥαντισμὸν αἵματος Ἰησοῦ Χριστοῦ⟩ 'Unto obedience and sprinkling-of-the-blood of Jesus Christ.' This is a hendiadys, the 'obedience' and the 'blood-sprinkling' being two aspects of a single thought. The blood of Christ is the seal of a new covenant between God and man, which requires the response of obedience. In a rather violent symbolism, the sprinkling with water in baptism is treated as figuring the sprinkling of the community with the blood of sacrifice. The figure is taken from the story of Exodus 24, where the people pledge their obedience to the Law of God, the Commandments which Moses has received on Mount Sinai; and Moses sprinkles over them the blood of the oxen offered in sacrifice (the peace-offerings). 'He took the book of the covenant, and read in the audience of the people; and they said, All that the Lord hath said will we do, and be obedient. And Moses took the blood, and sprinkled it on the people, and said, Behold the blood of the covenant, which the Lord hath made with you concerning all these words' (Ex. 24:7, 8). There is no thought here of atonement or of vicarious suffering. It goes back rather to the primitive idea of the sacrifice as a sacrament which binds the worshipper and his God together in vital communion, establishing between them a current of life in which both alike participate. In the Christian (as in the Hebrew) thought, this fellowship of man with God has the most profound moral consequences; it must issue in man's obedience to the revelation of the divine will for him. The blood of sacrifice, which is the sign and seal of the covenant made between God and man, is indissolubly linked with the obedience without which the communion cannot be maintained.

The threefold phrase, then, sets forth in splendid clarity, the eternal purpose of God, its effective operation through the power of the divine Spirit sanctifying the inward life, and its issuance in the obedience to Jesus Christ which is the fulfilment of the covenant sealed in His blood.

χάρις καὶ εἰρήνη⟩ 'Grace' and 'peace' are perhaps the most comprehensive words in the Christian vocabulary, summing up all that man receives by the free and unmerited gift of God, on the one hand; and on the other, the whole inward state that results from enjoyment of the divine goodness. 'Grace' includes forgiveness, and love, and mercy, and power, and whatsoever else God has to bestow in His goodness. 'Peace' includes the entire experience of the soul that is at one with God, and in harmony with itself and with its fellows. The prayer that 'grace and peace be multiplied' asks therefore that they receive more and more of the divine bounty, and that it may bear its perfect fruit in their lives.

II. THE BAPTISMAL DISCOURSE

A. The Exordium. A panegyric on regeneration and the glories of the Gospel (vv. 3-12).

B. The Body of the Discourse, in three parts:

Part I. The Fundamental Moral Demands of the New Life (1:13-2:10):

holiness, based on the knowledge of God as Father and as Judge and of Christ as Redeemer (1:13-21); and

love, the proper fruit of the holiness and immortality which belong to the new life, the bond of a sacred fellowship of priestly service to God, whereof Christ is the centre (1:22-2:10).

Part II. The Attitude and Conduct becoming to Christians in a pagan environment (The Haustafel) (2:11-3:12).

Part III. A Commendation of the life of goodness, as (1) the best safeguard against harsh treatment, or (2) if suffering nevertheless is inflicted, giving it a meaning akin to the meaning of the sufferings of Christ (vicarious and redemptive) (3:13-4:6).

C. The Peroration. A final exhortation to love and mutual service, concluding with a doxology (4:7-11).

This portion of the Epistle is complete in itself. It neither needs nor benefits from the epistolary setting. As Streeter remarks (*The Primitive Church*, p. 129), it 'reads, not like a letter, but like a *sermon*'. It will appear, as we proceed with the commentary, that the section as a whole finds its best interpretation when it is treated as a baptismal discourse, and that a number of passages stand out in a clear and vivid light only when they are seen to be addressed to a group of recent converts. Moreover, once the Discourse is separated from the remainder of the Epistle, and is read for its own message without reference to the burning words which follow it in 4:12ff., it becomes clear that its principal theme is not steadfastness under the pressure of persecution, but an exposition of the significance of Baptism as the sacrament of regeneration, a body of instruction and exhortation respecting the character and conduct which should accompany and flow from their profession of Christian faith, and from the spiritual experience into which they have entered.

The persons to whom the discourse is addressed are of course not the children of Christian parents, baptized in infancy, but converts from paganism for whom baptism is the seal of conversion, the act of public profession, and the symbol of admission to all the privileges of the Christian society. For such as they, baptism and confirmation are one; and the instruction to be given corresponds, *mutatis mutandis*, to that which would follow confirmation in circumstances akin to our own. Any grappling with problems of doctrine, any controversial exposition would be entirely out of place. A plain statement of the meaning of the sacrament and of the nature of the Christian life, with its ideals, its perils, its joys, and its unfailing resources — this is what the occasion requires and it is precisely this that the Epistle sets forth.

A very fine literary parallel is afforded by a letter of Professor Hort, which he wrote to his eldest son on the occasion of the latter's confirmation. I venture to quote at some length from this letter, partly as a modern example of the type of document that we are studying, but even more for its own sake, as a little gem of instruction in the elements of the Christian faith.

'The first thought that I would press upon you is that Confirmation is not the laying of a burden upon you. In so far as it has anything to do with burdens, it simply reminds you of a burden which is already there, and then gives you strength to bear it. But what is the burden? Simply the responsibility of a human being, a child of God, endowed with reason and conscience and affection that you may do the work of God, and in doing it grow more and more like to Himself, inheriting from your ancestors a constant liability to fall into evil, yet redeemed to good at an unspeakably costly price, and daily breathed upon by an invisible Power of good . . .

'You are reminded of temptations from three sources: from the evil customs and opinions of the people who surround you; from lawless indulgence of bodily cravings and desires; and from the spirit of evil, whispering pride and scorn and jealousy and hatred into your inner self. The means given you for turning all temptations into occasions of firmer and riper life is the recollection,

Whose you are and Whom you serve, and entire grasping at His love and help in prayer.

'Let the touch of the good old Bishop's hands upon your head dwell always in your memory as a sign of the Hands of blessing which are ever being laid upon your head out of heaven. Let nothing ever make you doubt or forget your heavenly Father's love and desire of your good, or dream that He can ever cease His patient working in and for you and all His children. Remember that you are called to share His work, and that everything which makes you useless, not to say mischievous, to others, makes you unworthy of that for which He created you. May his inexhaustible blessing be upon you always. . . .' (*Life and Letters of F. J. A. Hort*. By A. F. Hort. Vol. II. Macmillan's, London, 1896, pp. 272-4).

³ Εὐλογητὸς ὁ θεὸς καὶ πατὴρ τοῦ κυρίου ἡμῶν Ἰησοῦ Χριστοῦ, ὁ κατὰ τὸ πολὺ αὐτοῦ ἔλεος ἀναγεννήσας ἡμᾶς εἰς ἐλπίδα ζῶσαν δι' ἀναστάσεως Ἰησοῦ Χριστοῦ ἐκ νεκρῶν, ⁴ εἰς κληρονομίαν ἄφθαρτον καὶ ἀμίαντον καὶ ἀμάραντον, τετηρημένην ἐν οὐρανοῖς εἰς ὑμᾶς ⁵ τοὺς ἐν δυνάμει θεοῦ φρουρουμένους διὰ πίστεως, εἰς σωτηρίαν ἑτοίμην ἀποκαλυφθῆναι ἐν καιρῷ ἐσχάτῳ.

Blessed be the God and Father of our Lord Jesus Christ, who according to His abundant mercy has regenerated us unto a living hope, by the resurrection of Jesus Christ from the dead — unto an inheritance incorruptible and undefiled and unfading, which is kept in the heavens for you who are being guarded by God's power through faith — unto a salvation which is ready for its revealing at the Last Time.

³ αυτου ελεος) ελεος αυτου 33. 69 vg   ⁴ ουρανοις) pr. τοις ψ: ουρανω ℵ* υμας) ημας ϛ   ⁵ ετοιμην) ετοιμως ℵ

v. 3. The opening words of blessing to God are borrowed outright from St. Paul, who uses the same phrase in the beginning of 2 Corinthians. They occur again in the third verse of Ephesians, where they are followed by a participial clause, as here, to bring out the specific cause for which we bless Him. The phrase 'Blessed be God' occurs again and again in the Greek Old Testament, often with a clause attached to recall the particular action which inspires the utterance of adoration and thanksgiving; e.g., Psalm 66:20 — 'Blessed be God, which hath not turned away my prayer, nor His mercy from me'; 1 Maccabees 15:34 — 'Blessed be God, which hath kept His own place undefiled'. The Apostolic expansion of the blessing reminds us that Christians know God primarily as the 'Father of our Lord Jesus Christ', in whom He meets us also as *our* Father and makes known to us His nature and His will.

God is blessed, then, as the author of the grace received in baptism; he has regenerated us, created in us a new and divine life. The same connexion of thought, cast in strikingly similar language, is found in Titus 3:5 — 'according to His mercy He saved us, by the laver of regeneration and renewal by the Holy Spirit'. The thought, though not the technical language, still derives from St. Paul. The Apostle does not use the words 'regenerate', 'regeneration', etc., in any of the forms that are found elsewhere in the New Testament — παλινγενεσία, ἀναγεννάω, ἀναγέννησις, ἄνωθεν γεννηθῆναι. All these terms appear to have been introduced into the Christian vocabulary by Gentile teachers of post-Apostolic times, probably appropriating the language of the pagan mysteries to Christian uses. (See H. Windisch, *Die katholischen Briefe*, 2nd edition, Tübingen, 1930, p. 59, in an excursus on 1 Peter 1:23 and 2:1.) But it is only the particular words that are lacking in St. Paul's exposition of the sacrament; the underlying idea is manifestly present. In Romans 6:3-4, he teaches that baptism symbolizes death and resurrection, or more exactly, indeed, that it sacramentally effects the mystical union of the believer with Christ, in death to the life of this world and in resurrection to the life immortal. The καινότης ζωῆς — 'newness of life' — of which he there speaks, into which men enter through baptism, is the precise equivalent of the life to which men are 'begotten again', in the later terminology. Still more distinctly, the association of regeneration, or newness of life, with the resurrection-life of Christ, reflects the dependence of our writer upon St. Paul.

κατὰ τὸ πολὺ αὐτοῦ ἔλεος〉 'according to his abundant mercy' — As in the Titus passage, the words are to be taken as rejecting the thought that the grace received is in any sense a reward for our merits. It is 'not by works of righteousness which we have done, but according to His mercy'. In Titus, the thought is explicit: here it is implicit. ἔλεος — 'mercy', is the correlative of χάρις — 'grace': better, perhaps, it is grace itself seen under a particular aspect, grace exercised in forgiveness. In regeneration, when God by an act of grace makes us his sons, he mercifully forgives and removes all that makes us unworthy of sonship.

The blessing for our regeneration is followed by a threefold definition of the new life into which we have been brought; God has regenerated us εἰς ἐλπίδα ζῶσαν, εἰς κληρονομίαν . . . , εἰς σωτηρίαν 'unto a living hope, unto an inheritance, unto a salvation'. There is a progressive widening of the thought from (1) the nature of the inward life to (2) the spiritual possessions to which it gives title, and ultimately to (3) the total fulfilment of God's will in all his creation.

'Unto a living hope.' The words undoubtedly suggest a vigorous, firm, vivid hope, in contrast with any lifeless philosophical doctrine of immortality or any wavering anticipation of blessedness such as men may entertain apart from Christ; but this thought is far from exhausting the meaning of the phrase. We have here, rather, a pregnant paraphrase for the new life itself; the interpretation is to be sought along the lines of the θυσία ζῶσα — the 'Living Sacrifice' of Romans 12:1. As St. Paul entreats the Christians of Rome to 'present (their) bodies a living sacrifice', so this writer suggests that the regenerated man is himself, in the very essence of his new being, 'a living hope'. If we may be permitted to hark back at the same time to the ὕδωρ ζῶν 'living water' of John 4:10ff.(cf. 7:38), we might say that the life of the Christian is in itself 'a living hope'; in its attitude towards God, 'a living sacrifice'; and in its outflow, a springing fountain of 'living water' for the blessing of the world.

v. 4. The idea of the κληρονομία goes back to the Old Testament thought of the land which was promised to Abraham 'for an inheritance', and which became in due time the possession of his descendants; the 'inheritance' promised to Abraham becomes the patrimony of the

nation, and it is the sense of a divinely-given *patrimony* that is needed
here. But the patrimony of Christians is no earthly Land; it is the
spiritual reality of which the Promised Land of Israel was but a symbol.
(The contrast of Symbol and Reality is not, however, expounded here,
as it is in the Epistle to the Hebrews.) Those that are begotten anew by
God and admitted to the privileges of divine sonship thereby acquire
title to a share in the divine patrimony. (Cf. Rom. 8:17 — 'If children,
then heirs; heirs of God and joint-heirs with Christ'. In this context
also, the 'Inheritance' is conceived in terms of the future glory.)

ἄφθαρτον καὶ ἀμίαντον καὶ ἀμάραντον⟩ Hort thinks that ἄφθαρτον
may reflect the use of φθείρω in the military sense of 'ravage', and
suggests 'never ravaged by hostile armies'. The verbal can equally
well bear the meaning 'never to be ravaged' — suggesting 'a Promised
Land beyond the reach of ravaging armies'. It is more naturally taken,
however, in the more general sense of 'not corruptible, not perishable,
not liable to pass away', as in v. 23 ('begotten again not of corruptible
seed but of incorruptible'), where the thought is unquestionably of
immortality. Cf. 1 Cor. 15:48-53; *Ep. to Diognetus*, sec. 6 — ἀθάνατος
ἡ ψυχὴ ἐν θνητῷ σκηνώματι κατοικεῖ· καὶ χριστιανοὶ παροικοῦσιν ἐν
φθαρτοῖς, τὴν ἐν οὐρανοῖς ἀφθαρσίαν προσδεχόμενοι. — 'the soul, itself
immortal, dwells in a mortal tabernacle; even so Christians sojourn
among things corruptible, while they wait for the incorruptibility that
is in the heavens'; *Poimandres*, 27:28 — μεταλάβετε τῆς ἀθανασίας,
καταλείψαντες τὴν φθοράν. The word thus recalls the contrast between
the imperishable quality of the heavenly, and the evanescence of all
earthly goods, which finds frequent expression in the New Testament
(Matt. 6:19, 20; Lk. 12:16-21; John 6:27; etc.).

ἀμίαντον⟩ 'undefiled, unstained by evil (and unstaining)' — rarely
occurs in the New Testament. (In the Gospels, the Pauline Epistles,
and the Apocalypse, the Hebraic locutions κοινός, κοινόω — 'common',
'make common' — are used of defilement; e.g. Mark 7:15-23; Rom.
14:14; Apoc. 21:27.) The thought here is not in the least of ceremonial
defilement but of moral and spiritual evil. Cf. Plato, *Laws*, Book VI,
777E. ἀμίαντος τοῦ τε ἀνοσίου πέρι καὶ ἀδίκου — 'as touching im-
purity and injustice, undefiled'. There may also be a reminiscence of
the words of 2 Maccabees 15:34 — 'Blessed be God who has kept his
own place undefiled' — ὁ διατηρήσας τὸν ἑαυτοῦ τόπον ἀμίαντον —
where the thought of ceremonial defilement is certainly present, but in
connection with the intrusion of alien enemies; the word 'inviolate'
would be an exact rendering.

ἀμάραντον⟩ 'unfading', cf. the 'amaranthine flowers' of *Apocalypse
of Peter* 5:15 (τὴν γῆν ... ἀμαράντοις ἄνθεσιν ἄνθουσαν — 'the land
— with amaranthine flowers blossoming'); the word suggests a
supernal beauty which time does not impair. The paronomasia of the
three verbals is most effective; the inheritance is untouched by death,

unstained by evil, unimpaired by time; it is compounded of immortality, purity, and beauty. (See also the suggested interpretation of R. Perdelwitz, which is discussed in the Introduction, Section IV.)

τετηρημένην ἐν οὐρανοῖς) 'watched over, kept under watch, in the heavens'. τηρέω means basically, 'watch'; and thence 'keep watch over', or more generally 'keep'. The expression takes us back to Colossians 1:5 — 'the hope which is laid up for you in the heavens'. ἀποκεῖμαι, the verb used in the Pauline passage, is the ordinary business term, found many times in the papyri, of storage in a granary or other place of safekeeping; the substitution of τηρέω here conveys a more vivid apprehension of the active providence of God; the inheritance is not merely 'lying safely in store' (ἀποκειμένην) but kept under God's watchful care.

v. 5. 'Guarded by God's power'. φρουρέω — 'guard' — belongs to the military vocabulary, and the use of the present tense emphasizes our need for continual protection in the unending struggle of the soul. Christians are not removed from the arena of combat into a haven of safety. They remain in the field of spiritual battle, where dangers encompass them and they are subject to continual attack. But they are not left to their own resources; they are being guarded by God's power, and this is the guarantee of final victory. Their own part is the exercise of faith, which lays hold on the divine power.

εἰς σωτηρίαν ἑτοίμην ἀποκαλυφθῆναι ἐν καιρῷ ἐσχάτῳ) 'unto a salvation ready to be revealed in the Last Time'. This phrase has a double connection; it depends upon ἀναγεννήσας (v. 3) and also upon φρουρουμένους. Once begotten again unto salvation, Christians are perpetually guarded by God's power until the salvation is finally made manifest. σωτηρία — 'salvation', like σωτήρ — 'saviour', is one of the many words which Christianity took over from the current paganism to endow them with a deeper and richer content. (See the article 'Σωτήρ: eine religionsgeschichtliche Untersuchung', by P. Wendland, in *ZNTW*, V (1904), pp. 335ff.; and the Excursus on the meaning of σωτήρ in M. Dibelius' commentary on the Pastoral Epistles [Lietzmann's *Handbuch zum Neuen Testament*, 13], under 2 Tim. 1:10.)[1] Zeus and Asklepios were commonly given the title 'Saviour', and many other deities received it occasionally; Persephone, the Queen of Hades, is called Σωτεῖρα and this feminine form of the title is given to several of the great goddesses (Isis, Athena, Artemis, etc.). The same title could even be given to kings. (Ptolemy Soter, the founder of the Macedonian dynasty in Egypt; Eumenes II in Asia Minor, and others.) Thus it may mean Healer, or Redeemer from death, or Liberator; and in its application to our Lord, all these significations are united. In σωτηρία — 'salvation' — there is the same range of meaning; frequently, it means little more than 'health' or '(physical) safety' (inscriptions and papyri give numerous examples in this sense). But in Christian usage,

[1] See now A. D. Nock, 'Soter and Euergetes', in *The Joy of Study: Papers on N.T. . . . to Honor Frederick Clifton Grant* (New York: Macmillan, 1951), pp. 127-148.

it has the deepest and most comprehensive significance, embracing in itself all the great Christian thoughts of healing (spiritual and physical, which are not differentiated), reconciliation, deliverance (especially deliverance from the power of the demons), redemption, immortality, and the final universal triumph of God. In this verse, the word must be given the last of these senses; the thought moves from the personal (hope), and the social (inheritance), to the universal — the establishment of God's kingdom, the final triumph of love and truth. This 'salvation' is now ready; it awaits only the striking of the hour that God has appointed for its manifestation — it is 'ready for its revealing at the Last Time'. In keeping with the general atmosphere of the New Testament, the whole Epistle reflects the Church's belief in the imminence of the Great Consummation; the attitude of watchful waiting for the Day: the Kingdom of God is *near* (cf. 4:7).

⁶ ἐν ᾧ ἀγαλλιᾶσθε, ὀλίγον ἄρτι εἰ δέον λυπηθέντες ἐν ποικίλοις πειρασμοῖς, ⁷ ἵνα τὸ δοκίμιον ὑμῶν τῆς πίστεως πολυτιμότερον χρυσίου τοῦ ἀπολλυμένου, διὰ πυρὸς δὲ δοκιμαζομένου, εὑρεθῇ εἰς ἔπαινον καὶ δόξαν καὶ τιμὴν ἐν ἀποκαλύψει Ἰησοῦ Χριστοῦ· ⁸ ὃν οὐκ ἰδόντες ἀγαπᾶτε, εἰς ὃν ἄρτι μὴ ὁρῶντες πιστεύοντες δὲ ἀγαλλιᾶσθε χαρᾷ ἀνεκλαλήτῳ καὶ δεδοξασμένῃ, ⁹ κομιζόμενοι τὸ τέλος τῆς πίστεως ⟨ὑμῶν⟩ σωτηρίαν ψυχῶν.

In this prospect you rejoice, though now for a little while it may be necessary for you to be afflicted by manifold trials, that the fine metal of your faith — far more precious than gold, which though it is transient yet is tested by fire — may be found worthy of praise and glory and honour at the revelation of Jesus Christ; whom you love, though you have not seen Him; and believing in Him, though now you do not see Him, you rejoice with joy unspeakable and suffused with glory, receiving the end of the faith, the salvation of souls.

⁶ δεον)+εστιν AC minusc. pl. ς λυπηθεντες) λυπηθεντας אּ* L69   ⁷ πολυτι-μοτερον) πολυ τιμιωτερον ς χρυσιου) χρυσου B   δοξαν και τιμην) τιμην και εις δοξαν ς   ⁸ ιδοντες) אּ B 1739. vg sah syrr Polyc. Iren.: ειδοντες C: ειδοτες AKLP 33. 69. 2412. ς boh Oec Thphyl ἀγαλλιασθε) αγαλλιατε B   ⁹ υμων) om B 1. Cl^{al ex} Or

In this passage, the thought moves rapidly from the joy inspired by visions of the future glory, which is tempered by the burden of present tribulations, to the inexpressible joy which derives from their love of the unseen Master, and is a present experience of the salvation which is faith's ultimate consummation.

v. 6. ἐν ᾧ) the relative may be taken as masculine, attaching directly to καιρῷ ἐσχάτῳ; or, probably better, as neuter, attaching in a general way to the whole thought of the preceding sentence — 'In this regeneration with all the benefits and glorious prospects to which it leads'. The grace of God fills the believer with an abiding Joy, having its foundation in the contemplation of the eternal, which no hardness of temporal circumstances can destroy. εἰ δέον is best taken as having the effect of a concessive particle, defining the force of the participle — 'though it may be necessary for you to suffer grief' (so Oecumenius); it does not imply that the coming of grief is inevitable, and it clearly excludes any possibility that they are even now passing through a persecution of which the writer has knowledge. (An indication that this part of the letter was written before the writer received news of the persecution which inspired the burning words of 4:12ff.) But if the necessity should be laid upon them, let them remember that such trials are transitory — the suffering is 'now, for a little while'; and they have a purpose — to test and manifest the pure eternally-enduring quality of their faith.   There is a close verbal parallel in James 1: 2-3 (ποικίλοις πειρασμοῖς, τὸ δοκίμιον ὑμῶν τῆς πίστεως — note also the association of the thought of 'joy', though James uses a different word, χάρα, which is however coupled with ἀγαλλιᾶσθε in v. 9); but the phrase τὸ δοκίμιον τῆς πίστεως is used quite differently in the two passages. In James, it means 'the testing of your faith'; here it means 'the sterling quality of your faith'. δοκίμιον in the latter sense is attested by the papyri (see Moulton and Milligan, *Vocabulary of the Greek Testament, sub voc.*).

ἀγαλλιᾶσθε . . . λυπηθέντες⟩ Many commentators, beginning with Oecumenius, have somewhat woodenly asserted that ἀγαλλιᾶσθε must have the force of a future, on the ground that there is an incongruity in saying that they rejoice at the very time that they are burdened with grief. But this is the very paradox of Christian faith; cf. 2 Corinthians 6:8-10, especially v. 10, 'as sorrowful, yet always rejoicing'. Calvin has a very fine note on the passage. 'There is here a certain appearance of inconsistency, in that the faithful, who exult in joy, are said at the same time to be in grief; for these are contrary affections. But that these can be felt simultaneously the faithful know from experience, better than can be put into words. Nevertheless to treat the matter briefly, let us say that the faithful are not stocks of wood, and have not so put off natural human feelings, that poverty should not be troublesome to them, and persecutions difficult and hard to bear. Therefore they feel grief because of their ills, but it is so lightened by faith that they do not, for such a cause, cease to rejoice. Thus grief does not hinder the joy of the very ones that are afflicted, but rather gives place to it; and again, though joy overcomes grief, yet it does not wholly make an end of it, inasmuch as it does not rob us of our nature as men.'

ἀγαλλιάομαι⟩ This verb appears to be used always with the connotation of a *religious* joy, a joy which springs from the contemplation of God or of the salvation which comes from God. (See R. Bultmann's study of the word in G. Kittel, *Theologisches Wörterbuch zum Neuen Testament*, I [Stuttgart, 1933], pp. 18-20.)

v. 7. The comparison with gold as with the most precious of metals, and the highest standard of comparison (Cf. Pindar, *Olymp.*, I:1-4), yet less to be valued than the treasures of the spirit, is found frequently in the Old Testament (Ps. 19:10, etc.) and in Plato (δικαιοσύνη . . . πρᾶγμα πολλῶν χρυσίων τιμιώτερον — 'Justice . . . a thing more precious than many pieces of gold' — *Republic*, Bk. I, 336E); and the divine discipline of man is compared to the refining-furnace in Proverbs 17:3, probably by transference from the trying of hearts in the Judgment Day (Mal. 3:3) to the life of man in the world. The basic thought probably originates in Zoroastrianism, which teaches that Ahura Mazda will judge the world with a judgment of molten metal. In the thought of this writer, the testing of life in this world through the fiery trial of persecution is an anticipation, one might almost say a preliminary stage, of the fiery testing of the Last Judgment (4:17).

ἀπολλυμένου) Gold is 'perishable' in the sense that it belongs among the transitory things of this world, while faith belongs to the realm of the eternal, the heavenly.

'Unto praise and honour and glory, at the revelation of Jesus Christ.' 'The revelation of Jesus Christ' means, of course, His appearing in glory to judge the world; His coming means also the revelation of that salvation which is now 'ready to be revealed' (v.5). In Romans 2:5-11, Paul likewise links the search for 'glory and honour and immortality' (δόξαν καὶ τιμὴν καὶ ἀφθαρσίαν) and the attribution of 'glory and honour and peace' (δόξα τε καὶ τιμὴ καὶ εἰρήνη) to the 'day ... of the revelation of God's righteous judgment'. Similarly in 1 Corinthians 4:3-5, he links the attribution of 'praise' (ἔπαινος) to the coming of the Lord (Jesus Christ) in judgment. The thought here is a fresh presentation of the same attitude. The Christian believer seeks no honour or glory or praise in the present time, or from the judgment of men; he is concerned only with how he may show himself approved in God's sight in the divine judgment which is now hidden but in due time to be revealed.

The thought now turns to the present (partial) realization of the future glory. 'The Christ whose revelation you await, you love, though you have not seen Him; you believe in Him, though you do not behold Him with your eyes; and in thus believing you rejoice with a joy inexpressible and suffused with glory'. The repetition of the verb ἀγαλλιᾶσθε recalls the beginning of the passage (v.5), and binds the several thoughts together. The joy of the Christian is not wholly a joy of anticipation. The splendour of the divine inheritance, the pure imperishable beauty of heaven, penetrates the barriers of time and circumstance and the spiritual limitations of earthly life. Faith lays hold on the unseen Master and love embraces him; the anticipated joy is translated into an ineffable experience of the present; and thereby Christians are even now receiving the salvation for which they hope, which is 'the end of the faith'.

v. 8. ὃν οὐκ ἰδόντες ἀγαπᾶτε). One is tempted to think that the writer has in mind the words of the Gospel (John 20:29) — 'Blessed are they that have not seen, and yet have believed.' The contrast of 'faith' with 'sight' is to be found everywhere in the New Testament (esp. 2 Cor. 5:7; Hebrews 11 passim; Rom. 8:24, 25); accordingly, it seems far-fetched to see in the words οὐκ ἰδόντες an implication that the writer, unlike the readers, has seen Christ. ἄρτι — 'now' — as in v. 6, suggests a present experience which will be surmounted in the future; 'now' we see Him not, but 'then' we shall see Him with direct vision. Cf. 1 Cor. 13:12 — 'Now (ἄρτι) we see through a mirror in an enigma, but then, face to face'.

The reading εἰδότες is inferior both in attestation and in intrinsic probability. It would arise easily through an itacism (ει for ι) coupled with the failure of a copyist to observe the stroke (for ν) over the ο.

C actually has the form εἶδοντες, from which the corruption εἰδοτες has arisen.

ἀγαλλιᾶσθε χαρᾷ ἀνεκλαλήτῳ καὶ δεδοξασμένῃ⟩ 'Ye rejoice with joy unspeakable and suffused with glory.' The words are not to be taken as mere high-sounding hyperbole. ἀνεκλάλητος — 'unspeakable, inexpressible, ineffable' conveys the sense of a divine mystery exceeding the powers of speech or thought. It recalls the words used with such great effect by St. Paul in 1 Corinthians 2:9 (from Is. 64:4) — 'Eye hath not seen, nor ear heard, nor hath it entered into man's heart, what things God hath prepared for them that love Him.' δεδοξασμένη — 'suffused with glory' — takes up the δόξα of v. 7 — the glory to be manifested in the revelation of Jesus Christ; affirming that this glory of the manifestation of the heavenly is given already to the joy of Christian faith and love.

v. 9. κομιζόμενοι τὸ τέλος τῆς πίστεως ⟨ὑμῶν⟩ σωτηρίαν ψυχῶν⟩ 'receiving the end of the faith, the salvation of souls'. Here again, the future glory and the present experience are linked together. σωτηρία ψυχῶν — 'the salvation of souls' — is but one phase of the salvation which is 'ready to be revealed'; it is that final cosmic triumph of the divine will insofar as it is realized in the souls of men. In the nature of things it cannot be totally realized except in the future, and therefore the life of the Christian must be a life of hope, continually 'reaching forth unto those things which are before' (Phil. 3:13). Yet in this 'joy ineffable, suffused with glory', the future sheds its divine light into the present; and in such an experience, Christians are already 'receiving the end of the faith' — the culmination in which faith must find its issue — the 'salvation of souls', which can be nothing else than the transformation of man's whole being through communion with God and participation in His essence.

I have bracketed ὑμῶν in deference to the judgment of Hort, who had no doubt that it was an interpolation; but the arguments which he puts forward in his note on the passage (in his commentary) hardly seem strong enough to justify us in setting aside the all but unanimous testimony of the manuscripts and versions.

Professor E. J. Goodspeed holds that the governing verbs in this section should all be taken as imperatives: 'Rejoice ... love him ... rejoice ...' Similarly in 2:4, 5 — 'Come to him ... and build yourselves up.' Such a rendering intensifies the hortatory aspect of the epistle from the beginning.

'There is certainly much more point', he remarks, 'in calling upon the readers of the letter to rejoice over their salvation, and to love Christ though they have not seen him, than to tell them that they are already doing so; especially if they are "rejoicing with joy unspeakable and full of glory" (v. 8), they hardly need to be informed of the fact.' *Problems of New Testament Translation* (Chicago: U. of C. Press, 1945), p. 193.

¹⁰ περὶ ἧς σωτηρίας ἐξεζήτησαν καὶ ἐξηραύνησαν προφῆται οἱ περὶ
τῆς εἰς ὑμᾶς χάριτος προφητεύσαντες, ¹¹ ἐραυνῶντες εἰς τίνα ἢ ποῖον
καιρὸν ἐδήλου τὸ ἐν αὐτοῖς πνεῦμα Χριστοῦ προμαρτυρόμενον τὰ εἰς
Χριστὸν παθήματα καὶ τὰς μετὰ ταῦτα δόξας. ¹² οἷς ἀπεκαλύφθη ὅτι
οὐχ ἑαυτοῖς ὑμῖν δὲ διηκόνουν αὐτά, ἃ νῦν ἀνηγγέλη ὑμῖν διὰ τῶν
εὐαγγελισαμένων ὑμᾶς ἐν πνεύματι ἁγίῳ ἀποσταλέντι ἀπ' οὐρανοῦ·
εἰς ἃ ἐπιθυμοῦσιν ἄγγελοι παρακύψαι.

*Concerning this salvation prophets, who prophesied of the grace
destined to be bestowed upon you, made earnest quest and query,
seeking to learn to what time or what manner of time the Spirit of
Christ in them was pointing, when it bore witness beforehand to the
sufferings destined to befall Christ, and the glories to follow. It was
revealed to them that their ministry was not for their own benefit,
but for yours, in respect of these good tidings that have now been
proclaimed to you through those that brought you the Gospel by the
Holy Spirit sent down from heaven. Into these things angels fain
would glance.*

¹⁰ υμας〉 ημας K 33   ¹¹ η ποιον〉 om sah boh syrr   Χριστου〉 om B προ-
μαρτυρομενον〉—ουμενον AP minusc. nonnull. Oecum Thphyl   ¹² εν〉 om
BA 33

In this passage, the primary intention of the writer is to magnify
the salvation which is 'the end of the faith', by recalling that it was
foretold by the prophets in ages gone by, that the Spirit attends
upon its proclamation, and that it awakens the longing of angels.
At the same time he brings forward with deliberation and skill
the thought of the unity of the two Testaments; which he places
in (1) the witness to Christ, in humiliation and in glory, and (2)
the activity of the Spirit — then in the prophets, and now in the
preachers of the Gospel.

v. 10. 'Made earnest quest and query.' The rhetorical device of
paronomasia is a feature of this writer's style and is frequently employed with great effect. In this instance, however, the combination of
verbs is borrowed outright from 1 Maccabees 9:26 (ἐξεζήτουν καὶ
ἐξήραυνον) with a change only in the tense. The phrase reflects his
thorough familiarity with the Old Testament in the Greek Version, but
under the circumstances, we need not look for shades of difference in
meaning between the two verbs. Taken together, they give emphatic
expression to the earnestness with which enlightenment was sought.
Cf. Socrates' description of his lifelong search into the meaning of the
oracle which pronounced him the wisest of men (*Apol.* 23A) — ζητῶ
καὶ ἐρευνῶ κατὰ τὸν θεόν.

προφῆται) the omission of the article gives the noun a generic force — 'men who were prophets' — calling attention not to their persons, but to their function. (Cf. Westcott's note on ἐν υἱῷ in Hebrews 1:2, in his commentary on that Epistle.) The assumption is that the function of the prophet was *predictive*. This was the prevailing view of Old Testament prophecy held by the early church, which found a powerful apologetic in the correspondence of Old Testament prophecy and New Testament fulfilment, and sought for nothing more. Indeed, it is only in very recent times that any effort has been made to interpret the writings of the prophets in their historical setting. For this writer, the content of the prophetic message was essentially the advance proclamation of the coming of Christ (to suffer, followed by resurrection and exaltation to heaven), and of the blessings which He would thereby bring to His people.

περὶ τῆς εἰς ὑμᾶς χάριτος) 'Concerning the grace destined for you.' The grace destined for Christian believers, concerning which they prophesied, is the apprehension of the 'salvation'. χάρις — 'grace' — is here used *concretely*; it means not the divine favour in general, which is the usual New Testament force of the word ('by grace are ye saved'), but the specific consequences of the divine favour — the life, hope, joy, and glory which God in His grace purposed to bestow.

εἰς ὑμᾶς) 'destined for you' — this is the *pregnant* use of the preposition, as in τὰ εἰς Χριστὸν παθήματα just below — 'the sufferings destined for Christ'. This writer often puts great weight upon his prepositions, especially εἰς which he works very heavily (eleven times in these first twelve verses).

v. 11. (ἐραυνῶντες) εἰς τίνα ἢ ποῖον καιρὸν) (seeking to learn) 'to what time or what manner of time'. The second adjective softens the effect of the first[1] — τίνα suggests a defined period, almost a date to be fixed, while ποῖον suggests the general outward circumstances to be expected, the 'signs of the times' by which the arrival of the Messianic epoch may be discerned. The prophets, he believes, were interested to know whether their visions were to find fulfilment in their own lifetime or in a distant future. Such inquiry into the time of fulfilment of the prophet's own oracles is mentioned frequently in the apocalyptic writings of later Judaism, from which the writer derives his general view of the themes of prophecy and the nature of its inspiration. Among the canonical books, see especially Daniel from Chapter 8; and among the Apocrypha, 4 Esdras 4:33-5:13; cf. Philo's views of prophetic inspiration in the *De Vita Mos.* II. 188, 190 (pp. 163, 164).

τὸ ἐν αὐτοῖς πνεῦμα Χριστοῦ) 'the spirit of Christ that was in them'. The Spirit of prophecy is called the 'spirit of Christ', possibly in the sense that the pre-existent Christ is Himself the spirit, or that the

[1] A. Debrunner, *Friedrich Blass' Grammatik des neutestamentlichen Griechisch* (5th ed. revised: Göttingen, 1921) section 298, 2.

spirit was sent by Him. But it is not necessary thus to read into the passage the implication of the pre-existence of Christ; the words may mean only that the spirit of prophecy was the very Spirit that came upon Him in the baptism. An Old Testament expression like 'the Spirit of the Lord' (2 Sam. 23:2), would easily turn in Christian parlance into 'the Spirit of Christ', under the influence of the confessional saying 'Jesus is the Lord', and the familiar title 'the Lord Jesus Christ'.

ἐδήλου) The verb δηλόω is used in exactly the same way in Hebrews 9:8, of that which the Spirit *signifies* by what is revealed, the revelation in its externals being veiled in mystery.

προμαρτυρόμενον) In classical usage, the middle μαρτύρομαι means 'to call (another) to witness' to the truth of one's own affirmation. Hort therefore proposed to interpret the participle as meaning that the Spirit of prophecy called upon God to bear witness to the truth of the revelation. One is bound to feel that this is forced and unnatural in the extreme. The reading προμαρτυρουμενον, the middle of προμαρ-τυρέω, is a classical correction, to justify to the purist the sense that is obviously required in the context. However, the papyri offer instances of the use of μαρτύρομαι as equivalent to μαρτυρέω (= to bear witness; see Moulton and Milligan, *Vocabulary*, sub *voc.*), and the compound διαμαρτύρομαι is used intransitively in Lxx. In fact, it is impossible to maintain that μαρτύρομαι elsewhere in N.T. invariably means 'call to witness', not 'witness'. There is, therefore, nothing untoward in this intransitive use of the compound with προ — and the translation 'testify-ing beforehand' is amply justified.

τὰ εἰς Χριστὸν παθήματα καὶ τὰς μετὰ ταῦτα δόξας) 'the sufferings destined for Christ and the glories to follow them'. The phrase is constructed in careful parallelism with 'the grace destined for you' above, thus emphasizing the intimate relation of the two themes of prophetic utterance — the manifestation of Christ in humiliation and in glory, and the gifts bestowed upon men. The weighty εἰς in both cases brings out the thought of the divine foreordering; the sufferings of Christ, like the grace bestowed upon Christians, came upon him 'by the determinate counsel and foreknowledge of God' (Acts 2:23; cf. Acts 4:28).

Christian teaching in early times commonly summarized the message about Christ under the two heads of 'suffering' and 'glory'; this is the sum both of the prophetic witness in past ages and of the gospel pro-clamation now that the events have come to pass. Cf., for instance, Luke 24:25-27 — 'O fools and slow of heart to believe all that the prophets have spoken; ought not Christ to have suffered these things, and to enter into His glory? And beginning at Moses and all the prophets, He expounded unto them in all the scriptures the things concerning Him-self'. (Cf. also Acts 17:3 and 1 Cor. 15:3, 4). The birth, life and teach-ings of the Lord were secondary to the story of His 'sufferings and the glories that were to follow them'. The 'glories' would include the Resurrection and Ascension, the Session at the right hand of the majesty on high (as in Hebrews, especially), and above all, His final manifestation, still in the future, as the glorious King ruling over all the earth. His life and example and His teachings were not used as part of the missionary propaganda for the winning of converts; they were not included in 'the Gospel'. They were, of course, part of the *teaching* (διδαχή), which was subsequently given to converts (so in this Epistle — 2:21ff.; 3:21ff.).

v. 12. From the very beginning, the Church of Christ was possessed of the triumphant assurance that in its Master, His Gospel, and the fellowship of faith which was founded upon Him, all the purposes and promises of God were beginning to be realized. It claimed for its inheritance the whole Old Testament, and all the promised glories of the Messianic Age. 'These things were written for our sakes' (1 Cor. 9:10). Even the history of the Chosen People has significance chiefly as a detailed symbolism for the benefit of the Church. 'These things happened to them in symbol (τυπικῶς), and were written for the enlightenment of us, upon whom the consummation of the ages has come' (1 Cor. 10:11). The entire Old Testament, both in history and in prophecy, is an anticipation and a preparation for that which has now come into the world with Christ and the Church. This attitude had unfortunate consequences in one way, in that it led to a complete disregard of the historical treatment of the Old Testament, and a long-continued misinterpretation and a multitude of false applications of its words and of the institutions of religion which it portrays. On the other hand, it was perhaps the sole attitude that could have enabled the Church to continue to treasure the Old Testament, in the face of her long and sharp conflict with Judaism and the temptation to surrender to the unhealthy dualism of Greek thought. With all the errors and extravagances which resulted from the attempt to wrest everything in the Old Testament to Christian uses, the Church retained the fundamental values of the doctrine of the unity of God in Creation and in Redemption, of His transcendence, His glory and majesty, His love and mercy — a conception to which Greek philosophy at its highest and best never began to approach. The knowledge of the One Living and True God, the Father Almighty, the Creator of all things visible and invisible, of whom and unto whom are all things — this was the inestimable treasure which the Church inherited in the Old Testament, to make it available no longer to a single race but to all mankind. It is, of course, quite impossible to maintain the position that it was revealed to the prophets that they were ministers of promises intended not for their own nation, but for a catholic Church still to be created. This assertion of our writer is based upon a misunderstanding of the nature and purpose of the late-Jewish apocalyptic, which projected into the heroic past messages meant for the immediate situation and couched

them in the form of prophecies delivered by some ancient worthy
(Adam, Enoch, Noah, Moses, Daniel, etc.). Hort observes that there is
a fundamental general truth in the formula '*Not for themselves but for
you*', in that 'the privileges of a Divine revelation were of necessity held
in trust for the benefit of those who had not yet received it'.

νῦν⟩ 'now' — the present age, in contrast to the pre-Christian period
in which the prophecies were delivered.

διὰ τῶν εὐαγγελισαμένων ὑμᾶς ἐν πνεύματι ἁγίῳ⟩ 'through those
who brought you the Gospel by the Holy Spirit'. — Cf. 1 Thess. 1:5 —
τὸ εὐαγγέλιον . . . ἐγενήθη εἰς ὑμᾶς . . . ἐν πνεύματι ἁγίῳ.

εἰς ἅ⟩ The relative takes up the preceding ἃ νῦν ἀνηγγέλη — it refers
to the substance of the Gospel proclamation. It is certainly implied
that this remains veiled from the sight of angels. There is a similar
emphasis on the high privilege of Christian believers, a privilege to
which the angels themselves may not aspire, in Hebrews 2:16 —
'(Christ) lays not hold upon angels, but upon the seed of Abraham'.
ἐπιθυμέω in itself does not imply a desiring which cannot be fulfilled;
but it is not possible otherwise to give παρακύψαι its proper force (literally, 'to cast a quick glance, to peep' as through a door or window).
The thought is clearly that the angels are eager to win some slight
understanding of the mystery of salvation, but even this is not open to
them. By contrast, the readers may appreciate more fully the gracious
favour which God has shown to themselves. 'Selbst Engel, den Menschen von Natur weit überlegen, haben nicht, was ihr habt, sondern
möchten gern einen verstohlenen Blick hineintun' (Gunkel).

In most of the popular religion of the time, Jewish as well as pagan,
a great place was accorded to angelic beings of various grades and
dignities, and the most diverse functions were ascribed to them. The
Gospels reflect the extent to which the Christian imagination was
affected by similar ideas. In the Epistles, on the other hand, the powers
of the angels are greatly circumscribed; they tend on the whole to be
regarded as the representatives of the old order of things which is
passing away, to give place to the sole sovereignty of Christ. The
Epistle to the Hebrews, indeed, speaks of them as 'ministering spirits,
sent forth on service for the sake of those that are to inherit salvation'
(Heb. 1:14); but even these apparently honourable words are meant to
reject a higher conception of their functions, and to show them to be
not only subordinate to Christ Himself (vv. 6-8), but subsidiary to 'the
heirs of salvation' (in which they are not included). To St. Paul, they
are 'the rulers of this age' (1 Cor. 2:6-8), and have no knowledge of 'the
wisdom of God . . . which God fore-ordained before the ages, for our
glory'. Our writer in another passage (3:22) speaks of them as 'made subject to Christ', in His exaltation. He appears to think of them, therefore, not as resplendent spirits attendant upon God, but as emblems of
the dark spiritual forces that hold sway over the lower realms of being.

¹³ Διὸ ἀναζωσάμενοι τὰς ὀσφύας τῆς διανοίας ὑμῶν, νήφοντες τελείως, ἐλπίσατε ἐπὶ τὴν φερομένην ὑμῖν χάριν ἐν ἀποκαλύψει Ἰησοῦ Χριστοῦ.

Wherefore gird up the loins of your minds, live in perfect sobriety, and fix your hope upon the grace that is coming swiftly to you in the revelation of Jesus Christ.

In the close-knit and weighty exordium, the writer has magnified the new life, with its high hopes and promised glories. Now, in a series of exhortations, he sets forth the strenuous moral demands of the life into which they have entered.

• This verse effects the transition to the hortatory part of his discourse. As in v. 3, he lays the primary stress on hope. As God has 'begotten them again unto a living hope', their first duty, and in a sense their entire function is to *hope*. But observe that this hope is no vague and shallow optimism, no mere natural buoyancy of spirit that sees the future through rose-tinted spectacles. It is a strenuous moral exercise, requiring thorough discipline of mind and body, that all the faculties may be concentrated upon and directed toward it. To gird the loins of the mind is to prepare oneself mentally, as an athlete would prepare himself physically, for a sustained output of energy. The instruction to keep perfectly sober is to be taken first of all in its elementary sense, of avoiding drunkenness (cf. 1 Thess. 5:6-8); then more widely, in the sense of a true asceticism, refraining from self-indulgence of every kind, and keeping all one's powers under control that there may be no failure through dissipation or slackness in the pursuit of the highest and best.[1] The hope which calls for this earnest concentration of all the faculties is nothing less than the continual practice of laying hold upon the realities that are unseen, seeking the things that are above (Col. 3:1), and resolutely rejecting the ever-present temptations of earthly ambition and human glory.

νήφοντες) Sobriety is given a particular emphasis, as a necessary condition of the maintenance of that acute watchfulness of spirit which belongs to the hope of Christ's manifestation in triumph. More generally, it is used in the religious vocabulary, beyond the Christian circle, of those that are awake to the possibility of achieving immortality; while those that are wholly absorbed in this present life are described as 'drunken'. The words are frequently contrasted, in this sense, in the Hermetic literature; e.g. *Poimandres* 27 — 'O peoples, earth-born men, who have given yourselves over to drunkenness and sleep and the ignorance of God, become sober and cease from revelling, under the enchantment of irrational sleep. (28) Why, O earth-born men, have you given yourselves over to death, when you have the power to partake

[1] Cf. Ignatius, *Ep. to Polycarp* 2:3 νῆφε ὡς θεοῦ ἀθλητής. τὸ θέμα ἀφθαρσία καὶ ζωὴ αἰώνιος.

of immortality?' Professor Dodd (*The Bible and the Greeks* [London, 1935], p. 183) remarks, 'The Hermetist characterizes the two ways of life and death by a series of antithetical terms. The way of death is σκότος, ἀγνωσία, πλάνη, μέθη, φθορά: the way of life is φῶς, γνῶσις, ἀλήθεια, νῆψις, σωτηρία: . . .' It will be observed that the whole series occurs in First Peter, and may reasonably be interpreted in relation to the same circle of ideas. The injunction to 'keep perfectly sober' will then include the thought that they are to shun the intoxication of earthly things; true sobriety consists in having the affections 'set on things above, not on things on the earth' (Col. 3:1-2).

▸ ἐλπίσατε) 'fix your hope' — the aorist has ingressive force; not 'be hopeful' but 'start to hope', 'fix or set one's hope'; it implies the purposeful adoption of a new attitude of mind and heart. The 'grace which is coming swiftly', connected as it is with 'the revelation of Jesus Christ' is the manifestation of God's glory in all His creation, the 'salvation ready to be revealed' of v. 5. χάρις is used in this concrete sense, of the eschatological consummation, in the 'Teaching of the Twelve Apostles' (10:6) — 'May grace come, and this world pass away'. The participle φερομένην is taken by Hort (and others) as 'the passive of φέρω in its commonest sense "bring",' but this interpretation arises from the failure to appreciate the eschatological sense of χάρις here. The middle φέρομαι is commonly used in the sense of swift motion; here it suggests the vision of a triumphal procession sweeping upon the world with whirlwind speed; it is no 'far-off divine Event', but a rapidly approaching salvation, 'toward which the whole creation moves'; rather, which moves toward the whole creation.

'For lo! the days are hastening on
By prophet bards foretold.'

ἐν ἀποκαλύψει Ι.Χ.⟩ 'in the revelation of Jesus Christ' — again, as in v. 7, His manifestation in glory. Cf. Titus 2:13.

νήφοντες τελείως ἐλπίσατε⟩. It is grammatically possible to attach the adverb τελείως to ἐλπίσατε, which follows it, instead of to νήφοντες, which precedes; and it is this arrangement which leads to the rendering of the Authorized Version — 'be sober, and hope to the end'. But the Greek commentators attach it to νήφοντες, and as Hort points out, the author's 'prevalent usage elsewhere suggests a presumption in favour of taking an adverb with a verb that precedes rather than with a verb that follows' (as in 1:22; 2:19, 23). The rendering 'to the end' is in any case wrong; τελείως can only mean 'perfectly, completely, fully'. (See Moulton and Milligan, *Vocabulary*, sub voc. τέλειος).

Professor F. L. Cross, arguing that 'the Exodus theme underlies the whole of the section 1:13-21', finds an allusion to the Passover in 1:13, in the exhortation to 'gird up the loins of your mind' (cf. Ex. 12: 11). See his remarks in *I Peter: A Paschal Liturgy* (London: Mowbray, 1954), p. 25. It is more directly reminiscent of Luke 12:35 ('Let your loins be girded [περιεζωσμέναι as in the LXX of the Exodus passage] . . . and yourselves like men who are awaiting their lord'), where the figure is related, as here, to the eschatological expectation.

¹⁴ ὡς τέκνα ὑπακοῆς, μὴ συσχηματιζόμενοι ταῖς πρότερον ἐν τῇ ἀγνοίᾳ ὑμῶν ἐπιθυμίαις, ¹⁵ ἀλλὰ κατὰ τὸν καλέσαντα ὑμᾶς Ἅγιον καὶ αὐτοὶ ἅγιοι ἐν πάσῃ ἀναστροφῇ γενήθητε, ¹⁶ διότι γέγραπται· ἅγιοι ἔσεσθε, ὅτι 'ἐγὼ ἅγιος.

As children of obedience, do not continue to mould your life in accordance with the desires which formerly governed you in the time of your ignorance; but in likeness to the Holy One who called you, do you also become holy in all your active life, for it is written, 'Ye shall be holy, for I am holy'.

¹⁶ διοτι)διο ℵ C: om 33   γεγραπται) om 33   αγιοι) pr οτι B 69 syrr (?) εσεσθε) γινεσθε vel γενεσθε KLP minusc pler ç   οτι) διοτι ℵ minusc pauc αγιος)+ειμι CP ç

The passage reflects dependence upon Ephesians 2:1-3. The description of Christians as τέκνα ὑπακοῆς is suggested by the description of pagans as υἱοὶ τῆς ἀπειθείας — 'sons of disobedience', and τέκνα ὀργῆς — 'children of wrath'. Notice also the use of κατά in the sense of moral conformity to a model; the description of pagan life as governed by 'the lusts of the flesh' — ἐν ταῖς ἐπιθυμίαις τῆς σαρκός; and the occurrence of the verb ἀναστρέφω, in the Ephesians passage, with its cognate noun ἀναστροφή here.

v. 14. ὡς τέκνα ὑπακοῆς⟩ A reminder that they are called εἰς ὑπακοήν (v.2). The locution is Hebraic in form, and sounds as unusual in Greek as in English, but it is used in the sense required by Greek syntax, not according to the Semitic idiom. The genitive is *objective* — 'children *born for obedience*'.

μὴ συσχηματιζόμενοι⟩ This writer is exceptionally fond of using the participle as an imperative, whether in subordination to a main verb in the imperative mood (as in v. 13), or absolutely, as here (cf. ἔχοντες, 2:12; ὑποτασσόμενοι, 2:18; etc.). This usage easily passes over into an imperatival use of the adjective (3:8; 4:8-10). The same verb is used in the same sense of moral conformity in Romans 12:2.

ταῖς ἐπιθυμίαις⟩ 'desires' in the most general sense, not necessarily base or evil. In other New Testament writings the word is frequently coupled with τῆς σαρκός, τῶν καρδιῶν, in which case it is quite properly rendered 'lusts'. Here, however, the thought is not that their former life was vicious or depraved, but that it was morally unstable, lacking a governing principle of knowledge to control desire; it was a time of moral and spiritual ignorance, with no understanding of the true nature and destiny of man. 'Conduct ruled by desires is irregular and erratic, at the mercy of outward circumstances, not moulded by a consistent principle of life within' (Hort). The same thought seems to lie in the

● phrase κατὰ τὰς ἐπιθυμίας τῆς ἀπάτης 'according to the desires of deceit' (Eph. 4:22) — i.e., the desires, which are a deceitful guide, leading only to destruction; true conduct is modelled κατὰ θεόν (Eph. 4:24), as κατὰ τὸν . . . Ἅγιον here. Desires may in themselves be good or evil; in no case can they be allowed to guide conduct and determine character for the Christian.

v. 15. κατὰ τὸν καλέσαντα ὑμᾶς Ἅγιον⟩ 'In likeness to the Holy One who called you'. Not the vagrant impulses of desire, but the character of God Himself is to inspire and direct the conduct of those He has called into His fellowship. ὁ καλέσας (ὑμᾶς, ἡμᾶς, μέ) is a characteristic phrase of St. Paul's; he uses the participle as a substantive, but here it is more naturally taken as modifying τὸν Ἅγιον. The familiar Pauline usage has misled commentators into treating καλέσαντα as the substantive and Ἅγιον as a predicate adjective; but this would be a very awkward syntactical arrangement here. ὁ Ἅγιος is used in several well-known Old Testament passages as a name for God (cf. also 1 John 2:20) and is appropriate to the writer's purpose here. It is in his moral character as 'the Holy One' that God is the model for our imitation; to seek to be like Him in other ways may be presumption and sin.

καὶ αὐτοὶ ἅγιοι ἐν πάσῃ ἀναστροφῇ γενήθητε⟩ 'Do you also become holy (or, "show yourselves holy") in all your active life'. ἀναστροφή is used of public activity, life in relation to others — 'conversation' in the old sense. (E. L. Hicks, *Classical Review*, I [1887], p. 6; A. Deissmann, *Bible Studies*, trans. A. Grieve [Edinburgh, 1901], p. 194.) The rule of Christian conduct is holiness, modelled upon the holiness of God; the inward character must have a corresponding outward expression.

The use of ἅγιος to describe moral perfection is a debt to the Greek Old Testament, where it translates קָדוֹשׁ. The Hebrew word and its Greek equivalent have no necessary connotation of morality, etymologically; they derive their moral content from the conception of God as revealed and proclaimed in Old Testament Scripture. The root idea is merely 'separateness', for dedication to religion. That which is dedicated takes its character from that to which it is dedicated; women dedicated to Astarte, for instance, were temple prostitutes. (Cf. Sir J. G. Frazer, *The Golden Bough*, Part IV, Vol. I, *Attis, Adonis, and Osiris* [3rd ed., London, 1924], c. iv — 'Sacred Men and Women'.) That which was dedicated to the God of Israel was under obligation to conform to His essential purity and goodness; so Israel as a people 'holy unto the Lord', was to reflect in its national life the moral perfection of its God. The adjective 'holy' (ἅγιος, קָדוֹשׁ) and the noun 'holiness' (ἁγιωσύνη, קֹדֶשׁ) thus took on a far deeper meaning, and could be applied to God as expressing His complete and perfect purity, His essence as goodness.

The verb γενήθητε is not a mere equivalent for ἐστέ. The aorist may be taken as inchoative (ingressive) — 'begin to be', 'become' — and as an instruction to converts newly-baptized, this sense is most fitting.

γίνομαι may indeed have the sense 'prove oneself, show oneself', as Hort takes it — ' "show yourselves holy, as you are", "show forth in your lives the character of holiness, which you possess". Being holy as members of a holy people, they were to show themselves holy in every kind of dealings with other men'. It seems better, however, to take it as an injunction to a change of conduct, answering to the call to a new life which they have received.

v. 16. The injunction is supported by a reference to the Old Testament, which affords a further illustration of the notion of the Church as the true Israel; the command laid upon the ancient people of God is transferred automatically to the new.

γέγραπται⟩ 'It is written' — the regular Christian usage in introducing citations from the Old Testament, which in the first Christian century were the only Scriptures treated as sacred.

ἔσεσθε⟩ This is the reading of virtually all the best Greek witnesses, and of some of the Latin texts. The imperative γίνεσθε (or γένεσθε) appears to be a corruption induced by the presence of γενήθητε in the preceding verse. The sense is in any case imperative, not pure future. In the passage cited, the MSS. of Leviticus (Lxx) read ἔσεσθε without variant.

¹⁷ καὶ εἰ πατέρα ἐπικαλεῖσθε τὸν ἀπροσωπολήμπτως κρίνοντα κατὰ
τὸ ἑκάστου ἔργον, ἐν φόβῳ τὸν τῆς παροικίας ὑμῶν χρόνον ἀναστράφητε, ¹⁸ εἰδότες ὅτι οὐ φθαρτοῖς, ἀργυρίῳ ἢ χρυσίῳ, ἐλυτρώθητε
ἐκ τῆς ματαίας ὑμῶν ἀναστροφῆς πατροπαραδότου, ¹⁹ ἀλλὰ τιμίῳ
αἵματι ὡς ἀμνοῦ ἀμώμου καὶ ἀσπίλου Χριστοῦ, ²⁰ προεγνωσμένου μὲν
πρὸ καταβολῆς κόσμου, φανερωθέντος δὲ ἐπ᾿ ἐσχάτου τῶν χρόνων
δι᾿ ὑμᾶς ²¹ τοὺς δι᾿ αὐτοῦ πιστοὺς εἰς θεὸν τὸν ἐγείραντα αὐτὸν ἐκ
νεκρῶν καὶ δόξαν αὐτῷ δόντα, ὥστε τὴν πίστιν ὑμῶν καὶ ἐλπίδα
εἶναι εἰς θεόν.

*And if you invoke as Father Him who judges every man according
to his work without respect of persons, conduct yourselves with
reverent fear during your earthly pilgrimage, in the knowledge that
you were redeemed from the aimless way of life which you inherited
from your ancestors, not with perishable treasures of silver or gold,
but with precious blood, as of a spotless and unblemished lamb — with
the blood of Christ, who 'was foreknown before the creation of the
world, and manifested at the end of the ages' for your sakes, who
through Him are faithful to God who raised Him from the dead and
gave Him glory; so that your faith and hope are in God.*

¹⁷ κρινοντα) κρινουντα C boh   αναστραφητε) αναστρεφομενοι ℵ   ¹⁸ φθαρτοις
αργυριω) φθαρτου αργυριου ℵ   ¹⁹ τιμιω) pr τω C 69   ²⁰ εσχατου) εσχατων
KLP 69 ç vg   υμας) ημας A   ²¹ πιστους) BA vg: πιστευσαντας 33: πιστευοντας cett.   δι᾿ αυτου) δια του υιου αυτου sah (et post θεον posuit)   εγειραντα)
εγειροντα ℵ*

In vv. 14-16 the writer teaches that our new relationship to God
as His children should lead us to model our conduct upon His
character of holiness as revealed in Scripture. Now he turns from
the thought of God's moral character to the thought of his *function*
as Judge, and finds in this a further motive for holy living. Starting
again from the Christian relation to God as our Father, whom we
invoke by that name in our prayers, he impresses upon us the
reflection that He to whom we thus pray in filial confidence and
devotion is none other than the Judge of all the earth, who judges
every man according to his work, with no concern for special
privilege, though it be the privilege of sonship. Our knowledge of
Him as Father must not dispel our dread of Him as our Judge.
It must lead not to presumption, but to humility; it must not
induce moral laxity, as if by our new position we were exempted
from rendering an account to Him of the deeds done in the body;
rather, it should inspire in us all the greater moral earnestness, as

in those to whom is given the true knowledge of Him. The thought is finely illustrated in William Penn's words about George Fox — 'The most awful, living, reverent frame I ever felt or beheld, I must say, was his in prayer. And truly it was a testimony that he knew and lived nearer to the Lord than other men; for they that know him most will see most reason to approach him with reverence and fear'. In a different context, St. Paul writes in 2 Corinthians 5:10-11 — 'For we must all appear before the judgment seat of Christ; that every one may receive the things done in his body, according to that he hath done, whether it be good or bad. Knowing therefore the terror (properly, *fear* — φόβος, as in our own passage) of the Lord, we persuade men, but we are made manifest unto God'.

From the thought of God as Father and as Judge, the writer proceeds to the thought of Christ as Redeemer and as Mediator, who by the sacrifice of His own spotless life has delivered us from our vain ways and brought us into communion with God, in whom we now place our faith and hope. In the recollection of this costly sacrifice, he bids us find a further weighty motive for the holiness that befits children of God.

v. 17. εἰ πατέρα ἐπικαλεῖσθε) This verb in the middle voice implies more than the knowledge of God's fatherhood. It is not merely that we call Him by that Name, but that we pray to Him, exercising the privilege that He has granted us of invoking His gracious goodness. The writer may possibly have in mind the opening of the Lord's Prayer; in any case, he thinks of God's fatherhood not in terms of an abstract doctrine, but of an effective communion of spirits.

ἀπροσωπολήμπτως) the adverb is not found elsewhere in the New Testament, but its cognates occur several times. In them, we have an instance of the creation of religious and moral vocabulary through the medium of the Septuagint, the expression deriving from a literal rendering of the Hebrew נָשָׂא פָּנִים by λαμβάνειν πρόσωπον — 'to receive the face' of someone, in the sense of showing special favour to a suitor. In Acts 10:34 (οὐκ ἔστιν προσωπολήμπτης ὁ θεός) and in Romans 2:10-11 (οὐ γάρ ἐστιν προσωπολημψία παρὰ τῷ θεῷ), the thought is of the impartiality of God as between Jew and Gentile, in the offer of the Gospel and in the pronouncing of judgment. In this passage, however, the distinction of Jew and Gentile is not envisaged; the thought is rather that in God's judgment no special indulgence is extended to those who invoke Him as Father. A parallel is found in Deuteronomy 10:12-18, where Moses is represented as reminding the people that God has made them the object of His love and favour, exhorting them to respond with true inward consecration and obedience, and finally warning them that 'the Lord your God, He is the God of gods and Lord of lords, the great and mighty and terrible God, ὅστις οὐ θαυμάζει πρόσωπον οὐδ' οὐ μὴ λάβῃ δῶρον — who shows no partiality and takes no bribes' (Lxx). This passage may have been in the mind of our writer; but the same thought finds not infrequent utterance elsewhere in the Old Testament, receiving perhaps its earliest and most forceful expression in Amos 3:2 — 'You only have I known of all the families of the earth; therefore will I punish you for all your iniquities.' The favour which God bestows upon His people in choosing them to be *His* people does not entitle them to sin with impunity; His goodness is not a charter of licence, but the most powerful of motives for devotion to His will. This warning which the Old Testament prophets reiterated in the ears of the people of Israel is now sounded afresh for the benefit of the people of the new covenant. It should be observed that this is no contradiction of the doctrine that we are saved by grace through faith; it is, in fact, the necessary complement of that doctrine; for the life of faith, and that alone, will issue in the 'work' that God can approve, without partiality.

κρίνοντα) the present, not the future, because the thought dwells upon God's essential character and function, not upon a particular act or time of judgment. There is a sense, also, though it is not included here, in which God is continually judging our acts. They carry their consequences with them, for good and for evil. And certainly all our acts should be done as in His sight and under a profound sense of responsibility to Him.

τὸν τῆς παροικίας ὑμῶν χρόνον) 'the time of your sojourning'—i.e., the period of our life upon earth, conceived as a time of sojourn in an alien land, absent from our true home in heaven (cf. note on παρεπιδήμοις διασπορᾶς in 1:1).

ἐν φόβῳ ἀναστράφητε) 'conduct yourselves with reverent fear', 'let your life among your fellows be governed by the spirit of godly fear'. Like the noun ἀναστροφή above (v. 15), the verb is used of life in its relations with others, of outward conduct in social intercourse; this is to be determined by the Christian's attitude to God, to whom he is ultimately responsible. The 'fear' of which he speaks is of course not any craven terror of the Judgment Day, but the sense of awe which must be awakened by a true realization of the presence of God when we know ourselves to stand in His sight. It is that 'fear of God' of which the Old Testament writers often speak, which is at the heart of any true approach to Him, which dispels all pride and haughtiness and self-assertion; cf. the injunction of St. Paul in Romans 11:21 — 'Be not highminded, but fear'. A life which is governed by this acute sense of the awfulness of Him with whom we have to do will not succumb to the temptation to conform to the habits of the world about us; even in the most hostile environment it will be impelled to stand firmly by the moral principles which befit His children.

v. 18. εἰδότες ὅτι⟩ 'An appeal to an elementary Christian belief' (Hort). The locution is frequently used by St. Paul (Rom. 5:3 and 6:9; 1 Cor. 15:58; 2 Cor. 1:7; 4:14; 5:6 etc.). It appeals to a teaching that has already been given, recalling it to their memory as an incentive to action, or as a source of consolation, or as the basis of a true attitude towards life, as here. The relationship to God which must be the governing principle in the Christian's life among his fellows is made an even stronger motive for us by the constant recollection of the means by which we have been brought into this position of high privilege, and of the One who forms the link between us and the God whom we serve.

ἐλυτρώθητε⟩ 'you were redeemed', or perhaps more generally, 'you were delivered, you were rescued'. The verb is found only three times in the New Testament (always in the middle or passive); but has an important place in all parts of the Old Testament, occurring nearly a hundred times. It is infrequent in classical usage; in Homer's story of the ransoming of Hector (Iliad XXIV), the active of λύω is used for 'release upon payment of the ransom', and the middle for 'ransom', 'secure release upon payment of a ransom'. The noun λύτρον, formed on the stem of λύω, occurs fairly often (though not so early as Homer), for 'redemption-money', the price paid to secure release, usually in the plural λύτρα; and the verb λυτρόω is a denominative formed upon this noun, replacing λύω in this particular sense. In the active it means 'hold for ransom', or 'release upon payment of the ransom demanded'; and in the middle it means 'redeem', 'ransom', 'secure release of that which is held'. In the later vernacular (inscriptions and papyri) the verb and the noun are used, but infrequently, of the redemption of pledges, and of the manumission of slaves, and occasionally of release from a vow or from a legal obligation.

The use of the verb in the three N.T. occurrences is dependent wholly upon the usage of the Greek Old Testament, where, except for a very few instances, it renders either גָּאַל or פָּדָה. The former verb in* its primary sense has to do with the exercise of the rights of kinship, sometimes in relation to the avenging of blood, more often in the redemption of property which has been alienated through sale or mortgage, or of members of the family who have been enslaved; the latter verb is more general in its application. Both of them, however, have weakened, especially in the later literature, into the less precise idea of *deliverance*, not necessarily by payment of a ransom, but also by an act of power; and it is this looser and more general sense of λυτρόομαι which is most evident in the Greek version, and is taken over by the New Testament writers for this verb and for its cognates such as λύτρωσις and (the only form found in the Pauline letters) ἀπολύτρωσις. For instance, the verb is used frequently of the deliverance of Israel from Egypt, and again from the Babylonian captivity, where there is certainly no thought of a ransom paid to the enslaving power, but of the mighty intervention of God; as in Exodus 6:6, λυτρώσομαι ὑμᾶς ἐν βραχίονι ὑψηλῷ καὶ κρίσει μεγάλῃ — 'I will redeem you with a lofty arm and with a great judgment', where the verb is used in parallelism with ἐξάξω and ῥύσομαι — 'I will lead you out ... and will rescue you'; and again in Nehemiah 1:10 — καὶ αὐτοὶ παῖδές σου καὶ λαός σου, οὓς ἐλυτρώσω ἐν τῇ δυνάμει σου τῇ μεγάλῃ καὶ ἐν τῇ χειρί σου τῇ κραταιᾷ. — 'They are thy children and thy people, whom thou didst redeem by thy great power and by thy mighty hand'. In these and many like passages, the verb has lost most if not all of its proper force, accompanied by the thought that the deliverance is costly to God, but never that the cost is a ransom paid to the oppressor. (Cf. the remarks of Westcott in a note on this verb in his *Epistle to the Hebrews*, p. 296 — 'It will be obvious from the language of the Lxx that the idea of a ransom received by the power from which the captive is delivered is practically lost ... On the other hand, the idea of the exertion of a mighty force, the idea that the "redemption" costs much, is everywhere present'.)

In our own passage, the 'redemption' is really a moral transformation, effecting deliverance from the vain way of life which their fathers had followed and in which they themselves had been reared. It is costly, in that it has required the shedding of the 'precious blood' of Christ; yet it must be noted that he does not use for this the genitive of price, which would be the normal way of indicating the amount of the ransom, but the dative, which is not used at all of price (at least, not without a preposition), and seems therefore better taken as *instrumental*. Thus the thought of *power* is associated with the thought of cost.

This brings us to the problem, very difficult for us, of the primitive religious conceptions of the efficacy of blood, which lie behind much of the New Testament language about the 'blood of Christ'. To the people of the time, these conceptions were thoroughly familiar, not only to Jews who were acquainted with the sacrificial ideas of the Levitical law, but equally so to pagans. 'The blood' is not, as we too easily assume, a mere metaphor for the life given in sacrifice, as in our own usage when we acknowledge that we owe our freedom to the men who have defended it with their blood. In the religious thought of the ancient world, including that of the New Testament, the blood itself, especially the blood of a victim slain in sacrifice, is thought to possess a peculiar potency in the release of effective power in many different applications. In the story of Odysseus' visit to Hades (Odyssey XI), Homer tells how the hero summons the spirits of the dead to him with libations and prayers, and then cuts the throats of sheep and allows the blood to flow into a trench that he has dug in the earth; and as he allows them to drink of the blood, they are enabled to know him and speak to him. We have already had occasion to refer to the widespread idea that by the sacrifice a current of life is set up between the deity and the worshipper; often it is the blood itself which constitutes the effective medium of communication (see note on ῥαντισμὸν αἵματος, v. 2). And in the Levitical law, it is repeated again and again that the blood of the sacrifice is the means of atonement; the thought is not at all that the offering of the victim, or its death, is in itself efficacious, but that by the sacrifice the blood is released, as it were, and made effective for the purpose. (e.g., Lev. 17:11 — 'For the life of the flesh is in the blood; and I have given it to you upon the altar to make an atonement for your souls; for it is the blood that maketh an atonement for the soul'.)[1] The blood, then, is the channel or medium of living divine power, which is made effective in particular applications, whether for communion, for atonement, for the imparting of new life, or for deliverance from an alien (demonic) power, only when it is shed in sacrifice. The deliverance is costly, not in the sense that a ransom is paid, but in the sense that the power needed to effect it can be made available only through the sacrifice of the life. (Cf. Westcott, *The Epistles of St. John*, pp. 34-7, Additional Note on 1 John 1:7 — 'The Blood of Christ in the New Testament'.)

The thought of our passage, accordingly, is that deliverance from the vain life of ancestral tradition is effected by the living power of Christ, made available for us through His death.

οὐ φθαρτοῖς) 'not with corruptible things' (gold or silver) — cf. the description of gold as ἀπολλυμένου in v. 7. Gold and silver are 'corruptible' in the sense that they are mundane, material, not having that spiritual essence which alone is eternal, and thus incapable of effecting a moral and spiritual deliverance. There is possibly an underlying thought of the common practice of manumitting slaves through the legal fiction of a sale to a deity, the money being first paid into the temple treasury by the slave, and then remitted to the master. (Deissmann, *Light from the Ancient East*, E.T., c. 4, sec. 8, pp. 318ff.) Such a change in legal status could be effected by silver or gold, but not the transference of life itself from the mundane to the heavenly. In contrast, the Blood of Christ is conceived not as a material substance, but as a spiritual essence endued with liberating power, 'the power of a life not subject to dissolution' (Heb. 7:16).

Their former life, inherited from their ancestors (πατροπαραδότου), is termed 'vain', as lacking the reality and meaning that can only be given to life when it is lived in fellowship with the true God. Thus in Ephesians 4:17, the Gentiles (i.e., the heathen) are said to 'walk in the vanity of their minds' — ἐν ματαιότητι τοῦ νοὸς αὐτῶν — 'alienated from the life of God because of the ignorance that is in them'; and the apostles at Lystra, rejecting with horror the worship that is offered to them as to Zeus and Hermes, exclaim, 'We preach to you that you should turn from these vanities — ἀπὸ τούτων τῶν ματαίων — to the Living God.' There seems to be no suggestion that such a life is a form of slavery, but rather that in it men are subject to a false allegiance; the life is dominated by its worship of false gods; and by the living power of Christ, men are brought into a new allegiance, that they may henceforth live in the worship of the true God.

v. 19. The blood of Christ is called τίμιος — 'precious', or 'costly',

---

[1] Better 'by reason of the life (that is in it)'.

in that it becomes efficacious for the deliverance of men only through the sacrifice of his life.

ὡς ἀμνοῦ ἀμώμου καὶ ἀσπίλου⟩ 'as of a lamb without blemish and without spot' — bringing out definitely the thought of sacrifice, probably with particular reference to the Passover lamb. The sacrificial victim must always be unblemished (תָּמִים — sometimes rendered τέλειος, sometimes ἄμωμος). The adjective ἄσπιλος is not used by the Lxx, and is probably introduced here through the writer's fondness for paronomasia (cf. the first note on v. 10). There is a verbal reminiscence of Ephesians 5:27 — μὴ ἔχουσαν σπίλον . . . ἀλλ᾽ ἵνα ᾖ . . . ἄμωμος. The perfect holiness of Christ makes Him worthy to offer Himself unto God as the one sufficient sacrifice, of which the sacrifice of the lamb was an anticipatory symbol.

v. 20. The clause προεγνωσμένου . . . χρόνων has all the appearance of a liturgical distich, probably familiar to the readers, which is woven into the structure of the paragraph. The thought is often dwelt upon in the New Testament, most conspicuously in Ephesians (especially 1:3-12; 3:5, 9-11). Christianity is new in the world, but is rooted in eternity; it is the unfolding before men of the eternal counsel of God. Christ Himself has only now been revealed as the Saviour of the world, but He has been designated for this function, to redeem mankind by His Blood, from all eternity. The foreknowledge of God (see note on v. 2) conveys the thought of Will and Purpose; that Christ is 'foreknown' means that His work in the world was ordained of God, that the fulfil- ment of God's purpose for the world was destined to be accomplished through Him, through His sacrifice of Himself; God 'foreknew' Him in His *function as Saviour*. This does not of necessity imply His pre- existence; since in this sense, God 'foreknows' all whom He calls into His service (Rom. 8:29; 11:2).

καταβολή — the 'foundation' of the world. The verb καταβάλλω in the active usually means 'overthrow', 'cast down'; and this led Origen to interpret the noun as meaning the Fall, so that he used this phrase as a proof-text for his doctrine of the pre-temporal fall of souls. (*Comm. on St. John*, Tome 19, sec. 22; *De Principiis*, III, 5, 4, etc.) In the middle, however, the verb has the sense of 'lay' (a foundation — so Heb. 6:1); and the noun is used of a 'structure' in 2 Maccabees 2:29 and elsewhere (see Moulton and Milligan, *Vocabulary*, *sub voc.*).

ἐπ᾽ ἐσχάτου τῶν χρόνων⟩ 'at the end of the times'; cf. Hebrew 1:2 — ἐπ᾽ εσχάτου τῶν ἡμέρων τούτων — 'at the end of these days'; and Acts 2: 16ff., where the Descent of the Spirit is declared to be a fulfilment of the prophecy of Joel relating to 'the last days'. Such phrases reflect the conviction of early Christianity that human history is drawing to an end; the coming of Jesus Christ into the world, His Passion and Exaltation to heavenly glory, have set the term to the ages of the creation's bondage and alienation from God. In this last age, the 'powers of the world to come' (Heb. 6:5) are already present, and the final consummation which will usher in the New Age (of the Kingdom of God) is 'at hand' (cf. 4:7); the 'salvation' which has so long been awaited is 'ready to be revealed'. For this ultimate manifestation, the whole creation waits in hope, and even the Christian believers, who have received 'the firstfruits' of the coming glory in the gift of the Spirit, look forward in eager expectancy to the glorious transformation which God will effect in them and in the entire universe at 'the revelation of Jesus Christ'. Cf. Romans 8:18-25. 'The end of the times' is thus the immediate prelude to the 'Last Time' (1:5). From another point of view, the present age is itself the first stage in the realization of the promised Kingdom. 'For the New Testament writers in general, the *eschaton* has entered history; the hidden rule of God has been revealed; the Age to Come has come.' (C. H. Dodd, *The Apostolic Preaching and its Development*, p. 147.) Yet none of the writers expresses such a conviction apart from the complementary thought that we live by the hope of things not seen as yet; that what is already realized is no more than a firstfruit of the promised divine blessing; and that the present has meaning only in the light of the future, when Christ will 'appear' in glory.

δι' ὑμᾶς (v. 21) τοὺς δι' αὐτοῦ πιστοὺς εἰς θεὸν⟩ 'for your sakes, who through Him are faithful to God'. Christ was manifested for the sake of believers, that they might be brought through Him to the faith in God which they could never have known apart from Him. He seeks by these words to deepen our sense of gratitude, to make our minds dwell upon the thought that it was for the love of us that Christ was manifested to bring us into the new relationship to our Creator, in faith and fidelity.

πιστούς is to be preferred to πιστεύοντας, partly on the basis of attestation, for A and the Latin vulgate bring support to B from two independent lines of descent, and this combination of witnesses must be regarded as particularly strong; but even more for its intrinsic superiority. The change to the participle would be a natural accommodation to a commonplace of Christian language and thought; whereas no scribe would think of altering πιστεύοντας to the far more striking πιστούς. The adjective brings out the thought of faithfulness; through Christ, we are not only brought to have faith in God, but are enabled to show ourselves faithful to Him in all our life. It is this response in conduct that forms the theme of the entire paragraph.

'Who raised Him from the dead and gave Him glory.' The resurrection of Christ and His exaltation are a single thought. God 'glorified His Son Jesus' by raising Him from the dead (Acts 3:13-15). Similarly Paul, after speaking of the Death of Christ (Philippians 2:8) goes on immediately to say that 'God highly exalted Him', not directly mentioning the Resurrection but obviously including it in the Exaltation of which he speaks. When God raised Jesus from the dead, He 'set Him at his own right hand in heavenly places' (Eph. 1:20). The God whom we know through Christ is the God who raises from the dead and glorifies those who are faithful to Him.

ὥστε τὴν πίστιν ὑμῶν καὶ ἐλπίδα εἶναι εἰς θεόν〉 There is a good deal to be said for the view that ἐλπίδα here is to be taken as a predicate, after the infinitive — 'so that your faith is (or, so that your faith may be) also hope in God'. Those who believe in God also hope in Him, as in the One who promises resurrection from the dead, and future glory. If the phrase is construed in direct connection with the preceding words about God, this interpretation would seem to be necessary. It is possible, however, to take it as depending in a more general way upon the whole thought of the paragraph, as summing up the consequence for them of the work of Christ. The thought would then be, 'Christ has been manifested for your sakes — with the result that now you set your faith and your hope upon God'. But this is a rather lame ending, and the failure to repeat the article with the second noun offers some difficulty, if both stand in the same relation.

The section comprised in vv. 13-21 is centred in the exhortation to *holiness* of life. The following section develops the thought of *love* as the true expression of the life that has been purified inwardly, and that is immortal in its essence; this love leads us to the abandonment of everything harmful to others, and unites us in a living fellowship, of which Christ is the nucleus (1:22-2:10).

²² Τὰς ψυχὰς ὑμῶν ἡγνικότες ἐν τῇ ὑπακοῇ τῆς ἀληθείας εἰς φιλαδελφίαν ἀνυπόκριτον, ἐκ καρδίας ἀλλήλους ἀγαπήσατε ἐκτενῶς, ²³ ἀναγε-
γεννημένοι οὐκ ἐκ σπορᾶς φθαρτῆς ἀλλὰ ἀφθάρτου διὰ λόγου ζῶντος
θεοῦ καὶ μένοντος. ²⁴ διότι
  πᾶσα σὰρξ ὡς χόρτος,
  καὶ πᾶσα δόξα αὐτῆς ὡς ἄνθος χόρτου·
  ἐξηράνθη ὁ χόρτος,
  καὶ τὸ ἄνθος ἐξέπεσεν·
  τὸ δὲ ῥῆμα Κυρίου μένει εἰς τὸν αἰῶνα.
²⁵ τοῦτο δέ ἐστιν τὸ ῥῆμα τὸ εὐαγγελισθὲν εἰς ὑμᾶς.

*Now that you have purified your souls by obedience to the truth
unto unfeigned love of the brotherhood, love one another with earnest,
heart-felt love, since you are begotten again not of corruptible seed,
but of incorruptible, through the Word of the Living and Abiding
God (or, through the living and abiding Word of God).
For*

  All flesh is as grass,
  And all its glory as the flower of grass.
  The grass withers
  And the flower fades,
  But the utterance of the Lord abides for ever.

*And this is the utterance of the Gospel proclamation, which was made
for you.*

²² αληθειας)+δια πνευματος KLP 69 ς : αγαπης vg   καρδιας) pr καθαρας ℵ*
CKLP 33. 69. ς sah boh syrr: txt. BA vg   ²³ σπορας) φθορας ℵAC
μενοντος)+ εις τον αιωνα KLP 69. ς vg syrᴾ   ²⁴ ως¹°) om A   αυτης) αυτου
ℵ* ('quod magnam veri speciem habet'—Tisch.) : ανθρωπου KLP 69. ς
ανθος²°)+αυτου CKLP 69. ς   ²⁵ το ρημα το) om A

v. 22. ἡγνικότες⟩ The verb ἁγνίζω and the corresponding noun ἁγνισ-
μός are uniformly employed in the Greek Old Testament of the ritual
purification of worshippers or of vessels to be used in worship; and this
is the general New Testament usage also (Acts 21:24,26; 24:18, John
11:55). The adjective ἁγνός, however, appears always to be used of
moral, not of ceremonial purity; and this, together with the Christian
emphasis on inwardness in religion, makes easy the transition in the
verb also, to the sense of moral purification. So in James 4:8, we have
the phrase 'purify your hearts' (ἁγνίσατε καρδίας); and in 1 John 3:3 —
'Everyone that hath this hope in Him purifieth himself (ἁγνίζει ἑαυτόν)
even as He is pure'. In our own passage, the two senses are combined;
the ritual purification represented by baptism is efficacious in the
sphere of the moral life (cf. 3:21); in baptism, they have 'purified their
souls'. The use of the perfect makes it impossible to give imperative
force to this participle, as to those of vv. 13-14. He *affirms* that they have

purified their souls, and the fact of this accomplished purification is made the basis of the injunction to love one another, the purification being meant to issue in mutual love.

ἐν τῇ ὑπακοῇ τῆς ἀληθείας⟩ 'by obedience to the truth'. In view of the perfect participle, which cannot suggest a *process* of purification, the 'obedience' is to be understood not of a continuing attitude, but of a particular act. Their baptism, which is the response of faith to the proclamation, in public confession of their adherence to the truth, is the act of 'obedience to the truth', by which their souls have been sanctified.

εἰς φιλαδελφίαν ἀνυπόκριτον⟩ 'unto unfeigned love of the brethren'. The preposition again carries a great weight of meaning, as in vv. 10-11, setting forth the intended issue of obedience and purification. Christians are purified in heart, not for a solitary holiness, but for life in the divine society which is bound together by love; yet the transformation of the inward life of the individual is the necessary pre-condition of our entrance into the fellowship of God's people. Baptism, the response of obedience to the truth that we have been taught, means for us the purification of our souls, and this purification issues in the mutual love of the baptized, who now know one another as brethren, children of the same Father. Without the inward purification, there can be no love that is wholehearted, utterly sincere, with no element of simulation (ἀνυπόκριτον). φιλαδελφία does not mean 'brotherly love' in general, but quite specifically 'the love of the (Christian) brotherhood', the mutual love which binds together the children of God in one family. The language is again reminiscent of St. Paul (Rom. 12:9-10 — 'Let love be without dissimulation . . . Be affectionate to one another in the love of the brotherhood' — ἡ ἀγάπη ἀνυπόκριτος . . . τῇ φιλαδελφίᾳ εἰς ἀλλήλους φιλόστοργοι⟩.

ἐκ καρδίας⟩ 'from the heart' — This is the reading of A, B and the Latin Vulgate. The reading of the Byzantine text, on which the rendering of A.V. depends ('with a pure heart' — ἐκ καθαρᾶς καρδίας), is supported by a formidable array of authorities; it is clear, none the less, that the adjective is an interpolation, though an early one. ἐκ καρδίας gives the sense that is required — to love 'from the heart', i.e., sincerely, devotedly; in association with ἐκτενῶς — 'earnestly, intensely, perseveringly' — it must convey a similar thought. καθαρᾶς would be both redundant (in view of the preceding clause) and inappropriate. It 'was apparently suggested by the association of ἐκ καθαρᾶς καρδίας with ἀγάπη in 1 Tim. 1:5' (Hort).

ἀγαπήσατε⟩ The use of the aorist should be noted as supporting the interpretation that this is an injunction to newly-converted Christians. Otherwise the present would be more appropriate, as an exhortation to continue loving one another; the aorist (ingressive, cf. ἐλπίσατε in v. 13) has rather the force of inculcating the adoption of a new attitude, the necessary consequence of their admission to the Christian brother-hood.

v. 23. ἀναγεγεννημένοι〉 'begotten again'. The use of the perfect, as in ἡγνικότες just before, draws attention to the parallelism of thought in the two participles. Both set forth in different but complementary ways the state of life which follows upon baptism into the Christian society. Morally, it means inward purification; but more than that, it means the beginning of a new life, created in us by the Fatherly action of God. Here we return to the primary thought with which the Dis-course began (v. 3): God has begotten us again. There, the thought went on to the *issues* of the new life, in hope, in the heavenly inheritance, in the awaited salvation; here, it turns to the idea of the *essential character* of the life, the seed from which it develops, the immortal element from which it derives its being. The Christian believer experi-ences a moral transformation; but more than that, he finds implanted in him a new principle of life, immortal because it is divine.

οὐκ ἐκ σπορᾶς φθαρτοῦ, ἀλλὰ ἀφθάρτου〉 'not of corruptible seed, but of incorruptible'. The words have no moral connotation here; it is the contrast of permanence and impermanence. The natural life of man is 'of corruptible seed', in the sense that it is essentially transitory; it fades and withers away like the grass of the field; it does not spring from an immortal source. The new life of the Christian believer, on the other hand, springs from 'incorruptible seed', in that it is of God's sowing and is inherently immortal. Any thought that this immortality is a natural possession of man is clearly excluded. The immortality of the Christian is not achieved by giving true development to his natural capacities; it is the property of the new life which he receives by the creative act of God. So in the thinking of St. Paul, 'If any man be in Christ, there is a new creation (καινὴ κτίσις)' (2 Cor. 5:17).

It must be observed, further, that this thought also is linked to the central injunction to 'love one another from the heart, earnestly'. Immortality, like purity of soul, is set not in the context of an isolated individualism of experience and privilege, but in the mutual love of the Christian brotherhood. Precisely because the new life is immortal in its essence, it must find expression in the love of the brethren with whom we share it. For immortality is not truly conceived in terms of mere permanence, apart from the quality and function of the life which is to endure for ever; the immortal life which God bestows upon us through His Son is a life of holiness and of love, and it must be lived in the community which God has formed for it. In this social emphasis, Christianity is profoundly different from Neoplatonism and all such religions of solitary mysticism, which seek the salvation of the soul in isolation from the world and from its fellows, in a 'flight of the alone to the Alone'. In Christian thinking, the most sublime experiences of the soul are linked with the fellowship of all believers; and the higher we are drawn towards God, the closer is our communion with His people.

διὰ λόγου ζῶντος θεοῦ καὶ μένοντος) 'through the Word of the Living and Abiding God'. (The phrase εἰς τὸν αἰῶνα is an intrusion from v. 25.) God is 'the Living God' in the sense that He only has life in Himself and is the source from which all other life derives; the addition of 'Abiding' emphasizes the fact that this life of God is alone immortal. The Scriptural quotation (from Isaiah 40:6-8) brings out this contrast between human existence as transitory and evanescent, and the divine as alone enduring; the Gospel, because it is His utterance, likewise abides forever.

διὰ λόγου) 'through the Word'. The Word as the medium of regeneration is associated in thought with the ῥῆμα—the utterance of God, brought home to the hearts of men in the Gospel proclamation; but it is more than a mere equivalent. It suggests also the thought of the Logos of God, as in the Fourth Gospel and in the general religious conceptions of the time, as the Divine Essence emanating from God, and having its own substantive existence with Him, acting under Him and for Him in relation to the world and to human life. The adjectives ζῶντος and μένοντος may indeed be taken with λόγου instead of with θεοῦ, and should perhaps be attached to both. The Word also lives (cf. Hebrews 4:12) and abides. The change of preposition — ἐκ with σπορᾶς, διὰ with λόγου—indicates that the Logos is not itself the Seed, but rather the Sower, or the mediating agent in the sowing.

v. 25. εἰς ὑμᾶς) not merely 'to you', but 'for your benefit, for your salvation' (cf. τῆς εἰς ὑμᾶς χάριτος, v. 10).

2 ¹ Ἀποθέμενοι οὖν πᾶσαν κακίαν καὶ πάντα δόλον καὶ ὑπόκρισιν καὶ φθόνους καὶ πάσας καταλαλιάς, ² ὡς ἀρτιγέννητα βρέφη τὸ λογικὸν ἄδολον γάλα ἐπιποθήσατε, ἵνα ἐν αὐτῷ αὐξηθῆτε εἰς σωτηρίαν, ³ εἴ ἐγεύσασθε ὅτι χρηστὸς ὁ κύριος.

Put away, then, all malice and all guile and hypocrisy and envying and all slanderings; as new-born babes, crave the spiritual uncon-taminated milk, that by it you may grow unto salvation, now that you have tasted that the Lord is gracious.

¹ υποκρισιν⟩ B lat vet sah boh syrᴾ: υποκρισεις cett : pr πασαν sah boh φθονους⟩ φονους B : παντα φθονον sah boh πασας καταλαλιας⟩ πασαν κατα- λαλιαν ℵ* sah boh, (omisso πασαν) syrᴾ ² αρτιγεννητα⟩ – γενητα A εις σωτηριαν⟩ om ς ³ ει⟩ ειπερ ℵ* CKLP 69. ς vg Χρηστος⟩ Χριστος KL 33. 69. 614

These verses follow up the injunction to love one another, developing further the nature of the life of brotherhood into which they have now entered as children begotten of God. The evils which they are to avoid are precisely those which are incompatible with real brotherhood, those which are impossible to a life governed by love to others. All such things must be cast away, if our life is to have the proper spiritual development. They are then enjoined to seek the nourishment, spiritual in its nature, and unadulterated by any element of evil, which alone can enable them to grow from infancy to maturity, until they attain the 'salvation' which is the full flowering of that spiritual life into which they have now been born.

v. 1. ἀποθέμενοι⟩ The participle shares the imperative force of the governing verb; the aorist suggests that this is a moral decision to be made once for all. These vicious attitudes which tell against the well-being of our neighbour are to be discarded, as we cast off clothing for which we have no more use.

κακία–a wide and general term of the moral vocabulary, meaning 'vice' as opposed to 'virtue' (ἀρετή); sometimes used specifically to mean 'cowardice', but this would be pointless here. 'Malice' is perhaps too narrow a rendering; the word seems rather, in this leading position in the sentence, to gather up in one comprehensive term the several vices which are mentioned in detail after it, of all that is injurious to one's neighbour. Cf. the definition of Suidas ('probably taken from some Father'–Hort)–κακία δέ ἐστιν ἡ τοῦ κακῶσαι τὸν πέλας σπουδὴ παρὰ τῷ ἀποστόλῳ – 'κακία is the eagerness to harm one's neighbour'. It is the sum of all that is contrary to love. So St. Paul writes (Rom. 13:10) — 'Love does not work evil (κακόν) to the neighbour; therefore love is the fulfilment of the Law.'

Guile or deceit (δόλος) and hypocrisy are kindred vices, the former referring perhaps more to words spoken in order to deceive, the latter to a parade of outward conduct intended to impress others.

v. 2. ἀρτιγέννητα βρέφη⟩ 'newborn babes'—in strict literalness 'newly-begotten embryos'. The writer consistently thinks of the new life of the Christian in terms not of birth, but of begetting; the creative action of God as Father is never out of his mind. The complementary thought of the Church as the Mother of the faithful, in whose womb we are conceived and at whose breast we are nurtured, is not found earlier than the third century. The true meaning of βρέφος is 'embryo' (always used with this sense in Homer), not 'babe'; but in the usage of later writers it is extended to include sucklings and even small children generally (=νήπιος). The craving for milk is of course a figure that would be applicable only to the infant, but enough of the original sense remains to make possible the use of the adjective ἀρτιγέννητα— 'newly-begotten'.

Clearly, such a phrase could not be used with any appropriateness of the general body of Christians in the provinces mentioned in the salutation. In Asia and Galatia, at least, Christian missions had been conducted with marked success by St. Paul and his associates around the middle of the first century, more than fifty years earlier, so that by the time of this epistle the churches of the region would include many members of long standing, who had passed all their lives in the service of Christ and could in no sense be described as 'newborn babes'. On the other hand, the words are wholly appropriate to the condition of converts who have just been received into the Church by baptism.

C. Wordsworth, in *The New Testament in the Original Greek*, Vol. 2 (3rd ed., London, 1864), *ad loc.*, quotes a passage from Augustine, Sermon 353, an address to neophytes:

'These words are especially applicable to you, who are yet fresh in the infancy of spiritual regeneration; for to you mainly the Divine Oracles speak by the Apostle Peter "Having laid aside all malice . . . , earnestly desire the *rationabile et innocens lac ut in illo crescatis ad salutem*, if ye tasted that the Lord is gracious:" And we are witnesses that ye have tasted it.'

ἐπιποθήσατε⟩ He now bids them to crave for the nourishment which is best fitted to promote their development to spiritual maturity. Again the aorist imperative conveys the thought that the profession of Christianity must result in a new orientation of life. Hitherto they have craved the common objects of human desire, in ignorance of the spiritual possibilities revealed by the Gospel (cf. 1:14); now they must begin to cultivate the taste for spiritual things. The initial experience of the goodness of the Lord must lead them to long for more of the same food for the soul.

The new object of desire, the nourishment which the new life requires for its sustenance and growth, is described as τὸ λογικὸν ἄδολον γάλα. 'Milk' is a figure naturally suggested by the thought of 'newborn babes', but there is probably also a direct reference to the cup of milk which was given to initiates in the mystery-cults.[1] (Sallust. Philos. *De Deis et Mundo*, iv – ἐπὶ τούτοις γάλακτος τροφὴ ὥσπερ ἀναγεννωμένων; additional references in Perdelwitz [MR. pp. 57ff.], who comments 'Gewiss, Milch ist die Nahrung der Kinder — damit bleibt der Verfasser ganz in dem Rahmen des Bildes; aber genau dieselbe Beobachtung hatte man in den Mysterienkulten auch schon gemacht, und darum den neu geweihten Mysten Milch, oder Milch mit Honig zu trinken gegeben, weil man sie eben als Wiedergeborene betrachtete, in denen die Gottheit neu geboren war'.) But in the Christian cultus the letter is superseded by the spirit; and the 'milk' offered to the initiates is spiritual, just as the offering made by Christians is described as 'spiritual sacrifices' (πνευματικὰς θυσίας, v. 5; cf. Rom. 12:1 —θυσίαν ζῶσαν . . . τὴν λογικὴν λατρείαν ὑμῶν).

The adjective λογικός offers much difficulty, both in itself and in the determination of the significance of γάλα. The familiar rendering of A.V. — 'milk of the Word' is quite impossible. The Latin versions point the way to the true interpretation with the rendering 'rationale', 'rationabile' (rational, reasonable, conformable to reason, etc.), but this is still too narrow, for λόγος is not equivalent to 'ratio'. Part of the thought is indeed that the nourishment offered to the Christian by his religion is not the blind and senseless ritual of paganism, which any thoughtful man must either mock, or sublimate into the recondite imagery of spiritual instruction. As against this, the Christian cultus is in all its aspects eminently conformable to reason. But λογικός means more than this. On the whole, 'spiritual' is the best rendering that we can give for it in English. It is that which is proper to the Logos, and to the life which is mediated through the Logos (διὰ λόγου — 1:23); thus it is virtually equivalent to πνευματικός. Reitzenstein (*Hellenistischen Mysterienreligionen*[3], pp. 328-33) has shown how the word developed this sense in the technical terminology of the mysteries. He is not right, however, in giving it the meaning 'sündlos machend, heiligend' in this passage (p. 329); for here it is used of the quality, or the intrinsic character of the 'milk', not of its effect.

The second adjective — ἄδολος — is commonly used of corn, wheat, barley, oil, wine, and farm produce generally, in the sense of 'pure, unadulterated, uncontaminated'; and its use here, in application to the 'spiritual milk', is a natural employ of the everyday commercial language. At the same time, in so careful a writer, one who does not fall into clichés, the word must certainly be given much of its inherent sense of 'guileless', especially when the word δόλος 'guile', is used in the same sentence. The true nourishment for which the Christian must long has in it no element of moral contamination, nothing of the guile that he has been enjoined to cast away from him. This further points the contrast with the milk given to the initiate in the mystery-cults, which would be regarded as part of the apparatus of deceit by which the

[1] See supplementary note on p. 117.

devotee was led into false hopes. (Cf. Perdelwitz, MR. p. 62 — 'Es ist . . . möglich, . . . dass der Verfasser hier an einen ganz bestimmten Mysterienkult gedacht hat, bei welchem kein ἄδολον γάλα gereicht wurde, dass dort die Milch ein δόλος διαβόλου ist, mit dem er die Menschen zu fangen sucht'.) Certainly such an attitude to the sacraments of these religions is wholly in keeping with the general Christian teaching of the time; see, e.g., Justin Martyr, *First Apology*, sec. 66; Tertullian, *De Praescriptione Haereticorum*, sec. 40.

It is still not clear what he intends us to understand by this nourishment of the soul, which he describes as 'spiritual, uncontaminated milk'. The rendering 'milk of the Word' suggested that he meant the holy Scriptures, but a proper understanding of the words rules out this interpretation. It is not impossible that he is thinking of the Eucharist, and has been led to speak of the wine as 'milk' by his desire to maintain the thought of the 'newborn babes'. E. Lohmeyer defends this view in his article 'Vom Urchristlichen Abendmahl' II 'Das Mahl in der ältesten Christenheit', in *Theologische Rundschau*, IX (1937), p. 296. But it is perhaps better to take it of Christ Himself, in a more general sense than the reception of Him in the Eucharist. This interpretation is suggested by the concluding phrase 'if (not a condition, but as in 1:17, an assumption — "seeing that, now that") you have tasted that the Lord is gracious'. The expression is borrowed from Psalm 33 (34):9 (Lxx) — γεύσασθε καὶ ἴδετε ὅτι χρηστὸς ὁ Κύριος, and the verb certainly connects the thought with the idea of the nourishment which is sought. The soul is encouraged to seek more of that which it has already experienced in a measure, and found good; and that is Christ the Lord Himself. It may be observed that the word χρηστός is a play on the Name Χριστός, which would have the same pronunciation or something very close to it, at this period. Cf. the play on the words in Justin Martyr's *First Apology*, sec. 4 — Χριστιανοὶ γὰρ εἶναι κατηγορούμεθα· τὸ δὲ χρηστὸν μισεῖσθαι οὐ δίκαιον.

ἵνα ἐν αὐτῷ αὐξηθῆτε εἰς σωτηρίαν) 'that by it you may grow unto salvation'. The preposition need not be given as much weight as Hort suggests — 'in the power of it, in virtue of it'; ἐν with the dative is used as equivalent to the instrumental dative alone (cf. ἐν ξίφῳ, ἐν μαχαίρῃ etc.). 'Salvation' here, as in 1:9, clearly means the attainment of full spiritual development; it is eschatological only in the sense that this will become manifest at the 'Last Time', in the 'revelation of Jesus Christ'. (Cf. 1 John 3:2, 'Beloved, now are we the sons of God, and it doth not yet appear what we shall be. But we know that if He is made manifest, we shall be like Him, because we shall see Him as He is.') This salvation is to be attained through a process of growth, fostered by the continual nourishment of the newly-given life upon spiritual things.

The succession of ideas found in vv. 1-3 is paralleled in James 1:21 — 'Wherefore casting aside all filthiness, and overflowing of malice, receive with meekness the implanted Word, which is able to save your souls'. Here the nourishment of the soul is taken to be the divine principle that God has implanted within us — 'the ἔμφυτος λόγος cannot be taken without serious violence to language for any external word, Gospel or other, but must mean God's voice within' (Hort, p. 102). In both passages, the thought is substantially of Christ Himself under different aspects of His relation to us; it is by nourishing ourselves upon Him that we are brought to salvation.

Supplementary note on γάλα (v. 2).

Professor Cross (*op. cit.*, n. 75, p. 47) reproaches me, quite justly, with omitting the references in Christian writers. He himself refers to Tertullian *De Corona* 3, *Adv. Marc.* 1:14, and to Hippolytus *Apostolic Tradition* 23:2. The Hippolytus passage is confused (J. Crehan, *Early Christian Baptism and the Creed* [London: Burns, Oates and Washbourne, 1950], Appendix Five, 'Milk and Honey', p. 171, speaks of 'the stark incoherence of the Latin version'); but it is quite definitely *milk and honey* which are given to the newly-baptized after the first communion (so also in Tertullian). This is not a symbol of the nourishment appropriate to the newborn, however. It is explicitly said to symbolize the fulfilment of the promise to the fathers, that God would bring them into 'a land flowing with milk and honey'. The 'milk and honey' in turn become a symbol of 'the flesh of Christ through which those who believe are nourished like little children'. Here there is a mixture of *motifs*, a complexity that is not found in the simple figure of I Peter—milk as the appropriate nourishment of the newborn. I am not at all sure that the involved later symbolism throws light on the earlier passage; it seems more likely that the words of I Peter have been somewhat incongruously united in the later liturgical observance with the milk-and-honey (Promised Land) symbolism, which has no clear relevance to the imagery of the new birth.

The passages from *Odes of Solomon* cited by Dean Selwyn (*ad loc.*) seem to me to be quite irrelevant; and the citations from Clement of Alexandria are clearly echoes of I Peter.

⁴ πρὸς ὃν προσερχόμενοι, λίθον ϟῶντα, ὑπὸ ἀνθρώπων μὲν ἀποδεδοκιμασμένον παρὰ δὲ θεῷ ἐκλεκτὸν ἔντιμον, ⁵ καὶ αὐτοὶ ὡς λίθοι
ϟῶντες οἰκοδομεῖσθε οἶκος πνευματικὸς εἰς ἱεράτευμα ἅγιον, ἀνενέγκαι
πνευματικὰς θυσίας εὐπροσδέκτους θεῷ διὰ Ἰησοῦ Χριστοῦ. ⁶ διότι
περιέχει ἐν γραφῇ· ἰδοὺ τίθημι ἐν Σιὼν λίθον ἐκλεκτὸν ἀκρογωνιαῖον
ἔντιμον, καὶ ὁ πιστεύων ἐπ᾽ αὐτῷ οὐ μὴ καταισχυνθῇ.
    ⁷ ὑμῖν οὖν ἡ τιμὴ τοῖς πιστεύουσιν· ἀπιστοῦσιν δὲ
        λίθος ὃν ἀπεδοκίμασαν οἱ οἰκοδομοῦντες,
        οὗτος ἐγενήθη εἰς κεφαλὴν γωνίας,
⁸ καί,   λίθος προσκόμματος καὶ πέτρα σκανδάλου· οἱ προσκόπτουσιν
τῷ λόγῳ ἀπειθοῦντες· εἰς ὃ καὶ ἐτέθησαν. ⁹ ὑμεῖς δὲ γένος ἐκλεκτόν,
βασίλειον ἱεράτευμα, ἔθνος ἅγιον, λαὸς εἰς περιποίησιν, ὅπως τὰς
ἀρετὰς ἐξαγγείλητε τοῦ ἐκ σκότους ὑμᾶς καλέσαντος εἰς τὸ θαυμαστὸν
αὐτοῦ φῶς, ¹⁰ οἵ ποτε οὐ λαός, νῦν δὲ λαὸς θεοῦ, οἱ οὐκ ἠλεημένοι, νῦν
δὲ ἐλεηθέντες.

*In coming to Him, a Living Stone rejected by men but choice and
honourable in the sight of God, you yourselves also, as living stones,
are built up as a spiritual house for the duties of a holy priesthood,
to offer spiritual sacrifices acceptable to God, through Jesus Christ.
For it stands written,*
        *'Behold, I lay in Sion a choice and honourable cornerstone,
        And he that believes on Him shall not be put to shame.'*
For you, then, is the honour, you that believe; but for unbelievers
        *'The stone which the builders rejected, this was made the corner-
stone', and*
        'A stone to make them stumble, and a rock to foil them.'
*They stumble, in disobeying the Word; to this destiny they were
ordained. But you are*
        *'A chosen race, a kingly priesthood, a holy nation, a people for
God's prized possession',*
*that you may proclaim the mighty deeds of Him who called you out
of darkness into His marvellous light — you who aforetime were
'no people', but are now 'the people of God', who 'knew not God's
mercy', but now know His mercy.*

⁴ υπο) απο C   ⁵ λιθοι) λιθος ℵ* sah ϟωντες) οντες ℵ*   οικοδομεισθε) εποικ
ℵAᶜC vg πνευματικος) πνευματος ℵ εις) om KLP 33 69 ϛ vg syrʰˡ
πνευματικας) om ℵ θεω) pr τω ℵᶜ KLP 69 ϛ   ⁶ εν γραφη) η γραφη C :
εν τη γρ. KLP 69. ϛ εκλεκτον ακρογωνιαιον) transp. ℵAKLP 33. ϛ vg
sah syrʰˡ: txt BC 69. 1739. minusc. al. pauc. syrᵖ boh πιστευων)
πιστευσων vg sah αυτω) αυτον ℵ*   ⁷ απιστουσιν) απειθουσιν AKLP 69. ϛ
λιθος) λιθον ℵ* KLP 69. 1739. ϛ   ⁸ πετρα) πετραν ℵ οι) οσοι C ο) ην
παρεσκευασαν εαυτους ταξιν 69. 1739. 2412.   ⁹ υμεις) ημεις 69

v. 4. Many recent commentators and translators treat the main verb οἰκοδομεῖσθε as an imperative, which would impart the same force to the participle προσερχόμενοι — 'Come to Him, . . . and build yourselves up' (Goodspeed), 'Come to him then — . . . , come and be built' (Moffatt); similarly Bigg, Knopf, Windisch. It should be observed, however, that in such renderings, the idea of the main verb is subordinated to that of the participle — the real sense is 'Come . . . that you may be built'; and it is doubtful if this transference of the weight is justified. It seems better, therefore, to fall back upon the older practice of taking it as an indicative — 'In coming to Him . . . you are built', as above. (So Hort — 'Some good commentators take οἰκοδομεῖσθε as the imperative, but certainly wrongly'.)

The words will then be taken as introducing a second line of thought concerning the effects which follow upon the cultivation of the Christian life. He has just taught that by partaking of Christ as 'the spiritual unadulterated milk', we are enabled to grow to the attainment of spiritual maturity; now he brings forward the complementary thought, that this personal development is accompanied by a progressive incorporation into the spiritual household of Christ. Thus the thought of the brotherhood is again associated with the thought of personal holiness and attachment to Christ, and the whole passage culminates in a magnificent statement of the nature and function of the Church, wherein all the faithful, in living union with their Lord and with one another, serve God and proclaim His glories.

πρὸς ὃν προσερχόμενοι⟩ The new aspect of his teaching is introduced by another phrase borrowed from the same Psalm as the clause immediately preceding, and the figure under which Christ is presented is abruptly and radically changed. Psalm 33 (34):6 ('They looked unto Him and were radiant') is mistranslated in Lxx — προσέλθατε πρὸς αὐτόν, καὶ φωτισθῆτε — 'Come to Him, and be enlightened'. The passive of φωτίζω, and the cognate noun φωτισμός 'enlightenment' were commonly used of baptism in the second century (Justin Martyr, *First Apology*, sec. 61), and probably even in the first century (Hebrews 6:4; 10:32); and though the author makes use only of the first part of the line from the Psalm, its context must have been in his mind, so that for him, the 'coming' to Jesus would be in the first instance their baptism. The use of the present participle, however, indicates that his thought does not limit itself to that; the Christian keeps coming to Christ, and is progressively built into the living fabric of the holy society, in union with Christ.

In English, this phrase has an appearance of familiarity which it does not possess in Greek (See Hort's note, *ad loc*). The N.T. seldom speaks of 'coming' to Jesus, except for a few passages in the Fourth Gospel (5:40; 6:35, 37, 44, 45, 65; 7:37), where the verb ἔρχομαι is used, followed by πρός, in a sense only slightly different from πιστεύειν εἰς (note the parallelism of the two expressions in John 6:35, and 7:37-38).

The only other passage in which the expression occurs is the well known 'Come unto Me' — δεῦτε πρός με (Matt. 11:28), where it means 'Come as my disciples', being explained by the following 'Take my yoke upon you, and learn of Me'. The compound προσέρχομαι is not found elsewhere in N.T. with a following πρός, but always with the simple dative; and except in Hebrews, always in the literal sense of a physical approach to a person or place. In Hebrews, it is used of the approach to God in worship (4:6 — 'to the throne of grace'; 4:25 and 11:16 — 'to God'; 10:1 and 22 — absolutely, but with the implication that God is the object). In Hebrews 12:18, 22 — 'to the mount that might be touched ... to mount Sion' etc., we do indeed find 'Jesus, the Mediator of the New Testament' as one of the objects of the verb, but here the imagery is concrete, and based upon an idea of physical locality, and it is the whole figure, not alone the verb, that is applied to the realm of the spiritual. Thus there is no real parallel to this πρὸς ὃν προσερχόμενοι anywhere in the N.T., and it has to be interpreted partly in the light of the O.T. context from which it is borrowed, and partly in relation to the figure of the building-stones, which it introduces.

λίθον ζῶντα, etc.⟩ The figure is exceptionally complex. It sustains through a wider development several lines of thought arising out of applications which earlier Christian interpreters had already given to three separate passages of O.T., which have nothing in common but the word λίθος. There is, first, the passage in Psalm 117 (118): 22, which our Lord had Himself applied to His mission and destiny (Mk. 12:10; Matt. 21:42; Lk. 20:17; and again in a different context, Mk. 8:31; Lk. 9:22; cf. also Acts 4:11) — 'The stone which the builders rejected, this was made the head of the corner'. Part of the first phrase is employed in v. 4 ('rejected by men'), and the whole verse is introduced in v. 7. Next, there is the passage in Isaiah 28:16, which in Lxx has the form — ἰδοὺ ἐγὼ ἐμβάλλω εἰς τὰ θεμέλια Σειὼν λίθον πολυτελῆ ἐκλεκτὸν ἀκρογωνιαῖον ἔντιμον, εἰς τὰ θεμέλια αὐτῆς, καὶ ὁ πιστεύων οὐ μὴ καταισχυνθῇ. 'Behold, I lay for the foundations of Sion a valuable stone, a choice and honourable cornerstone for her foundations, and he that believeth shall not be put to shame.' (Cheyne comments — 'To understand the form of this prophecy, we must recollect the enormous size and cost of the foundation-stones of Eastern public buildings', and he cites 1 Kings 5:17 — 'great stones, costly stones, hewed stones, to lay the foundation of the house' — *Prophecies of Isaiah*, Vol. I, 4th ed., p. 166.) This verse is cited in an abbreviated form, partly borrowed from St. Paul's misquotation in Romans 9:33, in v. 6; and the words ἐκλεκτὸν ἔντιμον are taken up in v. 4, and ὁ πιστεύων in v. 7 (τοῖς πιστεύουσιν). ἐπ' αὐτῷ is a Christian gloss, which has been taken up into the Lxx text by the scribes of א AQ. The passage is not itself Messianic, but takes the great foundation-stone of the temple in Jerusalem as a symbol of the unchangeable, abiding firmness and adequacy of God, who is Himself the Rock on which His people is founded. It had, however, already been applied to Christ and the Church in a splendid passage of Ephesians (2:20-22), which is clearly laid under contribution here — ἐποικοδομηθέντες ἐπὶ τῷ θεμελίῳ τῶν ἀποστόλων καὶ προφητῶν, ὄντος ἀκρογωνιαίου αὐτοῦ Χριστοῦ Ἰησοῦ, ἐν ᾧ πᾶσα οἰκοδομὴ συναρμολογουμένη αὔξει εἰς ναὸν ἅγιον ἐν Κυρίῳ — 'Built upon the foundation of the apostles and prophets, Jesus Christ Himself being the cornerstone, by whom the whole edifice is fitted together and grows into a holy temple in the Lord'. The third passage employed is taken from Isaiah 8:14, which had already been combined with Isaiah 28:16 by St. Paul, who quoted erroneously, evidently translating the Hebrew from memory, and confusing the two passages in his mind — ἰδοὺ τίθημι ἐν Σιὼν λίθον προσκόμματος καὶ πέτραν σκανδάλου; and in First Peter the words are borrowed from this rendering given by St. Paul, not directly from the Lxx, which is quite differently phrased. The Petrine passage is thus not an independent application of the O.T. texts, but a development of the use already made of them in earlier writings; probably, indeed, the texts were familiar to all Christians in similar applications.

The transition from the figure of the 'Milk' to that of the 'Stone' is abrupt. Perdelwitz (MR. pp. 69-70) has attempted to show, however, that the two images were already connected in the mystery-cults; he refers to the black meteorite which was held to be the abode of the Phrygian mother-goddess, and to the widespread cult of the stone image in Syria (even the idea of 'animate stones'—λίθοι ἔμψυχοι); and points again to the cup of milk given to initiates in the same cults. A better illustration might be found in the images of Artemis of the Ephesians. The image in the great temple of Ephesus was evidently a meteorite, probably in its natural state (Acts 19:35 τοῦ διοπετοῦς); but the goddess, whose cult was widespread (cf. Acts 19:27 – ἣν ὅλη ἡ Ἀσία καὶ ἡ οἰκουμένη σέβεται), was regularly represented as a queenly figure with multiple breasts, capable of nourishing all her devotees with her milk. It is tempting to think that the words of the Epistle were meant to be understood against such a background. Instead of the dead stone image of the mother-goddess with manifold breasts, the Christians come to the living Christ, who feeds them with the 'spiritual milk'. But this line of interpretation is not convincing; for the Stone in the figure is not an image, but a building-stone.

ὑπὸ ἀνθρώπων μὲν ἀποδεδοκιμασμένον) 'rejected by men'–The change from 'the builders' to 'men' is deliberate. In the Gospels and Acts, 'the builders' is interpreted to mean 'the rulers of Israel' (Mk. 8:31 — δεῖ τὸν υἱὸν τοῦ ἀνθρώπου... ἀποδοκιμασθῆναι ὑπὸ τῶν πρεσβυτέρων καὶ τῶν ἀρχιερέων καὶ τῶν γραμματέων,–Acts 4:11 – ὁ λίθος ὁ ἐξουδενηθεὶς ὑφ' ὑμῶν τῶν οἰκοδόμων – addressed to the Sanhedrim). In the Psalm itself, it seems to mean rather the architects of the world-order, the Assyrians or the powerful nations generally, which had sought to crush Israel. In St. Paul, it is applied to unbelieving Israel as a whole, in reference to the national repudiation of Jesus. Now it is extended to men in general; the world as a whole is manifesting hostility to the Gospel and refusing to accept Jesus as the cornerstone of life.

παρὰ δὲ θεῷ ἐκλεκτὸν ἔντιμον⟩ Despite the hostility of the mass of mankind, the purpose of God stands firm. ἐκλεκτόν again has the double sense of 'choice' and 'chosen' (cf. note on ἐκλεκτοῖς 1:1); and in ἔντιμον, the sense of the underlying τιμή is strong, being emphasized by the introduction of the noun itself in v. 7 — not so much 'precious' (which would be rather the πολυτελῆ omitted from the citation, or τίμιον), but 'held in honour' (the usual classical sense), or even 'destined to honour'. The rejection by men cannot alter the fixed purpose of God, who has irrevocably chosen Christ for honour.

v. 5.   Those who come to Christ are 'changed into the same image' (2 Cor. 3:18). As He is the Living Stone, so they become living stones, as they are built with Him into the spiritual structure of the divine household.

οἶκος πνευματικός⟩ The word οἶκος combines the thought of 'house' and 'household'. The former sense is the more appropriate to the figure of the living building-stones. God's true house is spiritual, and its stones are the lives of those that believe. The contrast here is with 'temples made with hands', whether that of Israel or those of pagan deities. God dwells not in these, but in the society of the redeemed. (Acts 7:48; 17.24, etc., and 1 Cor. 3:16-17; 6:19; 2 Cor. 6:16). But the writer has deliberately chosen to use οἶκος in place of the ναός of these Pauline passages, and of Ephesians 2:21, which he has most in mind, in order that he may develop the secondary thought of 'household' (cf. Hebrews 3:1-6). The 'household' is 'spiritual' in that the bond which unites it is spiritual, in contrast with Israel, where the link of brotherhood was racial (cf. 'my brethren and kindred according to the flesh' — Rom. 9:3), and in that it exists to exercise spiritual functions.

εἰς ἱεράτευμα ἅγιον, ἀνενέγκαι πνευματικὰς θυσίας⟩ 'for a holy priest-hood, to offer spiritual sacrifices' — The noun ἱεράτευμα may have either of two senses: it may be a collective, meaning 'body of priests', like the similar formation στράτευμα — 'body of soldiers, army'; or it may be used concretely, of 'the exercise of priestly functions'. The latter is more appropriate here, both because of the preposition εἰς, which distinguishes it from the use in apposition which we have in v. 9, and because of the epexegetic infinitive ἀνενέγκαι which follows, defining the nature of the priestly function which is exercised. A group of authorities omit the εἰς here, probably through the influence of v. 9. The adjective ἅγιον is not to be taken as a commonplace, a 'permanent epithet' with ἱεράτευμα, as if all priesthoods or priestly services were 'holy'; but rather as distinguishing *this* priesthood from all others as alone having that relation to God which constitutes holiness. The 'spiritual sacrifices' must be understood in the light of the 'spiritual house' — not, therefore, of any kind of external acts, however devoutly offered, but of the perpetual offering of our lives (Rom. 12:1; Eph. 5:2), substance (Phil. 4:18), and thanksgivings, kind deeds, and generous sharing (Heb. 13:15-16), all of which are declared to be acceptable (δεκτός), or well-pleasing (εὐάρεστος) to Him. Here again, we find gathered together thoughts which had found varied expression in earlier literature.

Christianity in the second century tended to look upon all external rites of sacrifice, even those of the Jewish religion, as incompatible with the true knowledge of God. The anonymous *Epistle to Diognetus*, for instance, makes little distinction between them. It is folly to offer things in sacrifice to idols, because they are senseless objects, incapable of knowing that the offering is made, much less of profiting by it; but it is equally foolish to offer them to God, since He is Himself the Giver of all things and has no need of anything for Himself. 'Just as the Greeks exhibit folly in offering sacrifices to things senseless and deaf, so the Jews should realize that they are showing no piety, but rather folly, in supposing that they offer these things to God, as though He needed them. . . . Those who think that they are consecrating sacrifices to Him through blood and burnt fat and whole burnt-offerings . . . seem to me to be no better than those who show the same honour to deaf images' (*Ep. to Diog.*, sec. 3). The thought of any Christian rite as a sacrifice is foreign to the New Testament. The sacrifices of Christians are 'spiritual' as offered in the 'spiritual house' of God, and as being the inward response of the human spirit to the Spirit of God, in gratitude and faith. It is worship offered not 'in a pattern and shadow of the heavenly things' (ἐν ὑποδείγματι καὶ σκιᾷ . . . τῶν ἐπουρανίων — Heb. 8:5), but 'in spirit and in truth' (John 4:23-24).

εὐπροσδέκτους θεῷ⟩ 'acceptable to God', because spiritual — spiritual and so acceptable. The order of the words imposes this interpretation, and at the same time obliges us to take διὰ Ἰησοῦ Χριστοῦ with ἀνενέγκαι, not with εὐπροσδέκτους. That is to say, the thought is not that 'spiritual sacrifices' are acceptable to God because offered through Jesus Christ; but that the 'spiritual household', exercising its appointed functions of 'holy priesthood', offers sacrifices to God through Jesus Christ, and these sacrifices are acceptable to God because (unlike the sacrifices offered in Jewish and pagan worship) they are spiritual.

They are offered 'through Jesus Christ' because He is the Mediator, and apart from Him we cannot come before God in any capacity. The theology of the New Testament consistently teaches that we are never brought into an immediate relationship with God, which could dispense with the mediation of Christ. As we come to God through Him in the first instance, so we remain dependent upon Him for the continuance of our life with God. The mysticism which aspires to an immediate apprehension of God by the human soul in this life is found in Neo-platonism, Sufism, and Hinduism; but when it occurs in Christian circles it must be regarded as an aberration. 'Without Me, ye can do nothing.' Thus even the sacrifices which are spiritual and acceptable to God, cannot be offered to Him except through the mediation of His Son, our great High Priest who stands for us in the Holy of Holies, in the Presence of the Majesty on High.

v. 6. διότι περιέχει ἐν γραφῇ⟩ A fine example of the impersonal use of περιέχει is given in the Moulton and Milligan *Vocabulary*, from P. Oxy. II, 249, 24 — διαθήκη ὡς περιέχει — 'in the will as it stands written'. (The other examples offered are not true parallels to the usage here, for though they are intransitive they are not impersonal.) The verb properly means 'include', and in this impersonal use of the active (in passive sense) we have a parallel in the third singular to a usage that is fairly common in the third plural (Moulton-Howard, *Grammar of N.T. Greek*, Vol. II, Appendix on 'Semitisms in the N.T.', p. 447). This is not a Semitism, however, but an effect of the drift towards the disuse of the passive, which is rare in modern Greek.

v. 7. ὑμῖν οὖν ἡ τιμὴ τοῖς πιστεύουσιν⟩ 'To you, therefore, is the honour, you that believe'.[1] The phrase is exceedingly difficult. The οὐ μὴ καταισχυνθῇ of the citation is evidently taken as a *litotes*, the Greek literary device of understatement, the negative conveying the sense of a strong affirmation of the opposite (cf. τάραχος οὐκ ὀλίγος, Acts 12:18 and 19:23 — 'no small stir' = 'a very great stir'). Thus the writer takes from it the meaning 'shall be honoured', or 'shall receive honour', rather than 'shall not be put to shame', and this enables him to use ἡ τιμὴ in v. 7 in the corresponding relation with πιστεύω. But it is scarcely possible to deny that ἡ τιμή is also to be referred back to ἔντιμον, and the use of the article emphasizes this connection — 'the' honour which is accorded to believers is a share in the honour which God has accorded to Christ, with whom they are united in the building of the spiritual house. The thought is not at all eschatological; the honour is not that which is to be bestowed upon the faithful in the Judgment Day, but that which is given them here and now, in their incorporation into the divine temple which rests upon the 'honourable' cornerstone, Jesus Christ.

The interpretation of ὑμῖν as 'in your eyes', as in the translation 'to you he is precious' is impossible, for this would not be an application of the second line of the citation at all. It would in any case be quite without point, tautological, since the whole thought would already be included in the participle; faith, in the context, means precisely giving to Christ the honour which has been appointed for Him by God. The verse clearly sets in contrast the behaviour and destiny of the believing and the unbelieving — to the believing, the honour of a place in the spiritual house; to the unbelieving, shame and disaster, the wreckage of life upon the very Stone which was meant to be its foundation.

ἀπιστοῦσιν δέ⟩ With respect to the unbelieving, the two sayings of Scripture are proven true, for their discomfiture. The old proverb,

---

[1] So in the Vulgate and Old Latin (δ): vobis igitur honor credentibus.

applied by our Lord and by St. Paul to Israel and its rulers, is now given
a wider application, in keeping with the introduction of ἀνθρώπων in
v. 4, noted above. Christ is now seen as the key to all human destiny
and the touchstone of all endeavour; faith in Him leads to honour,
unbelief to disaster. 'The stone which the builders reject is made the
head of the corner.' 'The builders' now is taken to mean all who attempt
to build human society or to construct their own lives; in the latter
sense it will include all mankind, in the former it will have particular
reference to the civil authorities. The familiar words seem to be treated
as a proverb, which they probably were in the first place (cf. Duhm's
remark 'Der Satz ... klingt wie ein Volkssprichwort' — in *Die
Psalmen*², 1922, p. 414). The *Westminster Dictionary of the Bible* suggests that 'the head of the corner' means a massive cornerstone which
is set not in the foundation, but at the upper corner of the building, to
bind the walls firmly together. A huge stone suitable for this purpose
would be useless to the builders in any other position, and would have
to be 'rejected' while the walls were going up, yet its very size would
make it a continual stumbling-block to all concerned with the building
as long as it lay on the ground unused. Notice that the second saying —
λίθος προσκόμματος etc. — is not a predicate complement of ἐγενήθη but
is to be construed in parallelism with λίθος ὃν ἀπεδοκίμασαν. Unbelievers find, on the one hand, that the Stone which they reject is made
the keystone of the divine order of human society, from which they
are therefore excluded as long as they persist in their unbelief; and on
the other hand, that the same Stone is an insuperable obstacle to their
efforts at building an order of their own devising without it. There
is a superficial difficulty in the double thought of the Stone as at one
and the same time fixed in place in the building for those that accept it,
and yet lying in the path to hamper and foil the efforts of those that
reject it; but the double image is necessary and true. Christ is too great
to be neglected or avoided. For His followers, he becomes the foundation on which all life rests; where He is rejected, there is and can be only
chaos and anarchy. The Roman Emperors discovered this to be true
after three centuries of desperate struggle to build a stable society
without Him, and the same truth has been verified in all human
experience ever since. His Church survives through the wreckage of all
the systems which the world devises for itself.

v. 8. οἳ προσκόπτουσιν τῷ λόγῳ ἀπειθοῦντες⟩ A brief comment on
λίθος προσκόμματος, explaining the nature, or cause, of the stumbling.
λόγῳ is the object of ἀπειθοῦντες, not of προσκόπτουσιν; grammatically,
it could be taken with both, as Hort suggests, but not without disturbing
the natural flow of the thought. They stumble at the stumbling-stone
(Rom. 9:32), through disobeying the Word. τῷ λόγῳ ἀπειθοῦντες has
an Heraclitean-Stoic ring, as of rebellion against the fundamental divine
principle of the universe, the divine Reason which rules all things.
ὁ λόγος here, as in 1:23, means more than 'the Gospel message', though

it includes this, as the critical point of the divine-human encounter at which a decision must be made in response to the revelation of the Divine.

εἰς ὃ καὶ ἐτέθησαν⟩ 'To which also they were appointed' — by divine ordinance, as Christ was appointed (τίθημι, v. 6) to be the Stone. The will of God decrees the ruin of unbelief, as surely as the exaltation of faith. The words are to be taken with the main verb προσκόπτουσιν, rather than with the participle; it is the stumbling that is foreordained, rather than the unbelief which leads to it. Yet in the light of the Pauline passage on the unbelief of Israel (Romans 9), which he clearly has in mind throughout this section, it is perhaps better not to make such a separation between the unbelief and its consequences, and to take the thought of the divine decree of reprobation as including both. (Cf. especially Rom. 9:17-22 — 'What is there said ... is more explicitly awful than St. Peter's short phrase' — Hort.) The doctrine appals us, but we are not entitled to discard it, merely because it shatters and annihilates a too comfortable, and therefore inadequate conception which we entertain of God. Those that reject the Word are as truly in God's hands as those that believe, and His primal purpose embraces all alike. Knopf remarks with truth that 'The author has no thought whatever of offering a dogmatic theory in these few words, and the difficult problem of the relation between the freewill of man, and the foreknowledge and predestination of God is far from his mind'. But even in this passing reference, the underlying doctrine of predestination is manifest, reflecting the belief, so starkly expounded by St. Paul, that the fixed purpose of God is fulfilled in the unbelieving and disobedient, the 'vessels of wrath', as truly as in the 'vessels of mercy, which He had afore prepared unto glory'.

It should be kept in mind that for St. Paul, the total meaning and ultimate effect of the divine decrees is not yet revealed. The reprobation of Israel, their unbelief and stumbling, issues in the widening of the Church to embrace the Gentiles; and in due time, after 'the fulness of the Gentiles' has been gathered in, 'all Israel shall be saved'. In the splendid words of Hort, 'If we pursue St. Paul's argument to the end, we see that his purpose is to draw the utmost range of human perverseness within the mysterious folds of God's will, so that nothing should be left outside, that God's will may be seen at last in the far future accomplishing its purpose of good.... If it was an overwhelming thought that God Himself had appointed them unto stumbling, it was at last the only satisfying thought, for so it was made sure that they were in His hands and His keeping for ever'. In this respect also, the Pauline argument, which is directly concerned only with the unbelief, rejection, and ultimate salvation of Israel, may legitimately be extended in application to the whole world.

vv. 9-10. In concluding the section, the writer turns again to the thought of Christian believers in their corporate character and function.

The entire description is taken from the Greek Old Testament, with slight adaptation; he claims for the Church that place in the divine economy which the teachers of Israel had set before their nation as the destiny to which it was called. For him, Judaism is no longer a problem, and the relation of the Church to the historical Israel is not an issue. The Church is the Israel of God (cf. Gal. 6:16), and the scriptures of the Old Testament belong to her, not in any secondary or spiritualized application, but in their primary sense and purpose. He has gone far beyond the thought of St. Paul, that Israel is the parent stock on which Gentiles have been grafted (Romans 10) and also beyond the thought of the Epistle to the Ephesians, that the two strains of Jew and Gentile have now been merged in a new body. He has much less concern for Israel as a distinct historical and religious entity than either of these predecessors. He does not even think of the 'Gentiles' — τὰ ἔθνη — as non-Jews, but as unbelievers, and it never occurs to him that a religious problem is involved in the relation of the Church to Judaism. For him, God has been dealing with the Church — one might better say, has been forming the Church — from the beginning of His redemptive revelation of Himself to men. His thought is not that the Church has now supplanted or superseded Israel, but rather that the Church has been the object of God's concern all the while, though in earlier times she drew her membership from a single nation and is now open to all men. The Church which he knows is predominantly Gentile, and recognizes no distinctions of race, either as a privilege or as a problem, and it never occurs to him to imagine that Israel has a prior or peculiar right in the ancient Scriptures.

This appropriation of the Old Testament, which is not peculiar to First Peter, but reflects the common attitude of the Church once it had completely emancipated itself from the trammels of Judaism, had the most fruitful consequences. It imparted to the Church a profound social and political self-consciousness, and furnished the new society with a past history as well as an outlook on the future. The moral and spiritual factors making for Christian unity were thus supplemented by a powerful historical element, from which the Church derived the sense that she was not merely an association of like-minded persons co-operating with one another for certain specific purposes, but an enduring social organism, having a corporate life and a corporate significance not wholly expressed in her institutional forms and her moral and spiritual principles, but grounded in a continuum of historical experience and development.

The possession of such an inheritance of social history has saved her from becoming wholly subordinated to her own institutions of government, to the forms of doctrine in which from time to time she has expressed her faith, or to the Scriptures to which she has ascribed canonical authority. Highly as she has prized all three, and tempted as she has been to elevate one or all of them into constitutive principles of her existence, she has always had an underlying realization that these are the *products* of her life, not its formative causes or its ends. It has likewise saved her from the equally great danger of dissolving in the mists of a pure spiritualism divorced from the temporal and the concrete. The Spirit by which she lives informs her as a body manifest in history, one, holy, and catholic, growing in faith and knowledge till she attain her destined perfection, the realization of the ideal that is ever held before her, 'the measure of the stature of the fulness of Christ'.

γένος ἐκλεκτὸν . . . ὅπως τὰς ἀρετὰς ἐξαγγείλητε⟩ The framework of this passage is taken from Isaiah 43:20-21 — ἔδωκα ἐν τῇ ἐρήμῳ ὕδωρ . . . ποτίσαι τὸ γένος μου τὸ ἐκλεκτόν, λαόν μου ὃν περιεποιησάμην τὰς ἀρετάς μου διηγεῖσθαι. — 'I have provided water in the desert . . . to give drink to my chosen race, the people which I have acquired to declare my wonderful works'. For ὃν περιεποιησάμην, which could not have been employed without awkwardness, he has substituted εἰς περιποίησιν, and the infinitive διηγεῖσθαι is replaced by ὅπως . . . ἐξαγγείλητε, perhaps through the influence of Psalm 9:15 — ὅπως ἂν ἐξαγγείλω πάσας τὰς αἰνέσεις σου — (Have mercy upon me, O Lord) 'That I may proclaim all Thy praises'. Within this framework he sets two phrases from Exodus 19:6 — ὑμεῖς δὲ ἔσεσθέ μοι βασίλειον ἱεράτευμα καὶ ἔθνος ἅγιον — 'Ye shall be unto Me a kingly priesthood (for the Hebrew *mam'leketh koh'nim* — "a kingdom of priests") and a holy nation'. The terms are all corporate, and the thought is wholly concerned with the nature and function of the Church as a body, not with the activities of Christians as individuals.

There is considerable boldness in the language which describes the Christian Church as a γένος, ἔθνος, λαός — 'a race', 'a nation', 'a people' — when in literal fact it embraced members of many different races and nations — in principle, indeed, members of 'all races and peoples and kindreds and tongues' (Apoc. 7:9). Yet it must be remembered that there was a distinct tendency in the ancient world to think of religion as the essential basis of community, and of common religious observances as the determining feature of nationhood and the one really significant factor of homogeneity. The biological factor was involved only in so far as it was itself conceived to have a religious basis; and the lay state, which regards religion as irrelevant to its proper functioning and so leaves it to the discretion of the individual, was undreamed of. Even Rome, which accorded a wide tolerance to private cults of every description, and largely removed civil law from the sphere of religion, continued to look upon the official religion as the necessary centre and safeguard of the common life; and the ancient city-state was built upon the civic religion, in the rites of which all citizens participated. Undoubtedly, individuals might be slack in the performance of their religious duties; temples might be neglected, and the dues of sacrifice unpaid at times; and the spiritual impulses and desires might find satisfaction in esoteric cults and private brotherhoods. But when men withdrew purposefully and openly from participation in the rites of the official religion, as Christians were bound to do, then they ceased to be members of the community in any effective sense; the old ties of social relationship were broken. Negatively, therefore, those who became Christians had no more part in the race or nation of their birth; and positively, they formed new ties, and were united in a new community which was less a private brotherhood like those of the mystery-religions, than the unifying bond of all existence which we find in the nation or state. The Romans already regarded the Jews not as one race among many, but as a race apart, and they came in no long time to regard the Christians as a 'third race', distinct alike from the Jews and from the generality of the Empire's inhabitants, loosely designated 'Romans'. This description of the Christian society, therefore, was by no means an extravagant image, but a penetrating perception of the true situation and character of the Church.

[ἐπεὶ γὰρ οἱ ἀπὸ διαφόρων ἐθνῶν καὶ νομίμων κληθέντες ἀποβεβλήκασι πᾶσαν ποικιλίαν ἐν τῷ ἀναλαβεῖν μίαν γνώμην, μιᾷ πίστει καὶ διδασκαλίᾳ προσέχοντες, δι' ἣν ψυχὴ καὶ καρδία γίνεται μία, ἓν ἅγιον ἔθνος εἰσίν. 'For since those that were called out of many nations and cultures have cast aside all diversity in embracing one view, adhering to one faith and teaching, whereby they become one in heart and soul, they are now one holy nation.' (J. A. Cramer, *Catenae*, Vol. VIII, p. 53.)]

ἐκλεκτόν⟩ 'chosen', — previously applied to Christians as individuals (1:1), and to Christ as the Cornerstone (2:4), is now used of the Church as a whole. ἅγιον — 'holy' — in its primary sense of 'consecrated, dedicated, set apart' for the service of God.

βασίλειον ἱεράτευμα⟩ 'a kingly priesthood' — The Greek word ἱερεύς — 'priest' — was never taken over by the Church to denote any office or function in its own ministry. The word 'priest' in English derives from the Greek πρεσβύτερος — 'presbyter', 'elder', which has no sacerdotal significance in itself or in early Christian usage, and only acquires it in the third century, as the whole conception of the nature of the Christian Ministry changes. It is a remarkable fact that the Church of New Testament times, in developing the institutions necessary to its corporate life with great originality and boldness, refrained from creating an order of priests. It had apostles, prophets, teachers, evangelists, pastors, elders, bishops, and deacons. In the earliest times, these were hardly 'orders' in any formal sense, for men were not as a rule set apart by stated rites of consecration, or inhibited from the exercise of any function of ministry by the lack of ecclesiastical authorization. The varied ministries were exercised in the employment of the spiritual gifts of each for the benefit of all. The situation which prevailed in the Apostolic Age is set forth most clearly in 1 Corinthians 12:4-11; the χαρίσματα, διακονίαι, ἐνεργήματα do not accompany offices in the Church, but are individual gifts, distributed to each, severally, by the Spirit, as He wills (v. 11). The greater formality of appointment, with solemn ordinations and dedications of elders and other officers, which we find in the book of Acts and in the Pastoral Epistles, reflects the practice of a much later period. But the significant thing is not the degree of informality which prevailed, but the fact that none of these functions was sacerdotal; with all the 'diversities of gifts', there was no hieratical ministry. This is the more remarkable in view of the fact that Israel, though ideally 'a kingdom of priests', nevertheless had its priestly order, which was alone competent to offer sacrifice; and of course all the religions of the time had their priesthoods. But as the Christian religion had no use for rites of sacrifice, it had no place for a priesthood. Both sacrifice and priesthood were indeed retained in the Church, but as functions of the whole community; and the 'spiritual sacrifices' were, as we have seen, not external rites of any kind which could be performed by a priesthood, but the offering of ourselves to God in continual and entire dedication to His service, which could not be accomplished by surrogates designated for the purpose, but required that the community in its totality should be a priesthood.

The sense in which this priesthood is termed 'royal' is not easy to determine. As mentioned above, the phrase in the Septuagint is a mistranslation of the Hebrew, which would require to be rendered 'a kingdom of priests' — the word 'kingdom' being used in the general sense of 'national community' without regard to its form of government. The Lxx translators may have had a different text before them, and may have intended βασίλειον for a substantive, to which ἱεράτευμα would stand in apposition — 'a kingdom, priests' (cf. Apoc. 1:6 — ἐποίησεν ἡμᾶς βασιλείαν, ἱερεῖς τῷ θεῷ — (Christ) 'has made us a kingdom, priests to God'; which may be an independent translation of the Hebrew text). However that may be, it is unquestionably used as an adjective here, and there is no suggestion of the saints reigning as kings upon the earth (as in Apoc. 5:10). Probably the writer was content to take the phrase as it stood in his Greek Old Testament, as a divinely-given title of the people of God, without feeling himself under any necessity to define its significance more precisely in Christian terms; at all events he does not develop the thought of the 'kingly', as he does that of the priesthood, and without such help from him, we can only guess at what may have been in his mind. Hort suggests that 'the kingship of Him to whom the priesthood here spoken of is consecrated is intended and alone intended'. It would perhaps be better to seek to understand the phrase in the light of the fundamental notion of the kingly office itself. In origin, priesthood and kingship are not separate from one another; on the contrary, priesthood is a function, perhaps the principal function, of the Kingship, and the officiating priests are merely the King's surrogates in local and limited duties. The divine virtue that maintains effective contact between the community and the mysterious Powers on which its welfare depends, resides in the King alone; and the royal priesthood therefore embraces all others, and is alone complete and ultimate. Some element of this way of thinking may underlie the words both in this passage and in Exodus. The holy community is to be a 'kingly priesthood' in relation to the whole world, not as ruling it (though this aspect easily intrudes, and at times becomes dominant), but as mediating the divine power and blessing to all mankind.

λαὸς εἰς περιποίησιν⟩ 'a people for God's possession' — The expression conveys rather more than the phrase ὃν περιεποιησάμην of the Septuagint Isaiah, which it replaces — not merely 'a people which God has acquired', but a people which finds the end of its existence in its possession by God; it becomes a 'people', a true community, only through the action of God in making it His own, and it is brought into being in order that it may be His, a community distinguished from all others by its unique relation to Him. The phrase is used in the same sense in Malachi 3:17 — καὶ ἔσονταί μοι . . . εἰς ἡμέραν ἣν ἐγὼ ποιῶ, εἰς περιποίησιν — 'They shall be mine . . . on the day that I am about to make — my very own'. (Translation of J. M. Powis Smith, in *The Complete Bible: An American Translation*, Chicago, 1939.)

ὅπως τὰς ἀρετὰς ἐξαγγείλητε τοῦ ἐκ σκότους ὑμᾶς καλέσαντος εἰς τὸ θαυμαστὸν αὐτοῦ φῶς⟩ The final clause, like the infinitive in the Isaiah passage, states the purpose for which God has made this people His possession. διηγέομαι in Isaiah and ἐξαγγέλλω in the Psalms represent the same Hebrew word (ספר — to narrate, declare); but to a Greek διηγέομαι would have rather the sense of 'explain', and ἐξαγγέλλω of 'proclaim'; the latter is preferred here as more appropriate to the proclamation of the Gospel. The thought is certainly of preaching, not of the testimony borne silently by life and conduct. He who calls us is God, as in 1:15 and 5:10, and in the general usage of the N.T. (1 Cor. 7:15ff.; Gal. 1:6, 15; Heb. 5:4, etc.). Christ is not said to 'call' us; God calls us 'in Christ', or 'through the grace of Christ'.

τὰς ἀρετάς⟩ not 'virtues', or 'excellencies', or 'praises' but 'wonderful works'. In contemporary pagan usage, the ἀρεταί of a god are his miracles; and the compound ἀρεταλόγος is used in Greek and borrowed in Latin, of the wandering story-tellers who went about recounting the marvellous deeds of some saviour-god, or of famous men. (S. Reinach, 'Les Arétalogues dans l'Antiquité' — in *Bull. de Corr. Hell.*, IX (1885), pp. 257ff.) Deissmann brought forward some evidence of the use of the word in this sense (*Bible Studies*, E.T., pp. 95-6), and still better evidence from inscriptions is offered in M. and M. The 'wonderful works' of God to be proclaimed, would be first of all His calling them out of darkness into light, and then more generally, the mighty acts which He wrought in Christ when He raised Him from the dead and gave him glory (1:21).

ἐκ σκότους, etc.⟩ Conversion from paganism to Christianity is frequently described in the New Testament under the figure of the contrast of darkness and light. Thus in Acts 26:18, the purpose of St. Paul's mission to the Gentiles is set forth as 'to open their eyes, to turn them from darkness unto light, and from the power of Satan unto God, that they may receive the forgiveness of sins and a portion among the sanctified'. Pagans are said to 'walk in the vanity of their minds, darkened in understanding — ἐσκωτισμένοι τῇ διανοίᾳ, — alienated from the life of God, because of the ignorance that is in them, because of the hardness of their hearts'. (Eph. 4:17-18.) Conversion is en-lightenment, which brings 'the knowledge of the glory of God in the face of Christ', like the primal light of the creation dispelling the darkness. (2 Cor. 4:6 — ὁ θεὸς ὁ εἰπών· Ἐκ σκότους φῶς λάμψει, ὃς ἔλαμψεν ἐν ταῖς καρδίαις ἡμῶν πρὸς φωτισμὸν τῆς γνώσεως τῆς δόξης τοῦ θεοῦ ἐν προσώπῳ Χριστοῦ.) The contrast is moral, intellectual, and social — knowledge in place of ignorance, obedience in place of dis-obedience, virtue in place of vice, love in place of hate, fellowship in place of alienation. (Eph. 5:1-14; 1 John 1:6-7; 2:9-11.) This light is 'marvellous', 'wonderful' (θαυμαστόν), not only as evoking our wonder, but even more as exhibiting the wonders of God's power, the ἀρεταί, which we are to proclaim.

This contrast of φῶς and σκότος, σκοτία is not peculiar to the religious vocabulary of Christianity, but is widely employed in the contemporary paganism;[1] cf., e.g., the words of Tractate VII of the Hermetic Corpus, Section 2a—'Seek a guide to lead you to the doors of Knowledge, where is the radiant light, that which is pure of darkness.' ζητήσατε χει-ραγωγόν, τὸν ὁδηγήσοντα ὑμᾶς ἐπὶ τὰς τῆς γνώσεως θύρας, ὅπου ἐστὶ τὸ λαμπρὸν φῶς, τὸ καθαρὸν σκότους. Perdelwitz (MR. 77ff.) seeks to relate the entire clause to the ritual of the mysteries. From varied sources he collects the information that in an advanced stage of his mystic progress, the initiate waits in the darkness of the inner temple for the revelation of the deity, not venturing to enter the sanctuary itself, the ἄδυτον, until the god calls him in a vision. Then, in the climactic experience of the rite, a blaze of light bursts forth upon him and dispels the darkness; — he is 'called out of darkness into wonderful light'. It is not to be denied that here, as in many other aspects, Christianity exhibits striking parallels of vocabulary and imagery with the cults that were its principal rivals for the spiritual allegiance of mankind. Though the language of our passage can, as we have seen, be sufficiently explained and illustrated by earlier Christian usage, it does unmistakably reflect forms of religious thought that were generally familiar in that age. This observa-tion should neither surprise nor dismay us, but should rather lead us to reflect that if the Gospel is to win the hearts of men in any age, it *must* clothe itself in contemporary forms and bring into its service every thought, imagination, and aspiration of man that is congenial to its own inner spirit. The glory of Christianity indeed, lies in this very power to draw enrichment from every source, and to become all things to all men.

v. 10. οἵ ποτε οὐ λαός, νῦν δὲ λαὸς θεοῦ, οἱ οὐκ ἠλεημένοι, νῦν δὲ ἐλεηθέντες⟩ 'Who were aforetime' 'Not a people', but are now 'God's people', who 'knew not God's mercy', but now 'have obtained His

---

[1] The Dead Sea Scrolls have now given us evidence of its characteristic use by the sectaries of Qumran.

mercy'. The phrases are taken, with the necessary adaptation, from
Hosea 1:6; 1:9; and 2:1; and are influenced in application by the use
made by St. Paul (Rom. 9:25-26) of other verses from the same part of
the book of Hosea (1:10 and 2:23). Hosea's daughter is given the name
Lo-Ruhamah — οὐκ ἐλεημένη — 'Not shown mercy', and his son is
called Lo-Ammi — οὐ λαός μου — 'Not my people', in token of God's
repudiation of Israel for her unfaithfulness to Him; and the names are
subsequently changed to Ammi — λαός μου — 'my people', and Ruha-
mah — ἐλεημένη — 'Shown mercy', in token of God's promise of future
reconciliation and forgiveness. The substitution of λαὸς θεοῦ for λαός
μου is made necessary by the context, and the change in the tense of the
participle from the perfect to the aorist fixes the thought not upon the
new state of the converted as contrasted with their former state, but
upon the action of God in regenerating them 'according to His abundant
mercy' (1:3). Though in Hosea, the words have nothing to do with the
conversion of Gentiles to the faith of the true God, they had been taken
out of their context by St. Paul and treated as a prophecy of God's
intention to create a 'people', who should be called 'sons of the living
God', of those who had formerly not been His people in any sense. This
Pauline passage paves the way for a similar application here.

¹¹ Ἀγαπητοί, παρακαλῶ ὡς παροίκους καὶ παρεπιδήμους ἀπέχεσθαι τῶν σαρκικῶν ἐπιθυμιῶν, αἵτινες στρατεύονται κατὰ τῆς ψυχῆς· ¹² τὴν ἀναστροφὴν ὑμῶν ἐν τοῖς ἔθνεσιν ἔχοντες καλήν, ἵνα ἐν ᾧ καταλαλοῦσιν ὑμῶν ὡς κακοποιῶν, ἐκ τῶν καλῶν ἔργων ἐποπτεύοντες δοξάσωσιν τὸν θεὸν ἐν ἡμέρᾳ ἐπισκοπῆς.

Beloved, I beseech you as foreigners and sojourners to abstain from the fleshly desires which make war against the soul. Let your conduct among the Gentiles be excellent, in order that, in the very matter wherein they slander you as evil-doers, they may by your excellent deeds attain spiritual insight and glorify God in the Day of His visitation.

¹¹ απεχεσθαι⟩ απεχεσθε ACL 33 syrr : + απο C* ¹² εν τοις εθνεσιν⟩ post καλην KL syrᴾ boh pos. εχοντες⟩ om B εποπτευοντες⟩ εποπτευσαντες AKLP ꝗ δοξασωσιν⟩ δοξας ου τρεμουσιν (ex 2 Pet. 2:10) ℵ

These verses introduce the second main section of the body of the Discourse. In the first section (1:13-2:10), the writer has spoken in a general way of the principles of holiness and love which govern the life of those whom God has regenerated and brought into the fellowship of the Church. In this section (2:11-3:12), he deals with particular issues of Christian conduct in a heathen environment. The effect of their conduct upon their pagan neighbours is to be kept in mind, both for the sake of their own good name, and for the hope of winning converts. Vv. 11-12 form the transition to the new theme and announce its tenor. He then proceeds to teach the necessity of obedience to constituted authority in the State (vv. 13-17); the duty of servants towards their masters (vv. 18-25); of wives towards their husbands, especially pagan husbands (3:1-6), and of husbands towards their (Christian) wives (v. 7); and the mutual relations which are to prevail among Christian brethren (vv. 8-9). The section is concluded, according to his custom, with an Old Testament citation to drive home his admonitions by the authoritative words of the Holy Scripture.

v. 11. ἀγαπητοί⟩ 'Beloved' — This form of address to Christian readers is used frequently by all the N.T. writers, with or without ἀδελφοί, and was probably the usual vocative in sermons also. It reflects the love which is the central motif of all Christian thought and life, and expresses both the teacher's love for his disciples and God's love for all in Christ. Its introduction at this point shows that the author is consciously passing to a new element in the Discourse.

παρακαλῶ, etc.⟩ The construction offers a certain difficulty, which is evaded in some MSS. by the insertion of ὑμᾶς. As the text stands, the verb is used absolutely, and the accusatives are to be taken as subjects of the infinitive ἀπέχεσθαι. (The variant ἀπέχεσθε, though well-attested, is nothing but an itacism, ε and αι having almost identical sounds.)

παροίκους καὶ παρεπιδήμους⟩ The words differ little in meaning. He probably had in mind the ξένοι καὶ παρεπίδημοι of Hebrews 11:13, and the words of Abraham in Genesis 33:4 (Lxx) — πάροικος καὶ παρεπίδημος ἐγώ εἰμι μεθ' ὑμῶν — 'I am a foreigner and a visitor with you' (cf. Ps. 38:12). Abraham uses the words in their literal sense; he is at the time a foreigner, temporarily sojourning in the land of the Hittites. The Psalmist has given them a spiritual application; and in Hebrews they are applied to the earthly life of the great heroes of faith. The paronomasia of the Septuagintal phrase appeals to our author (cf. 1:10, *note*), and he applies it in a spiritual sense to the earthly life of all Christians. (Cf. his use of παροικία, in 1:17, and of παρεπίδημοι in the salutation.) The thought is that the true homeland of Christians is in heaven, and that on earth they are in foreign territory, is now made the basis of a moral appeal. The indulgence of the 'fleshly desires' belongs to the order of earthly existence, now alien to them, and must be given no place in their new, heaven-centred life.

ἀπέχεσθαι τῶν σαρκικῶν ἐπιθυμιῶν⟩ 'abstain from the fleshly desires'. The vocabulary derives in part from St. Paul, and in part from the general inheritance of Greek moral philosophy — in the first instance from Plato. ἀπέχομαι with the genitive, in the sense of 'abstain from', 'do not indulge', is used several times by Plato — τῶν κατὰ τὸ σῶμα ἐπιθυμιῶν ἁπασῶν (Phaedo 82C); τῶν ἡδονῶν τε καὶ ἐπιθυμιῶν καὶ λυπῶν καὶ φοβῶν (Phaedo 83b); τῶν πολλοὺς δὴ καὶ πολλὰς ἐπιθυμιῶν εἰς ἔσχατα βαλλουσῶν —'The desires which reduce many men and women too, to the uttermost depths' —(*Laws* VIII, 835E). In all these passages, the thought is that the lives of wise men will be governed by basic principles of reason and knowledge, not by impulse. 'Desires' — ἐπιθυμίαι — are not evil in themselves, any more than are the 'pleasures and griefs and fears' which are mentioned along with them; wise men — 'true philosophers' — will 'abstain from' them, in the sense that they will refuse to indulge them, or to allow them to dominate life. That is the sense here also — 'Refuse to indulge the fleshly desires' — do not submit to their domination. σαρκικός — 'fleshly' — is used 'strictly in the Pauline or ethical sense' (Hort). St. Paul occasionally employs σάρξ and σαρκικός in the literal sense, of the physical body of man (Rom. 2:28 — 'circumcision in the flesh'; 1 Cor. 15:39ff., etc.), or by an easy extension, of the external, the mundane, the treasures of earthly life, as contrasted with the spiritual treasure of the Gospel (Rom. 15:27; 1 Cor. 9:11). But when he transfers the words to his ethical vocabulary, they have no longer any but the most remote connection with this primary, literal sense. Here they are used, not of the material body as such, but of the whole nature of man in its unredeemed condition, with its inherited tendencies towards evil, which remain even in the redeemed as a legacy from the past life and involve us in a ceaseless inward struggle to overcome them by the power of the Spirit which God imparts to us. (Rom. 8:1-14; Gal. 5:16-25.) The 'flesh' in this sense is not a material conception; there is no implication that the physical part of the human constitution is particularly predisposed to evil, or incapable of sanctification for the service of God. It is rather the Ego, the self-centred natural disposition, which must be 'crucified', or 'mortified', that the new life which Christ gives may have its full manifestation. (Gal. 5:24 — 'They that are Christ's have crucified the flesh, with its passions and desires'; Gal. 1:19-20 — 'I am crucified with Christ, and it is no longer I that live, but Christ that liveth in me' (cf. Rom. 8:13; and, in a different figure, Col. 3:9-10.) 'The works of the flesh', accordingly, are all the forms of wickedness to which the unredeemed, self-centred nature of man is prone — not merely the gross sins of licentiousness, but such sins of the mind and spirit as idolatry, heresy, envy, quarrelsomeness, etc. (Gal. 5:19ff.). In keeping with this Pauline terminology on which it is based, the 'fleshly desires' of our passage will mean the evil impulses of our own nature as men, which prompt us to deeds and thoughts incompatible with the new life into which God has brought us through Christ.

αἵτινες στρατεύονται κατὰ τῆς ψυχῆς⟩ 'which make war against the soul'. The thought of the Christian life as a warfare against spiritual foes occurs several times in the New Testament (2 Cor. 10:3ff.; Eph. 6:10-20; 1 Tim. 1:18, etc.). The thought of a warfare within man, which we have here, is found also in James 4:1ff.; and in a context more closely akin to our passage, in Romans 7; cf. especially vv. 22-23 — 'I delight in the law of God after the inward man; but I see another law in my members warring against — ἀντιστρατευόμενον — the law of my mind' (i.e., 'the law of God, which my mind approves'). In the writings of St. Paul, the warring elements within man are 'flesh' and 'spirit' (πνεῦμα); e.g., Galatians 5:16-17 — 'Walk in the Spirit, and you will not fulfil the desire of the flesh; for the flesh pits its desires (ἐπιθυμεῖ) against the Spirit, and the Spirit against the flesh, and these two are in opposition the one to the other'. The 'soul', on the other hand, appears to mean 'the life', 'the inward nature', not in its aspect as evil, or as disposed to evil, but as lacking the capacity for the divine, as limited to the sphere of the earthly. (So especially in the adjective ψυχικός, which A.V. renders 'natural' — as, 'The natural man receiveth not the things of the Spirit of God', being contrasted in this respect with 'the spiritual man' — ὁ πνευματικός.) In this respect, however, our writer has not followed St. Paul. For him, it is the ψυχή which is set over against the 'flesh', in the conflict which is waged within man. This is not to say that he uses ψυχή in the sense which St. Paul reserves for πνεῦμα. It would be nearer the truth to say that while he borrows the adjective σαρκικός from St. Paul, with the same notion of the σάρξ underlying it, he uses in general a different conception of the elements of which man is constituted. The ψυχή is for him the essential being of man, the true life. It is 'purified' in baptism (1:22); its salvation is 'the end of the faith' (1:9); it is under the care of Christ as Shepherd and Bishop (2:25); it is to be committed to God's keeping by those who are called to suffer in accordance with His will (4:19). Hort remarks that 'This whole class of words has in truth a variable force in accordance with the context'. Certainly, the connotation of ψυχή was by no means fixed in popular or in philosophical usage. Every school had its own doctrine of the soul, and in the popular mind, primitive notions of multiple souls existed still, side by side with such elements of the higher speculations as had filtered down into the general understanding. The looseness and variety with which the word is employed in the New Testament merely reflects the fluid state of psychological doctrine at the time.

v. 12. The language and thought here rest upon the saying of Jesus in Matthew 5:16 – 'Let your light so shine before men that they may see your good works and glorify your Father which is in heaven'. In the final clause, the dependence in vocabulary is unmistakable; ἵνα . . . ἐκ τῶν καλῶν ἔργων ἐποπτεύοντες δοξάσωσιν is certainly formed upon the reminiscence of ὅπως ἴδωσιν ὑμῶν τὰ καλὰ ἔργα καὶ δοξάσωσιν . . . There is also a clear parallelism of thought in the main clauses. 'Let your light so shine before men' is interpreted and applied to a particular situation in the new phrasing, 'Let your behaviour among the Gentiles be excellent'. In both, the thought is that the beauty of inward character is to be given manifest expression in the outward life for the spiritual benefit of others. The passage here applies the wide and general thought of our Lord's words to the life of the Asian Christians in their relations with the pagans among whom they live.

τὴν ἀναστροφὴν ὑμῶν ἐν τοῖς ἔθνεσιν⟩ 'your behaviour among the Gentiles'—not of religious activities, but of general outward conduct in relations with their fellows, the everyday life of regular social intercourse (cf. 1:15, 17, notes).

ἔχοντες⟩ Here again the participle is used with imperative force.

καλήν⟩ The word unites aesthetic with moral elements. It is used of goodness which commends itself to the beholder by its evident quality, goodness that manifests itself in beauty, in nobility, in attractive power.

ἐν ᾧ καταλαλοῦσιν ὑμῶν ὡς κακοποιῶν⟩ 'in the very matter wherein they slander you, saying that you are evil-doers'. ὡς κακοποιῶν explains ἐν ᾧ. Popular slander bears upon the conduct of Christians; it is to be disproved by the exhibition of conduct that approves itself as good (cf. v.15 below). καλὰ ἔργα are the best answer to calumny.

In some quarters, Christians were suspected of the vilest crimes. It was commonly reported that in secret gatherings they practised incest, murder, and cannibalism. The writer, however, seems to have in mind rather the accusation that they were given to disturbing the public peace, fomenting sedition, and fanning the fires of social unrest. The word κακοποιός is very general in meaning, and does not of itself suggest vice, but rather mischief-making. The technical sense of the Latin *maleficus* — 'sorcerer' — does not appear to suit the context, though it suggests itself to some commentators.

ἐποπτεύοντες⟩ The verb ἐποπτεύω is nearly always used transitively, as in 3:2. Used absolutely as it is here, it can hardly have the ordinary meaning of 'observe'. 'Your good works, which they behold' (A.V.) does not give the true force. The thought is rather of spiritual insight, which is to be gained in the future *through the influence of* (ἐκ) the 'good works'. The participle is to be taken closely with the verb, sharing its future force. The recollection of the good works of the Christians is to have its effect 'in the Day of visitation', as the means of awakening those who now indulge in scorn and slander to a vision of the God who has inspired in His followers such goodness, so that they too will glorify Him. ἐποπτεύω (with its cognates ἐπόπτης and ἐποπτεία) belongs to the technical language of the mysteries, marking the highest grade of initiation, when the candidate was permitted to 'behold' with joy and adoration the symbolic objects which represented the ultimate revelation. The ἐποπτεία was thus the vision of the heavenly, the attainment to mystic knowledge of the divine. Something of this sense pertains to the word here. The 'beholding' is the attainment of such an understanding of the nature and will of God as to lead men to 'glorify' Him.

ἐν ἡμέρᾳ ἐπισκοπῆς⟩ 'in the Day of visitation'—The ultimate source of the phrase is probably Wisdom 3:7 — ἐν καιρῷ ἐπισκοπῆς αὐτῶν or Isaiah 10:3 — τῇ ἡμέρᾳ τῆς ἐπισκοπῆς. The writer surely has in mind the Day of Judgment, which he believes to be close at hand (4:7); but it should be recalled that God 'visits' mankind for redemption also (Gen. 50:24; Lk. 1:68). The words here suggest the attractive thought that even in the dread hour of Judgment there may be mercy for those whose eyes are at last opened to the revelation of the divine glory in the beauty of the Christian character which they now slander.

¹³ Ὑποτάγητε πάσῃ ἀνθρωπίνῃ κτίσει διὰ τὸν κύριον, εἴτε βασιλεῖ ὡς ὑπερέχοντι, ¹⁴ εἴτε ἡγεμόσιν ὡς δι' αὐτοῦ πεμπομένοις εἰς ἐκδίκησιν κακοποιῶν, ἔπαινον δὲ ἀγαθοποιῶν. ¹⁵ ὅτι οὕτως ἐστὶν τὸ θέλημα τοῦ θεοῦ, ἀγαθοποιοῦντας φιμοῦν τὴν τῶν ἀφρόνων ἀνθρώπων ἀγνωσίαν. ¹⁶ ὡς ἐλεύθεροι, καὶ μὴ ὡς ἐπικάλυμμα ἔχοντες τῆς κακίας τὴν ἐλευθερίαν, ἀλλ' ὡς θεοῦ δοῦλοι. ¹⁷ πάντας τιμήσατε, τὴν ἀδελφότητα ἀγαπᾶτε, τὸν θεὸν φοβεῖσθε, τὸν βασιλέα τιμᾶτε.

Be subject to every human institution for the sake of the Lord, whether to the Emperor as supreme, or to Governors as sent under his commission for the punishment of malefactors and the praise of upright men. For thus is the will of God carried out, in that by upright living you put to silence the ignorance of foolish men. Comport yourselves as free men, not as men who make their freedom a pretext for trouble-making, but as God's slaves. Give honour to all. Love the brotherhood. Fear God. Honour the Emperor.

¹³ υποταγητε)+ουν KLP ς vg clem syrhl ανθρωπινη) om ℵ* κυριον) θεον vg   ¹⁴ ηγεμοσιν) ηγεμονι sah   εκδικησιν)+μεν CP 1739. syrhl ¹⁵ φιμουν) φιμοιν ℵ* (W-H) : pr υμας C 69 syrr   ¹⁶ θεου δουλοι) transp. AL 33. ς vg   ¹⁷ την αδελφοτητα) αλληλους sah

With v. 13 we come to a pronouncement on the Christian's duty towards the civil authority, which is the first section of the 'Haustafel' in this epistle. K. Weidinger (*Das Problem der urchristlichen Haustafeln*, Leipzig, 1928), following a suggestion of Dibelius (in an Excursus to Col. 3:18ff., in his Commentary on that Epistle in Lietzmann's *Handbuch*, Tübingen, 1912, pp. 91-2), has shown that in several passages of this general description in the New Testament, we have to do with the Christian adoption of a literary form already well-established in Hellenistic philosophical literature, both Jewish and Greek.¹ It sets forth in ordered arrangement a code of practical conduct in keeping with the principles of the philosophy, following a scheme which is fixed in its broad lines but capable of adaptation in particulars, of expansion, abbreviation, and omission of some of the sections, as the purpose of the teacher or the needs of the people addressed may require. In such passages of the Christian Epistles (e.g., Col. 3:18ff., Eph. 5:22ff., Tit. 2:1ff.), the material belongs in the main to a common stock of ethical instruction, and critical observation can perceive how and where Christian pointing has been given to phrases and sentences which have been taken over by the writer from a non-Christian source. It follows that we must be very

¹ I am no longer convinced of the validity of this position, despite the strength of its supporters. See the essay on 'First Peter in Recent Criticism', pp. 212ff.

cautious about drawing inferences from such passages with respect to the particular situation of the group which is addressed. (See also W. K. L. Clarke, *New Testament Problems* (London, 1929), c. XIX (review of Weidinger); and the excellent essay by J. W. C. Wand in his *Commentary on the General Epistles of St. Peter and St. Jude* (London, 1934), Introduction, Part II, 'Moral Codes'.) In First Peter, however, it must be observed that the element drawn from the common store is relatively small, and is not only brought into significant relationship with fundamental Christian teaching, but even made the point of departure for an exposition of the character of our Lord and the meaning of His earthly life.

This passage undoubtedly stands in some close degree of literary relationship to Romans 13:1-7, with which it shares certain elements of vocabulary. The differences, however, are more significant than the resemblances, and this had led Weidinger to suggest (p. 63) that there is no direct dependence of our author upon St. Paul at this point, but that the two writers make use, each in his own way, of a clause on civil duties which was contained in an earlier (non-Christian?) 'Haustafel'. In view of the familiarity with Romans which is displayed elsewhere in this Epistle, it seems better to suppose that here also the Pauline writing is laid under contribution, but that the teaching is consciously, though tacitly, modified. The doctrine that 'the powers that be are ordained of God' is not repeated here, though it is not directly challenged. The Christian duty of subjection is enjoined, but is not based upon the doctrine that the authority of human government itself derives from God. No particular theory of the State emerges in the passage, and we are not entitled to read into it the well-defined ideas of St. Paul, when the author himself passes them over in silence. The duty of the Christian is based wholly upon his relation to God and to Christ, not upon any intrinsic quality of the State and of its established authorities. It is the will of God that the Christian should recognize the duty of civil obedience; he is to submit 'for the Lord's sake'. His obedience is to be yielded, not under compulsion, but freely. In the exercise of the freedom which God has bestowed upon him, he is to accept the duty of submission to earthly authority. In receiving from God inward freedom, he acknowledges himself God's slave; and in obedience to his Master in heaven, he freely submits to the authorities which are established upon earth. Knowing himself to be free, the Christian freely accepts God's will for the entire direction of his life, and that will requires his submission in earthly things to the governmental authorities under which he dwells. The writer feels himself under no necessity to adduce the Pauline doctrine that civil authority derives ultimately from God, or to offer any other elementary principle in its place, to justify his injunction to obedience. For him, it is sufficient that God requires of us submission to the authority, whatever its source and ultimate sanction may be. The most complete inward freedom is by no means incompatible with voluntary submission to an external authority.

v. 13 πάσῃ ἀνθρωπίνῃ κτίσει⟩ 'to every human institution'. An ἀνθρωπίνη κτίσις can mean nothing else than a governmental institution in human society. There is nothing in the words to suggest or imply a divine origin for human institutions. κτίζω is commonly used of the founding of cities or colonies, with their constitutions; it is not particularly applied to the divine activity in the world; and the corresponding noun 'is ascribed to men far oftener than to God' (Hort). No useful parallel can be cited for the meaning of κτίσις that we have here. Yet it is most unlikely that the writer is coining a new usage for the word; in all probability, he is employing a common expression for which we happen to have no example in extant documents. Certainly the notion that it means an institution created by God ('such elements of God's universal κτίσις as are characteristically human' — Hort), though it has commended itself generally to commentators, has no basis in the passage itself; if the Pauline passage were not at hand, no one would think of such an interpretation.

βασίλει⟩ 'the Emperor'; literally, 'the King'. Official documents use the title 'Autocrat' — Αὐτοκράτωρ. Roman prejudice against the kingship forbade the use of the title 'Rex'; in Latin, the civil title was Princeps, and the military, Imperator. In the Greek world, however, there was no such prejudice against the title βασίλευς, and though it was not taken up into formal state documents, it was common in popular usage.

ὡς ὑπερέχοντι⟩ 'as supreme' — as the head of the public administration, not as a divinity; for his high office, not for any sanctity attaching to his person.

ἡγεμόσιν⟩ 'Governors' — the usual Greek title for the head of the administration in the province, regardless of his rank.

ὡς δι᾽ αὐτοῦ πεμπομένοις⟩ 'as sent under his commission', holding delegated authority under him. Hort finds implied here (in the preposition διά) the theory that the Emperor is not the ultimate source of the governor's authority, but the mediator through whom it is transmitted from the divine source; but such an exegesis carries us far beyond the plain meaning of the words, and is in fact an anachronism. Even the Romans passage, with its uncompromising insistence that 'all power is of God', does not suggest that the Emperor is to be regarded as the primary depository of the power, through whom it is mediated to others.

In all strictness, only the Governors of such provinces as were under the direct authority of the Princeps could be said to be 'sent by him'; the words would not properly apply to the Governors of senatorial provinces. In Bithynia and Pontus, Pliny was the first governor to be sent by an Emperor in the Flavian period; until that time, the province was under Senatorial administration. Asia was always under the Senate, and Galatia was in the same position until Vespasian transferred its administration to the legate of Cappadocia in A.D. 76. This observation would tend to confirm the later dating of the Epistle, to which other considerations have already pointed us, but it is not possible to lay too great weight upon the expression. Outside Italy, the authority of the Senate was a shadowy thing at the best; the jealous regard paid to constitutional forms at Rome meant little to the provinces. A provincial writer, therefore, may have thought of all governors as commissioned by the Emperor, even though many were actually sent by and responsible to the Senate.

εἰς ἐκδίκησιν κακοποιῶν ἔπαινον δὲ ἀγαθοποιῶν⟩ 'for the punishment of malefactors and the praise of upright men (or benefactors)'. In this twofold phrase he summarizes what St. Paul had said in Romans 13:3-4, omitting (significantly) the twice-made assertion of the Apostle that the ruler is 'God's servant' — θεοῦ διάκονος — in both respects. Words like these could hardly be written at a time when the authorities in question were using their power for the persecution of the Christian brotherhood, least of all to the very people who were enduring persecution; they are one more indication that the Discourse to which they belong was composed before the persecution broke out, and is thus prior to the Letter in which it is embodied.

The words pay well-deserved tribute to the integrity and beneficent spirit which generally marked the work of the Roman governors, especially in the Imperial provinces; where the Senatorial administration prevailed, the record is much less commendable. The Emperors, in the provinces for which they were themselves responsible, made a consistent effort to provide efficient and honest administration, to punish peculation, and to remedy the worst abuses of an oppressive local administration. The correspondence which passed between Trajan and Pliny affords abundant evidence of the efforts made, and of the difficulties which confronted a governor who was sincerely desirous of promoting the welfare of the governed.

The 'praise' which is to be given to the upright is to be taken concretely, of the rewards which were bestowed from time to time upon public benefactors, at the instance of the governor. It would apply most naturally to laudatory inscriptions, and then more broadly, to the award of crowns, or of citizenship. Such 'praise' from the State was much coveted and was doubtless a stimulus to beneficence. But few Christians can have entertained any great hope of winning such public distinction, or have set much store by these earthly honours; and it seems likely that the words are a stock phrase taken over from some current formula of instruction in civic duty.

v. 15. ὅτι οὕτως ἐστὶν τὸ θέλημα τοῦ θεοῦ⟩ literally, 'because thus is the will of God'. The verb is more than a mere copula; it is not adequately rendered by 'is', but has the sense of 'is given effect' (in the sphere of human life), 'is recognized and carried out'. οὕτως is retrospective (see Hort's discussion of the construction), harking back to the initial injunction. It is further defined by the participle ἀγαθοποιοῦντας, which in the context must mean primarily 'by showing yourselves to be good subjects', and then more widely 'by active beneficence'.

φιμοῦν ... ἀγνωσίαν⟩ 'to silence ... ignorance' is a difficult phrase. ἀγνωσία is not equivalent to ἄγνοια (1:14). The latter is used of the ignorance which is a mere lack of knowledge, which is therefore pardonable and may be overlooked (cf. Acts 17:30 — 'God overlooked the times of ignorance, but now commands men that all everywhere should repent'). ἀγνωσία on the other hand means culpable ignorance, the ignorance that shuts out and rejects knowledge which is offered; thus it involves moral delinquency. Here the thought is of such ignorance venting itself in slander of the good.

τῶν ἀφρόνων ἀνθρώπων⟩ 'the foolish men' — those who set themselves against the will of God. ἀνθρώπων is not otiose; it stands in explicit opposition to θεοῦ. ἄφρων is used frequently in the Greek O.T., especially in the Psalms and the Wisdom literature, of the 'fool' who sets himself against truth and right; cf. Proverbs 1:22 —

οἱ δὲ ἄφρονες, τῆς ὕβρεως ὄντες ἐπιθυμηταί,
ἀσεβεῖς γενόμενοι ἐμίσησαν αἴσθησιν.

'Fools, having their hearts set upon insolence, show themselves impious and hate discernment.'

v. 16. ὡς ἐλεύθεροι ... ἔχοντες ... δοῦλοι⟩ This clause is not dependent upon anything in the foregoing sentence, nor is it to be taken as subordinated to the imperatives in the following verse. The adjectives and the participle stand independently, with a clear imperative force, not substantially different from the imperative use of the participle which we find in ὑποτασσόμενοι (v.18), and frequently in the Epistle. The general sense is clear. To submit to constituted authority is not the annulment of freedom, but its true expression; obedience is yielded voluntarily, not compelled. The Christian man is indeed free, as none can be free who know not the liberating power of the Gospel; but this freedom is degraded, is made to put forward claims not proper to it, when it is made a pretext for defying authority. In the exercise of his freedom in Christ, the Christian remains bound by his responsibility to God, the common Master of all.

The thought is based upon St. Paul's bold definition of the Christian's twofold status, in 1 Corinthians 7:22 — ὁ γὰρ ἐν κυρίῳ κληθεὶς δοῦλος, ἀπελεύθερος κυρίου ἐστίν· ὁμοίως ὁ ἐλεύθερος κληθεὶς δοῦλός ἐστιν χριστοῦ — 'For he that is called in the Lord, being a slave, is the Lord's freedman; likewise the freeman who is called is Christ's slave'. The warning against the misuse of freedom is closely paralleled, though in a different context and application, in Galatians 5:13 — 'For, brethren, ye have been called for liberty; only use not liberty for an occasion to the flesh, but in love serve as slaves one to another'. Cf. also Ephesians 5:5-7, where the duty of slaves to masters is similarly viewed as a secondary expression of the obedience due to God. The spirit which casts off the irksome burden of compulsion by accepting the service voluntarily, is given still more emphatic expression in the words of our Lord, 'Whosoever shall compel thee to go a mile, go with him twain'. And the fundamental doctrine receives classic exposition in Luther's great Reformation treatise, 'Concerning Christian Liberty', with its twin propositions, 'A Christian man is the most free lord of all, and subject to none; a Christian man is the most dutiful servant of all, and subject to everyone'.

ἐπικάλυμμα) 'a veil, a covering' presenting evil in a false guise of goodness.

ὡς δοῦλοι θεοῦ) 'as slaves of God' — not as under compulsion, but in the voluntary bondage of love, which finds its joy in doing His will.

v. 17. τιμήσατε…ἀγαπᾶτε…φοβεῖσθε…τιμᾶτε) The change of tense from the aorist in the first of these four verbs to the present in the other three, is not easy to explain. The first impression would be that the initial phrase is meant to be a comprehensive injunction, which is then applied particularly in the three following phrases. As against this, it must be said that it is hard to imagine that the injunction to 'fear God' could be thus reduced to one particular among others. A much more natural sense is given by a different grouping, taking the first two phrases together, and the last two. The aorist is probably to be taken of definite action — not merely of an attitude of respect, but of its translation into the specific words and especially deeds that are called forth by the desire to do appropriate honour to all. Towards the brotherhood, the honour which we owe to all deepens into the love which binds us to those who share our fellowship of faith. ἀδελφότης occurs again in 5:9, but is not used by any other N.T. writer; in the Greek O.T. it is found only in 1 and 4 Maccabees, and then not in this collective sense, but in the abstract sense of 'brotherliness' (∥ φιλίαν, 1 Macc. 12:10). Though Christians are frequently called 'brethren' — ἀδελφοί, we seem to have here the coining of a new collective title. (Perdelwitz suggests, not too confidently, the possibility of some influence derived from the Mithraic terms — φρατόρες, φρατρίαι — *op. cit.*, p. 80.) It is remarkable that this writer, though so much attached to the Epistle to the Ephesians, and despite his strong sense of the unity of Christians in one 'spiritual house' (v.5), never employs the word ἐκκλησία. He seems to prefer expressions which suggest the mutual relations of the members, rather than the call of God, as the unifying element.

τὸν θεὸν φοβεῖσθε, τὸν βασιλέα τιμᾶτε) 'Fear God. Honour the Emperor.' Here he takes up the injunction of Proverbs 24:21 — φοβοῦ θεόν, υἱέ, καὶ βασιλέα — but modifies it, perhaps under the influence of St. Paul's τῷ τὸν φόβον τὸν φόβον, τῷ τὴν τιμὴν τὴν τιμήν (to which he now gives specific application), to emphasize that even the proper respect for the Emperor is still something quite different from the reverence which is to be paid to God alone.

¹⁸ Οἱ οἰκέται, ὑποτασσόμενοι ἐν παντὶ φόβῳ τοῖς δεσπόταις, οὐ μόνον τοῖς ἀγαθοῖς καὶ ἐπιεικέσιν, ἀλλὰ καὶ τοῖς σκολιοῖς. ¹⁹ τοῦτο γὰρ χάρις, εἰ διὰ συνείδησιν θεοῦ ὑποφέρει τις λύπας πάσχων ἀδίκως. ²⁰ ποῖον γὰρ κλέος, εἰ ἁμαρτάνοντες καὶ κολαφιζόμενοι ὑπομενεῖτε; ἀλλ᾽ εἰ ἀγαθοποιοῦντες καὶ πάσχοντες ὑπομενεῖτε, τοῦτο χάρις παρὰ θεῷ. ²¹ εἰς τοῦτο γὰρ ἐκλήθητε, ὅτι καὶ Χριστὸς ἔπαθεν ὑπὲρ ὑμῶν, ὑμῖν ὑπολιμπάνων ὑπογραμμὸν ἵνα ἐπακολουθήσητε τοῖς ἴχνεσιν αὐτοῦ· ²² ὃς ἁμαρτίαν οὐκ ἐποίησεν οὐδὲ εὑρέθη δόλος ἐν τῷ στόματι αὐτοῦ· ²³ ὃς λοιδορούμενος οὐκ ἀντελοιδόρει, πάσχων οὐκ ἠπείλει, παρεδίδου δὲ τῷ κρίνοντι δικαίως· ²⁴ ὃς τὰς ἁμαρτίας ἡμῶν αὐτὸς ἀνήνεγκεν ἐν τῷ σώματι αὐτοῦ ἐπὶ τὸ ξύλον, ἵνα ταῖς ἁμαρτίαις ἀπογενόμενοι τῇ δικαιοσύνῃ ζήσωμεν· οὗ τῷ μώλωπι ἰάθητε. ²⁵ ἦτε γὰρ ὡς πρόβατα πλανώμενοι, ἀλλ᾽ ἐπεστράφητε νῦν ἐπὶ τὸν ποιμένα καὶ ἐπίσκοπον τῶν ψυχῶν ὑμῶν.

You that are slaves, be subject to your masters in all fear (of God), not only to those that are good and kindly, but also to those that are harsh. For this is excellence, if from a sense of duty to God a man endures his pains when he suffers unjustly. For what manner of glory is there in enduring, if you are beaten for doing wrong? But if you endure when you suffer for doing good, this is excellence in the sight of God. For this is the patience to which you were called, because Christ too suffered for you, leaving you an example that you might follow in His footsteps. He 'did no sin, nor was guile found in His mouth'; when He was reviled, He did not answer by reviling; when He suffered, He did not threaten, but committed Himself to Him that judges justly. He 'Himself carried our sins' in His body on the cross, in order that we might die to sins and live to righteousness; 'by His gashes you were healed'. For you were 'straying like sheep', but you have now returned to the Shepherd and Bishop of your souls.

¹⁸ εν παντι φοβω) antⁱ ὑποτασσ. pos. ℵ δεσποταις)+υμων ℵ ¹⁹ χαρις)+ παρα τω θεω C (33, om τω) syrr θεου) pr αγαθην C syrᴾ : +αγαθην A* Ψ 33. ²⁰ κολαφιζομενοι) κολαζομενοι ℵᶜ P lat vet syrᴾ υπομενειτε²°) om C : υπομενετε (bis) 69. vg τουτο)+γαρ (ex v. 19) A 33. ²¹ και) om A syrʰˡ Χριστος) pr ο ℵ επαθεν) απεθανεν ℵ syrᴾ υπερ) περι A υμων υμιν) ημων ημιν ꞯ syrᴾ ²³ αντελοιδορει) ελοιδορει ℵ* vg sah boh δικαιως) αυτον αδικως vg Claᶫᵉˣ Cypr ²⁴ ημων) υμων B εν) om ℵ αμαρτιαις)+ημων A ζησωμεν) συνꝫ. C : συꝫ. 1739 μωλωπι)+αυτου ℵ* ꞯ ²⁵ ητε γαρ) om B πλανωμενοι) πλανωμενα CKLP ꞯ

If he speaks first to slaves, it is probably because most of the converts whom he addresses were slaves. The word οἰκέται is not so general as δοῦλοι, the usual N.T. word for 'slaves', but means particularly the slaves of the household. In the society of that age, this would include not only the domestic servants and farm labourers but also some professionally-trained men — scribes, teachers, and doctors. The slave, whatever his qualities as a person, was a mere chattel in the hand of his master. He had no civil rights; his testimony had no value in a court of law, unless it were extracted under torture; and there were no limits, except those set by custom and public opinion, to the punishment that his master might cause to be inflicted upon him, even to flogging him to death or crucifying him. It ought to be said, however, that most masters were relatively humane, and the worst punishments were rarely inflicted. Even so, beatings were common, were indeed the normal punishment for the ordinary faults of the slave — pilfering and impudence. The surly and unreasonable (σκολιοί), who would have a slave punished for a trifling fault, or for no fault at all, were the exception.

The writer, like all the Christian teachers of the time, refrains from criticizing the institution of slavery itself, and does not question, much less attack, the right of the master to have the slave beaten if he does wrong. Since 'the end of all things is at hand' (4:7), he is not concerned to reform the Society of the time, or to encourage men to seek to better their lot within it. His teaching is directed solely to making clear the duty which is incumbent upon the Christian within the existing framework. For the slave, this means that his conduct is to be governed not by the character of his master, whether he be kindly or brutal, but upon his own inward sense of what God requires of him. His relationship to God is to determine his behaviour in all earthly relationships.

v. 18. οἱ οἰκέται⟩ The nominative with the article is often found as a vocative, from classical times.

ἐν παντὶ φόβῳ⟩ 'in all fear' — not fear of the masters to whom they are subject, but fear of God. Throughout the epistle, it is always the fear of God that is enjoined (1:17; 2:17; cf. 3:2, 15); any other fear is not to be entertained. 'All fear', then, will mean, 'the fear of God which governs all your conduct'; it is the spirit of reverence towards Him that induces respect and faithfulness to duty in the sphere of human relationships.

v. 19. χάρις⟩ In this context, the word is best taken in its primary sense of 'excellence' — that which is admirable, enhancing the esteem in which those who display it are held.

διὰ συνείδησιν θεοῦ⟩ θεοῦ is to be taken as an objective genitive — 'because of a conscience responsive to God' — not in any fawning desire to curry favour with the master.

v. 20. The last two words of the preceding verse — πάσχων ἀδίκως — are now made the theme of his teaching. Mere endurance is no cause for pride. Slaves, like schoolboys, sometimes vied with one another in demonstrating the ability to endure corporal punishment without flinching. The writer warns them against boasting of a mere stoicism. If the beating is deserved, there is no glory in bearing it; but to show patience in the face of injustice is true evidence of Christian character — the kind of excellence that God esteems.

v. 21. ἐκλήθητε⟩ 'you were called' — by the 'call' of God. In calling us 'to His eternal glory' (5:10), 'out of darkness into His marvellous light' (2:9), God also calls us to the exercise of this patient endurance of suffering that we have done nothing to deserve. In this very respect, Christ has given us a model of Christian conduct; for He too was called to endure an undeserved punishment. It must be kept in mind that the writer is still addressing himself to the slaves. In the ancient world, nothing noble was expected of the slave, and it is impossible to lay too much emphasis upon the new dignity that Christianity conferred upon him when it taught him to take Christ for the pattern of his life. The slave was now called to live by the same standards of conduct as the noblest of all. Conversely, Christ Himself is set before us as μορφὴν δούλου λαβών (Phil. 2:7). In the words of Bishop Wordsworth, 'The μώλωψ is the wound produced by the *chastisement of slaves*, and the ξύλον is the instrument of the *death of slaves*. Mark the Humility of Him, who being Lord of all, stooped to be the servant of all, and to suffer scourging and the cross *as a slave*; and was especially exemplary to that class which St. Peter is here addressing'.

ἔπαθεν ὑπὲρ ὑμῶν⟩ 'suffered for you' — the preposition is given a wide range of significance. The phrase is applied first in the sense that belongs most closely to the context — He suffered 'for us', in that He showed us how to bear wrong, setting us an example to follow. The manner of His conduct under injustice is developed in the multiple suggestions of vv. 22-23. Then in the next two verses, he applies the phrase in the redemptive sense; He suffered 'for us' in that He sacrificed His life for our sins. With this, the words go beyond the circle of slaves immediately addressed, and are meant for all Christian believers.

ὑπογραμμόν⟩ 'example' — in the literal sense, the model of handwriting to be copied by the schoolboy; then, figuratively, of a model of conduct for imitation, amplified by the epexegetic ἵνα clause.

v. 22. Cited from Isaiah 53:9 with modifications. In Lxx (Bℵ) the rendering is ἀνομίαν οὐκ ἐποίησεν, οὐδὲ δόλον ἐν τῷ στόματι αὐτοῦ — 'He did no lawlessness, nor (did he do) guile with his mouth.' (The reading εὑρέθη δόλος, found in ℵ^{c.a.} AQ, derives almost certainly from this

Petrine text.) The alterations here are not made deliberately, but are the easy corruptions apt to occur in a citation made freely, from memory; in fact, all through this passage, the writer is expressing his own thoughts in the familiar language of the ancient scripture, rather than citing it in support of his teaching. ἁμαρτίαν οὐκ ἐποίησεν, then, need not be regarded as a conscious modification, intended to introduce the idea of the sinlessness of Christ. In the context, it means only that he committed no offence to justify the sufferings inflicted upon him. He was in the very position of the slave who suffers an undeserved punishment.

v. 23. There is no trace of literary dependence on the passion story as we have it in the Gospels, and it is possible that he is still drawing upon the picture of the Suffering Servant of Isaiah 53, though not reproducing the words. The first two phrases reflect the general thought of Isaiah 53:7 as it appears in Lxx — καὶ αὐτὸς διὰ τὸ κεκακῶσθαι οὐκ ἀνοίγει τὸ στόμα . . . καὶ ὡς ἀμνὸς ἐναντίον τοῦ κείροντος ἄφωνος, οὕτως οὐκ ἀνοίγει τὸ στόμα αὐτοῦ. The third phrase is his own statement of the positive counterpart to the negative description of Christ's attitude under injustice. 'He committed Himself to Him that judges justly' — i.e., he accepted without rebellion the unjust treatment meted out to him, ~~confident of vindication before God.~~

Harnack (*Zur Revision*, pp. 89-90) argues in support of the remarkable variant offered by the Latin Vulgate — iudicanti se iniuste (τῷ κρίνοντι αὐτὸν ἀδίκως) 'to him that judged Him unjustly', i.e., to Pilate. This is undoubtedly an early variant; though it is not found in any Greek MS., there is testimony for its use by Cyprian and by Clement of Alexandria. If this reading were accepted, the phrase would be interpreted as emphasizing by one more example the duty of humility and submission to human authority, even when it is unjustly exercised, which is the theme of the passage. But the evidence for the variant is very weak, and it seems likely that ἀδίκως is merely a scribal error, induced by the presence of the same adverb at the end of v. 19.

v. 24. ἁμαρτίας . . . ἀνήνεγκεν⟩ from Isaiah 53:12 — αὐτὸς ἁμαρτίας πολλῶν ἀνήνεγκεν; cf. Hebrews 9:28 — ἅπαξ προσενεχθεὶς εἰς τὸ πολλῶν ἀνενεγκεῖν ἁμαρτίας. 'Having come once to bear the sins of many.' It is hard to define with precision the significance of ἀναφέρω. The idea of the scapegoat (Leviticus 16) does not appear to be in his mind; the scapegoat was not slain in sacrifice, but driven away into the wilderness. Nor is it remotely conceivable that the verb should have its usual sense of 'offer in sacrifice', seeing that 'our sins' could not constitute the offering made to God; for this reason, too, it is wrong to draw a parallel between ἐπὶ τὸ ξύλον and the frequent ἀναφέρειν τι ἐπὶ τὸ θυσιαστήριον of Lxx. Deissmann's elaborate note (*Bible Studies*, pp. 88 ff.), in which he seeks to establish the meaning 'he carried our sins up to the cross', is dependent for its force upon his erroneous supposition that ἐπὶ with the accusative can only mean 'up to', not 'upon'. In fact, the accusative at this period is invading the territory of the other cases and is well on the way to the victory which it has won in modern Greek and ἐπὶ with the accusative frequently does mean 'upon'.

The best meaning for the verb here seems to be 'bear the consequences'. This use is rare, but a parallel is found in Numbers 14:33 — οἱ δὲ υἱοὶ ὑμῶν . . . ἀνοίσουσι τὴν πορνείαν ὑμῶν — 'Your sons . . . shall bear the penalty of your wantonness'. The idea of expiation is not directly brought out, but it certainly underlies the whole passage.

ἐν τῷ σώματι αὐτοῦ⟩ 'in his body' — is reminiscent of Colossians 1:22 νυνὶ δὲ ἀποκατήλλαξεν ἐν τῷ σώματι τῆς σαρκὸς αὐτοῦ διὰ τοῦ θανάτου — 'He has now reconciled you in his body of flesh through death'. It is emphasized that the saving acts of Christ are accomplished within the sphere and under the conditions of the human life which He shares with us, not in a timeless drama.

ξύλον is used of anything made of wood, as staves (Matt. 26:47 and ‖s), the stocks (Acts 16:24), wooden building materials (1 Cor. 3:12), and trees (Apoc. 2:7; 22 *passim*). Apart from this passage, it is used in the N.T. of the Cross only in Acts (3 times in all; twice in speeches of Peter, once in a speech of Paul) except for the O.T. quotation in Galatians 3:13 (Deut. 21:23) — ἐπικατάρατος πᾶς ὁ κρεμάμενος ἐπὶ ξύλου — 'Cursed is everyone that is hanged on a tree'. This scripture obviously referred originally to hanging by the neck, or possibly to impaling, but not to crucifixion, of which the Deuteronomist had never heard; but Paul applied it to the death of Christ on the cross, and this is apparently the origin of this use of ξύλον in the later Christian writings.

ἵνα . . . ζήσωμεν⟩ The clause clearly reflects dependence upon Romans 6, especially vv. 10-14, 18-19. There is some thought of 'moral influence' here, but it is subordinated to the Pauline thought of the effective power which brings us through death into a new life. The doctrine of baptism as the sacrament through which we enter into Christ's experience of death and resurrection is again brought to their remembrance. The ultimate meaning of the cross is realized in us only when we die to the old life of sin and alienation from God, and enter, united with Christ, into the new life that God causes to spring forth out of the death of the old, the regenerate life which is no longer enslaved to sin but devoted to righteousness.

οὗ τῷ μώλωπι ἰάθητε⟩ from Isaiah 53:5 — τῷ μώλωπι αὐτοῦ ἰάθημεν. By the change from the first to the second person of the verb, he brings the thought sharply back to its particular application to the slaves. μώλωψ means strictly a cut which bleeds; he thinks here of the lashing which draws blood. The slave who is thus brutally lashed finds 'healing' in the remembrance that Christ too was scourged.

v. 25. He concludes his admonition to the slaves with another reference to Isaiah 53, this time to v. 6 — πάντες ὡς πρόβατα ἐπλανήθημεν, again putting the verb into the second person, and changing it from the aorist to the compounded form of the imperfect (not 'went astray', but 'were straying, were going astray').

ἐπεστράφητε νῦν⟩ Note the aorist, which suggests not their new state, but the action which effected their 'return'. The words are most vivid, if they are taken as a direct reference to the baptism — 'In the sacrament now administered, you returned'.

ἐπὶ τὸν ποιμένα⟩The thought of Christ as the Shepherd is not found in the earlier strata of traditional Christian teaching. It does not occur in the Synoptics (the quotation from Zechariah 19:7 in the Passion story is not really an exception), or in the Pauline Epistles. The depiction of Christ as the Good Shepherd who lays down His life for the sheep, so beautifully set forth in John 10, may rest upon some saying of Jesus Himself, but is more likely to be a theme created and developed by the Evangelist. Elsewhere in the New Testament, it occurs only in Hebrews 13: 20 — 'that great Shepherd of the sheep'. Our writer may have drawn upon this last passage, but it is not necessary to seek so far; the thought of Christ as the Shepherd is a natural counterpart to the thought of the disciples as sheep who had been straying, and it rests ultimately upon O.T. conceptions of God as the 'Shepherd of Israel'. It is, indeed, not altogether certain that the writer himself does not think of God, rather than Christ, as 'the Shepherd and Bishop'.

ἐπίσκοπον⟩ It is hard to say what this word is intended most to suggest. It was, of course, already in use as a title of church leadership, though without the precise official significance which it later acquired. The church at Philippi had 'bishops and deacons' from its first foundation (Phil. 1:1); and the letters of Ignatius, written about the same time as First Peter, indicate that the organization of the local churches under the headship of a single minister, called the 'bishop', was rapidly developing. The writer might, then, have in mind some thought of Christ as the spiritual head of the Christian community — 'the bishop of souls' *par excellence* — the 'chief bishop' as He is called the 'chief Shepherd' in relation to the elders in 5:4. More probably, he is using the word in its primary sense of 'one who inspects, keeps watch over', and is bringing out this particular function of Christ as the Shepherd, watching over His flock, His eye ever upon them to guard them from harm, and to keep them from straying yet again.

3 ¹ Ὁμοίως γυναῖκες, ὑποτασσόμεναι τοῖς ἰδίοις ἀνδράσιν, ἵνα ⟨καὶ⟩ εἴ τινες ἀπειθοῦσιν τῷ λόγῳ, διὰ τῆς τῶν γυναικῶν ἀναστροφῆς ἄνευ λόγου κερδηθήσονται, ² ἐποπτεύσαντες τὴν ἐν φόβῳ ἁγνὴν ἀναστροφὴν ὑμῶν. ³ ὧν ἔστω οὐχ ὁ ἔξωθεν ἐμπλοκῆς τριχῶν καὶ περιθέσεως χρυσίων ἢ ἐνδύσεως ἱματίων κόσμος, ⁴ ἀλλ᾽ ὁ κρυπτὸς τῆς καρδίας ἄνθρωπος ἐν τῷ ἀφθάρτῳ τοῦ πραέως καὶ ἡσυχίου πνεύματος, ὅ ἐστιν ἐνώπιον τοῦ θεοῦ πολυτελές. ⁵ οὕτως γάρ ποτε καὶ αἱ ἅγιαι γυναῖκες αἱ ἐλπίζουσαι εἰς θεὸν ἐκόσμουν ἑαυτάς, ὑποτασσόμεναι τοῖς ἰδίοις ἀνδράσιν· ⁶ ὡς Σάρρα ὑπήκουσεν τῷ Ἀβραάμ, κύριον αὐτὸν καλοῦσα· ἧς ἐγενήθητε τέκνα ἀγαθοποιοῦσαι καὶ μὴ φοβούμεναι μηδεμίαν πτόησιν.

⁷ Οἱ ἄνδρες ὁμοίως, συνοικοῦντες κατὰ γνῶσιν ὡς ἀσθενεστέρῳ σκεύει τῷ γυναικείῳ, ἀπονέμοντες τιμὴν ὡς καὶ συγκληρονόμοις χάριτος ζωῆς, εἰς τὸ μὴ ἐγκόπτεσθαι τὰς προσευχὰς ὑμῶν.

You that are married women, likewise, be subject to your husbands, that any who disobey the Word may be won without a word through the behaviour of their wives, when they mark the purity of the life that you lead in the fear (of God). Not for you be the outward adornment that consists in elaborate hairdressings and flaunting of gold ornaments or the wearing of (rich) clothes; let yours be the beauty of the heart, the inward beauty of personality that lies in the incorruptible blessing of a mild and tranquil spirit, which is precious in the sight of God. For it was in this manner that the holy women of old, who put their hope in God, adorned themselves. So Sarah obeyed Abraham, calling him 'Lord', and you have become true daughters of hers, if you keep doing good, without falling prey to terror.

You that are married men, in turn, live with them in accordance with the knowledge (of God), remembering that they are the weaker sex, holding them in the honour due them as fellow-heirs of the grace of life, that your prayers may not be hindered.

¹ γυναικες⟩ txt Bℵ*A : pr αι cett   και⟩ om B 2412 : post ει CK 69 transp. κερδηθησονται⟩—σωνται ς   ³ τριχων⟩ om C Ψ Cl alex   ⁴ πραεως και ησυχιου⟩ ησυχ. και πρα. B vg boh   ⁵ εις⟩ επι τον ℵ ς   εκοσμουν εαυτας⟩ post γυναικες ℵ pos.   ⁶ υπηκουσεν⟩ υπηκουεν B 69. vg syrᴾ   ⁷ οι⟩ om B   συνοικουντες⟩ συνομιλουντες ℵ*   κατα γνωσιν⟩ om ℵ*   συγκληρονομοις⟩ txt Bℵᶜ 33. 69. 1739. 2412. vg sah boh syrᴾ : —μους ℵ* per errorem : —μοι (pro μωι cj. Tregelles) AC ς syrʰˡ   χαριτος⟩ pr ποικιλης Aℵᶜ² 2412. syrʰˡ boh εγκοπτεσθαι⟩ εκκοπτ. C² 33. 69. ς   τας προσευχας⟩ ταις προσευχαις B syrᴾ

v. 1. ὁμοίως⟩ 'likewise' — here (and in v. 7) has the force merely of '*item*'. It is to be construed with γυναῖκες, 'wives', the next group to which he addresses himself; not with ὑποτασσόμεναι (Knopf, et al.), which would force upon the writer a thought which is not in his mind, of a likeness between the position of a wife and that of a slave. Subjection, thus inculcated in a third context (with 2:13 and 18) as a duty incumbent upon all Christians, is for him a necessary part of the Christian attitude in his earthly environment. The Christian is to accept willingly, without inward or outward rebellion, that subordination which his place in the society of the time requires.

τοῖς ἰδίοις ἀνδράσιν) 'to their own husbands'. The same phrase occurs in Ephesians 5:22, cf. Colossians 3:18. ἰδίοις is not emphatic; it is perhaps needed to prevent ambiguity, to make it clear that it is subjection in the marital relationship, not a general subjection of women to men, that is required.

εἴ τινες ἀπειθοῦσιν τῷ λόγῳ) literally, 'if any disobey the word'. This is not a truly conditional clause, but an example of the indefinite use of εἰ (τις) as, e.g., in Philippians 4:8, where εἴ τις is not substantially different from ὅσα (ἀληθῆ . . . σεμνά, etc.). The meaning is, therefore, 'any who disobey', or even, 'those who disobey'. There is no suggestion that these are exceptional cases; the implication of the whole passage, on the contrary, is that the women whom he is addressing are nearly all married to pagan husbands.

The troubles of a household divided against itself in religion are many, under the best of circumstances. When the wife, without her husband's consent or good will, had embraced the Christian faith, while he continued to despise it as a 'deadly superstition' (exitiabilis superstitio — Tacitus *Annales* xv. 44) there cannot have been much peace in the home. (A vivid picture of the strife that often ensued is given by Tertullian, in his treatise *Ad Uxorem*, Bk. II, cc. 4-7.) Pagan moralists, moreover, taught that it was the duty of the wife to follow her husband in religion (Plutarch, *Praecepta Conjugalia* 19.) Many a husband will have felt that his wife was failing in her proper fidelity to him when she became converted to another religion, especially one which compelled her to refuse to worship his gods or to take part in the ordinary religious rites of the household, let alone the public ceremonies.

'The Word' may be taken to mean 'the Gospel preaching', which the husband might have heard at the same time as the wife, though not to the same effect; or he might hear it from a Christian teacher visiting the home after the wife's conversion; or in some cases, the converted wife might prevail upon him to accompany her to a Christian gathering. (For conversions of unbelievers at the meetings of Christians, see 1 Cor. 14: 24-25.) ἀπειθέω 'disobey' frequently means little more, in N.T., than ἀπιστέω 'disbelieve'; in fact, wherever the one occurs in the text, the other is usually found as a variant reading. (Similarly, the corresponding nouns ἀπειθεία, ἀπιστία are seldom found with undivided support; cf. note 2, p. 386, in my article on 'The Text of the Epistle to the Hebrews in P⁴⁶', in *Journal of Biblical Literature*, Vol. LXIII, December, 1944.) But as in 2:9 (τῷ λόγῳ ἀπειθοῦντες, *note*), the phrase seems to suggest the thought that refusal to believe the Gospel is evidence of

disobedience to the Logos, the divine Principle of life and truth that
inhabits all things.

ἀναστροφῆς (–φήν, **v. 2**)⟩ 'behaviour'—the life led in converse with
others, the entire deportment of the wife in all the affairs of every day
(cf. 1:15, note). A favourite word of this writer (6 occurrences, as against
7 in all the rest of the N.T.). Again, as in 2:12, he insists that Christian
conduct, the outward life that is formed by Christian faith and love,
may be the most effective means of overcoming hostility and even of
turning opponents into disciples.

St. Augustine's story of his mother Monica has often been adduced
as a perfect illustration of the passage. 'When she came to marriageable
age, she was bestowed upon a husband and served him as her lord, and
she did all she could to win him to Thee, speaking to him of Thee by
her deportment, whereby Thou madest her beautiful and reverently
lovable and admirable to her husband ... Finally, when her husband
was now at the very end of his earthly life, she won him unto Thee.'
(*Confessions* IX. 19, 22.)

ἄνευ λόγου⟩ 'without a word'—by the silent testimony of Christian
life and character.

κερδηθήσονται⟩ 'may be won'—The same use of κερδαίνω, in the
sense of 'winning' men to Christ, is found in 1 Corinthians 9:19-22; cf.
Matthew 18:15. On the use of the future indicative in a final clause with
ἵνα, see Moulton's remarks on the general closeness of relationship
between the subjunctive and the future, (*Proleg.* p. 240); and L. Rader-
macher, *Neutestamentliche Grammatik*, p. 178, on the use of the future
in place of the subjunctive. In the active and middle, the future is little
more than a specialized form of the aorist subjunctive. In the passive,
the relationship is not so close: but the usage could easily be extended
to this voice by analogy with similar constructions in the active and
middle.

v. 2. ἐποπτεύσαντες (ἐποπτεύοντες ℵ*, from 2:12)⟩ 'marking', 'ob-
serving'. The aorist may be intended, as frequently, to indicate time
before the main verb. Though not used absolutely, as in 2:12, ἐποπτεύω
seems still to have an undertone of the technical cultic meaning (2:12,
note), for the thought is that the husbands' eyes are opened to the truth
of the Gospel by their observation of the wives' conduct.

ἐν φόβῳ ἁγνήν⟩ The adjective is to be taken in close connection with
the prepositional phrase. ἁγνός, closely related to ἅγιος, is a distinctively religious word. It suggests a purity charged with piety and
commanding reverence; and this purity is the expression of a life led 'in
fear', i.e., in the fear of God (cf. 2:18).

v. 3. Protests against luxury and ostentation were common to pagan
moralists as well as to Jewish and Christian teachers. Simplicity and
frugality in dress, as in food and drink, were regarded especially by the

Cynics, and after them by the Stoics, and indeed by most of the later philosophical schools, as a necessary part of that asceticism which was essential to the cultivation of the higher life.

It is implied that the Christian communities included among their members women of wealth and position. Slave girls and women of the poor might indeed try to make themselves attractive by putting up their hair in braids and by giving some attention to their dress, but they would hardly need the warning against flaunting golden jewellery. Even the ἐμπλοκῆς τριχῶν — 'braiding of hair' — suggests the services of the hairdresser, and the ἐνδύσεως ἱματίων — literally 'the putting on of garments' — clearly implies sumptuousness, and perhaps even such elaborate dressing as would require the help of maids. The point in any case is that Christian women are not to take pride in such adventitious aids to beauty, but are to cultivate rather the graces of the soul.

v. 4. ὁ κρυπτὸς τῆς καρδίας ἄνθρωπος⟩ 'the hidden man of the heart' — i.e., the inward beauty of character — is contrasted with ὁ ἔξωθεν ... κόσμος, 'the outward adornment' (of hair, jewels, clothing, etc.). This use of ἄνθρωπος is unusual; no precise parallel seems to be available. It is, however, loosely related to such Pauline phrases as ὁ παλαιὸς ἡμῶν ἄνθρωπος (Rom. 6:6); κατὰ τὸν ἔσω ἄνθρωπον (id. 7:22); ὁ ἔξω ἡμῶν ἄνθρωπος ... ἀλλ' ὁ ἔσω ἡμῶν (2 Cor. 4:16), etc. It might be rendered 'character', or even 'personality'. It is not an adornment (κόσμος), but the true nature of the Christian woman.

τῆς καρδίας⟩ is explanatory of κρυπτός. The Christian character is 'hidden' in the sense that it is not exhibited in the outward appearance, but belongs to 'the heart', in contrast to the ἔξωθεν ... κόσμος, which has to do with styles of hair and clothing.

ἀφθάρτῳ⟩ 'incorruptible' — best taken as a neuter substantive, not as an adjective in the masculine, agreeing with (κόσμῳ). Here again, the word has the sense of 'immortal', — 'in the immortal part'. It suggests the thought of that which is given by God in regeneration (cf. ἐκ σπορᾶς ... ἀφθάρτου, 1:23, note).

πνεύματος⟩ genitive of definition. The 'incorruptible part', the Christian's immortal possession, is the 'spirit' that God has given. πνεῦμα is used almost exclusively, not of the natural disposition, but of that which comes from God. (See Knopf's note on the passage.) Most commentators, however, take it here in the sense of 'inward nature', 'essential character', 'disposition of the heart and mind'; and this sense is not so rare as Knopf supposes. (Cf. Matt. 5:3 — οἱ πτωχοὶ τῷ πνεύματι; 1 Cor. 4:21 — ἐν ἀγάπῃ πνεύματί τε πραΰτητος.)

ὅ⟩ The relative in the neuter may be attached directly to πνεῦμα, or to ἀφθάρτῳ, but it is better to take it as attaching to the entire preceding clause (cf. ἐν ᾧ, 1:6, note). That which is precious in the sight of

God is the immortal, imperishable beauty of the inward life, not the richness of outward adornment.

On the whole passage, cf. 1 Timothy 2:9-12.

v. 5. By 'the holy women' we are to understand simply the women of the Old Testament, who were 'holy' as belonging to the people of God and dedicated to His service. As in Hebrews 11, the men and women of Israel's sacred literature are regarded as the heroic predecessors, the famed spiritual ancestry of the house of faith, supplanting in the imagination of the faithful the heroes of Greek and Roman history and legend whom they had been taught to honour and to emulate in the days of their pagan upbringing. Cf. the remarks on the value to the nascent Church of the sense of historic continuity with the ancient people of God, in the note on 2:9-10.

αἱ ἐλπίζουσαι εἰς θεόν⟩ 'who hoped in God' — sharing the 'living Hope' to which the women now addressed had been regenerated. The participle in the present tense is durative — hope was the continuing attitude of their life. The phrase sums up the thought of Hebrews 11:13 (which also stands in juxtaposition to the mention of Sarah) — 'These all died in faith, not having received the promises, but having perceived them afar off, and embraced them'.

ὑποτασσόμεναι⟩ 'subjecting themselves' — He seems to look upon the exhibition of a loyal 'subjection' to husbands as a cardinal element — almost as *the* cardinal element — in the inward, spiritual adornment which he commends.

v. 6. ὡς Σάρρα, etc.⟩ As Abraham was looked upon as 'the father of all them that believe' (Romans 4:11), it was a natural parallel, in an address to women, to present Sarah in similar terms, as the 'mother' of believing women, and they as her spiritual daughters. The Scripture which he introduces — κύριον αὐτὸν καλοῦσα — 'Calling him lord' — is, we must feel, introduced quite arbitrarily; it has at most a verbal connection with the thought here advanced, not a genuine pertinence. (Gen. 18:12 — of Sarah's incredulous reception of the promise that despite her barrenness, she should bear a son to Abraham at his advanced age — οὔπω μέν μοι γέγονεν ἕως τοῦ νῦν· ὁ δὲ κύριός μου πρεσβύτερος. 'It has never yet happened to me until now, and my lord is too old.') Sarah's use of κύριος here has certainly no significance in the way of exhibiting an attitude of subjection to her husband.

ἐγενήθητε⟩ The aorist is difficult. It may be taken as one of the rare examples of the truly 'timeless' aorist, which has survived chiefly in the gnomic usage; in that case, it would be best rendered by the English present — 'You show yourselves true daughters of Sarah', etc. If it be taken of past time, we might look upon it as another reference to the baptism — 'You became her daughters' — in the baptism, when you embraced her faith and became members of the spiritual household. This is perhaps somewhat forced; it becomes easier to accept, if the punctuation of W-H (margin) be adopted, setting apart ὡς Σάρρα . . . τέκνα in a parenthesis.

ἀγαθοποιοῦσαι καὶ μὴ φοβούμεναι οὐδεμίαν πτόησιν⟩ With the negative μή, it is natural to take the participles as conditional. However, the distinction between οὐ and μή is not maintained as rigidly by Hellenistic writers as by the masters of Attic prose, and there is a tendency to use μή as the regular negative with the participle in almost all its varieties of force. The clause might, then, mean not '*if*', but '*in that* you do good and are not a prey to terror'. With the punctuation suggested in the margin of W-H (see above), these participles would be dependent not upon ἐγενήθητε but upon ἐκόσμουν, in parallelism with ὑποτασσόμεναι.

The concluding phrase — μὴ φοβούμεναι, etc. — is adapted from Proverbs 3:25 — οὐ φοβηθήσῃ πτόησιν ἐπελθοῦσαν — 'Thou wilt not fear the terror that sets upon thee (the onset of terror)'. In our passage, however, πτόησιν seems to be used as a cognate accusative, like the frequent φοβεῖσθαι φόβον. The writer can hardly be thinking of anything else than the intimidation that might be attempted by a husband displeased with his wife's new faith.

v. 7. The counsel for wives assumes that they are, for the most part, married to pagan husbands; the counsel for husbands, that they are married to Christian wives. Doubtless it would be easier for a husband to carry his wife with him into the Christian society, once he had himself become a member, than for a wife to win her husband. In the former case, the great authority possessed by the husband in ancient society was thrown into the balance in favour of the new faith. The brevity of the address to husbands reflects both the fact that they are not faced with the same tragic problem as the wives of hostile pagans, and also that the men were much less numerous than the women in these early communities.

κατὰ γνῶσιν⟩ 'according to knowledge' — certainly, the knowledge of God is meant. γνῶσις is one of the key words of the contemporary philosophy of religion, always in the sense of γνῶσις θεοῦ, the knowledge which is light, truth, and immortality; frequently set over against the indulgences of the body, as it is (tacitly) here. (Cf. Reitzenstein, HMR³, pp. 285ff.) The relationship to God determines the nature of the marriage relationship; through the knowledge of God, the husband learns to set a new value on the wife, not merely as the mother of his children (which even in so exceptional a person as Plato is virtually the only consideration), but as the partner in his eternal hope and in his prayers.

σκεύει⟩ literally, 'vessel' — cf. 1 Thessalonians 4:4 — εἰδέναι ἕκαστον ὑμῶν τὸ ἑαυτοῦ σκεῦος κτᾶσθαι ἐν ἁγιασμῷ καὶ τιμῇ, μὴ ἐν πάθει ἐπιθυμίας — where the thought runs along the same general lines as here; the passage is probably in the writer's mind. σκεῦος is not used of the

wife in any derogatory sense; the man is a 'vessel' in the same sense. Cf.
Acts 9:15, where St. Paul is called σκεῦος ἐκλογῆς; and 2 Timothy 2:21.

ἀσθενεστέρῳ⟩ 'weaker'. ἀσθένης is used both of physical infirmity
(Matt. 25:43; Acts 5:15f.), and of moral and spiritual weakness (Rom.
5:6; 1 Cor. 8:7ff.; cf. the similar use of the verb ἀσθενέω — Rom. 14:1,
etc.). The latter sense may be intended here; if so, we should have to
see in it a vestige of the low estimation of the moral stamina of women,
common to Jews and Greeks. (Cf. 1 Tim. 2:14; and for a typical
expression of the Greek point of view, Plato, *Laws*, Book VI, 781b —
'The female nature, in mankind, is inferior in virtue to that of the males'
— ἡ θήλεια ἡμῖν φύσις ἐστὶ πρὸς ἀρετὴν χείρων τῆς τῶν ἀρρένων.) But
it is perhaps better to take the word in the sense of physical weakness in
this passage; this would be more in keeping with the thought of the
clause which follows, where husbands are bidden to remember that
wives are called to share in the same spiritual privilege as themselves.

ἀπονέμοντες τιμήν⟩ An unusual phrase, but its significance is clearly
illustrated by a striking passage in the *Laws* (Book VIII, 837b-c) —'For
he that loves the body and hungers for its bloom, as it were for a peach,
urges himself on to satisfy his desire, according no honour to the
beloved's character of soul (τιμὴν οὐδεμίαν ἀπονέμοντες τῷ τῆς ψυχῆς
ἤθει τοῦ ἐρωμένου). But he that holds the desire for the body as a
secondary thing ... holding in awe and revering that which is temperate
and brave and noble and discreet, will desire ever to live chastely with
the chaste beloved'. In both cases, the thought is that the only true
and worthy affection is that which rests not primarily upon physical
attraction, but upon respect for character and personality. τὸ τῆς ψυχῆς
ἦθος τοῦ ἐρωμένου — 'the character of the soul of the beloved', in
Plato's phrase, is defined by the Christian writer in terms of the divine
grace which has been bestowed upon the married pair — they esteem
one another, or rather, the husbands are to esteem the wives, as 'fellow-
heirs of the grace of life'. (Plato is not writing here of the marriage
relationship, but of the love of men for men; the difference of context
does not diminish the aptness of the language as throwing light upon
the meaning of the Petrine phrase.)

χάριτος ζωῆς⟩ χάρις, here, is concrete, having the sense of 'gift of
grace', the imperishable inheritance that awaits the regenerate (1:4);
and ζωῆς is the genitive of apposition (or of definition) — 'the gift of
grace, which is life', i.e., the true life, life eternal.

εἰς τὸ μὴ ἐγκόπτεσθαι τὰς προσευχὰς ὑμῶν⟩ 'that your prayers may
not be hindered'. ὑμῶν may be taken as meaning 'of you husbands' or 'of
husband and wife', probably the latter. The thought appears to be that
unless the esteem for the spiritual quality of the mate be given the
primacy over the physical desires, it will be hard to maintain an earnest
mutual life of communion with God. Cf. 1 Corinthians 7:1-7, especially
v. 5.

⁸ Τὸ δὲ τέλος πάντες ὁμόφρονες, συμπαθεῖς, φιλάδελφοι, εὔσπλαγχνοι, ταπεινόφρονες, ⁹ μὴ ἀποδιδόντες κακὸν ἀντὶ κακοῦ ἢ λοιδορίαν ἀντὶ λοιδορίας, τοὐναντίον δὲ εὐλογοῦντες, ὅτι εἰς τοῦτο ἐκλήθητε, ἵνα εὐλογίαν κληρονομήσητε.

¹⁰ ὁ γὰρ θέλων ζωὴν ἀγαπᾶν
καὶ ἰδεῖν ἡμέρας ἀγαθὰς
παυσάτω τὴν γλῶσσαν ἀπὸ κακοῦ
καὶ χείλη τοῦ μὴ λαλῆσαι δόλον·
¹¹ ἐκκλινάτω δὲ ἀπὸ κακοῦ καὶ ποιησάτω ἀγαθόν,
ζητησάτω εἰρήνην καὶ διωξάτω αὐτήν·
¹² ὅτι ὀφθαλμοὶ Κυρίου ἐπὶ δικαίους
καὶ ὦτα αὐτοῦ εἰς δέησιν αὐτῶν·
πρόσωπον δὲ Κυρίου ἐπὶ ποιοῦντας κακά.

Finally, let all be one in mind and in feeling, and in the love of the brotherhood. Be tender-hearted, and humble-minded. Do not return evil for evil, or reviling for reviling, but on the contrary, bless; for to this you were called, that you may inherit a blessing.

For　　　　*'He that desireth to love life*
　　　　　And to see days that are good,
　　　　　Let him keep his tongue from evil
　　　　　And his lips from speaking guile;
　　　　　Let him depart from evil and do good,
　　　　　Seek peace and pursue it.'

Because　　*'The eyes of the Lord are upon the righteous,*
　　　　　His ears are open to their prayer,
　　　　　But the face of the Lord is against them that do evil.'

⁸ ταπεινοφρονες⟩ φιλοφρονες ϛ : pr φιλοφρονες L　　⁹ οτι⟩ pr ειδοτες ϛ syrʰˡ ᵐᵍ
¹⁰ γλωσσαν⟩+αυτου ℵ 69. ϛ syrr boh　χειλη⟩+αυτου ϛ　ιδειν ημερας⟩ transp. C　¹¹ δε⟩ om ℵ 33 ϛ　¹² δεησιν⟩ pr την C

The 'Haustafel' is concluded with a general admonition; and the whole teaching of the section is supported, according to his fashion, by a passage of Old Testament Scripture to drive it home.

v. 8. ὁμόφρονες, συμπαθεῖς, φιλάδελφοι⟩ These three adjectives all bear upon the attitude of Christians to one another. None of them occurs elsewhere in N.T. or in Lxx, except for one occurrence of φιλάδελφος in 2 Maccabees 15:14; but the thoughts which they convey find frequent expression in other forms.

ὁμόφρονες⟩ 'like-minded' – of that inward unity of attitude in spiritual things, which makes schism unthinkable. St. Paul prefers the phrase τὸ αὐτὸ φρονεῖν — literally, 'to think the same (thinking)', i.e., as A.V. renders, 'to be like-minded' (Rom. 15:5; Phil. 2:2; et al.; cf. 1 Cor. 1:10). No pride in 'private judgment' should cause us to forget the obligation which rests upon us to seek unity of mind with our brethren in Christ.

συμπαθεῖς⟩ 'sharing in feelings' — united alike in sorrow and in joy. Cf. Romans 13:15 — 'Rejoice with them that rejoice, and weep with them that weep'. The verb συμπαθέω is used twice in Hebrews, once of Christ ('touched with the feeling of our infirmities' — 4:15), and once of the Christian community, of all the members sharing the feelings of those that are in chains (10:34; cf. the entire thought of vv. 32-34).

φιλάδελφοι⟩ like φιλαδελφία (1:22, note) — 'loving your (Christian) brethren'. The Vulgate renders accurately fraternitatis amatores. The thought is of the mutual love which is the bond of brotherhood in Christ, not of an all-embracing 'brotherly love'.

εὔσπλαγχνοι, ταπεινόφρονες⟩ more widely, of the spirit that is to govern Christians in all their relationships.

εὔσπλαγχνοι⟩ 'tender-hearted'. τὰ σπλάγχνα — literally, 'the bowels' — is used in classical literature as betokening the seat of violent passion, whether of love or (more frequently) of anger. In N.T. and Lxx, it is used of the deepest inward feelings, usually of love or compassion ('bowels of mercy, bowels of compassion'; Paul calls Onesimus 'my own bowels' — Philemon, v. 12). The verb σπλαγχνίζομαι occurs frequently in the Synoptic Gospels, usually of Jesus, in the sense of 'deeply touched', 'moved with compassionate tenderness'. The adjective occurs again in N.T. only in Ephesians 4:32 — 'Be ye kind, tenderhearted, forgiving', etc.

ταπεινόφρονες⟩ 'humble-minded' — The only occurrence of the adjective in N.T. The noun ταπεινοφροσύνη, however, occurs several times, sometimes of a false humility (Colossians 2:18, 23). The true humility of mind is expounded in Philippians 2:3, as that attitude in which each esteems the other more highly than himself.

v. 9. μὴ ἀποδίδοντες . . . ἀλλὰ . . . εὐλογοῦντες⟩ He turns now to the attitude in which Christians are to meet hostility. There is to be no retaliation; the Christian's whole profession is to bless. Our attitude towards others is not to be determined by the attitude which they adopt towards us, but by our relationship to God and our recollection of the kind of life to which He has called us.

It is most remarkable that even in such a passage as this, where the teaching is most distinctly that of Jesus Himself (Matt. 5:43-48), the Christian teacher makes no appeal to the words of his Master, while the words of the Pauline Epistles are taken up almost verbatim. (Rom. 12:17 — μηδένι κακὸν ἀντὶ κακοῦ ἀποδιδόντες; cf. 1 Thess. 5:15; 1 Cor. 4:12 — λοιδορούμενοι εὐλογοῦμεν; Rom. 12:14 — εὐλογεῖτε τοὺς διώκοντας ὑμᾶς· εὐλογεῖτε καὶ μὴ καταρᾶσθε.) Is this remotely conceivable in such a one as St. Peter, to whom, after all, we must be indebted at least as much as to any single man for such knowledge of our Lord's sayings as we possess?

vv. 10-12. The Scriptural citation is from Psalm 33 (34) vv. 13-17. The ordinary text of Lxx is its basis, but it has been not so much freely quoted as skilfully re-phrased in a better Greek style. The changes are greatest in the first two lines, where Lxx reads

$$\text{τίς ἐστιν ἄνθρωπος ὁ θέλων ζωήν,}$$
$$\text{ἀγαπῶν ἰδεῖν ἡμέρας ἀγαθάς;}$$

'Who is the man that desires life, that loves to behold good days?' The crude barbarity of the Alexandrian version has not been wholly surmounted, but it has at least been greatly softened by our writer. (A strong indication that he was a Greek, or at least that his native tongue was Greek. A Jew whose primary language was Aramaic would hardly have been so offended by the barbarisms of Lxx as to feel himself compelled thus to revise.) In O.T., of course, the thought was simply of long life and prosperity; but to the N.T. writer and his readers, ζωή would have the deeper sense of 'true life', 'life in God', 'life eternal', as in v. 7 above; and the 'good days' would mean to them the days of the future glory. (So St. Basil; see Cramer's *Catenae*, vol. VIII, p. 61.) The change from the second to the third person in the five imperatives which followed was necessary to the sense, once the first two lines were altered. The last three lines show no change from the text of Lxx.

¹³ Καὶ τίς ὁ κακώσων ὑμᾶς, ἐὰν τοῦ ἀγαθοῦ ζηλωταὶ γένησθε;
¹⁴ ἀλλ' εἰ καὶ πάσχοιτε διὰ δικαιοσύνην, μακάριοι. τὸν δὲ φόβον
αὐτῶν μὴ φοβηθῆτε μηδὲ ταραχθῆτε, ¹⁵ κύριον δὲ τὸν Χριστὸν ἁγιάσατε ἐν ταῖς καρδίαις ὑμῶν, ἕτοιμοι ἀεὶ πρὸς ἀπολογίαν παντὶ τῷ
αἰτοῦντι ὑμᾶς λόγον περὶ τῆς ἐν ὑμῖν ἐλπίδος, ¹⁶ ἀλλὰ μετὰ πραΰτητος
καὶ φόβου, συνείδησιν ἔχοντες ἀγαθήν, ἵνα ἐν ᾧ καταλαλεῖσθε καται-
σχυνθῶσιν οἱ ἐπηρεάζοντες ὑμῶν τὴν ἀγαθὴν ἐν Χριστῷ ἀναστροφήν.
¹⁷ κρεῖττον γὰρ ἀγαθοποιοῦντας, εἰ θέλοι τὸ θέλημα τοῦ θεοῦ,
πάσχειν ἢ κακοποιοῦντας.

*And who is there that will harm you, if you be full of zeal for the
good? If even you were to suffer for righteousness' sake, you would be
blessed. Be not terrified by the fear of them; be not shaken; but
sanctify Christ the Lord in your hearts, and be ever prepared to make
a reasoned defence before anyone that summons you to give an
accounting in the matter of the hope that is in you. But (make your
defence) with gentleness and fear, keeping your conscience clear, so
that those who revile the good life which you lead in Christ may be
put to shame in the very matter wherein you are slandered. For it is
better for you to suffer, should the will of God require it, for doing
right, rather than for doing wrong.*

¹³ εαν) ει B   ζηλωται) μιμηται ⸃   γενησθε) γενοισθε B   ¹⁴ μακαριοι)+εστε 𝕏
μηδε ταραχθητε) om BL   ¹⁵ Χριστον) θεον ⸃   ετοιμοι)+δε A ⸃   αει) om A
αιτουντι) απαιτουντι 𝕏ᶜ A   ¹⁶ αλλα) om ⸃   καταλαλεισθε) txt B 206. 1518.
1739. 2412. sah (latt) syrʰˡ ᵐᵍ : καταλαλουσιν υμων ως κακοποιων (ex 2:12)
𝕏AC 33. 69. ⸃ boh   ¹⁷ θελοι) θελει ⸃

v. 13. τίς ὁ κακώσων⟩ The participle takes up the last phrase of the
Scripture passage — ποιοῦντας κακά — and makes it the point of
departure for a new line of thought. The question is obviously rhetorical; he is asserting boldly (and somewhat naively), that if their lives are
wholly devoted to goodness, no one will do them harm. Nevertheless,
he has recognized in his admonition to the slaves (2:19ff.) that they
may suffer unjustly, that they may be beaten without having done
anything to deserve it, as Christ suffered. Even so, he appears to feel
that this is quite abnormal; his words imply that there is seldom an
utter lack of provocation, that the hostility which could be disarmed by
meekness, submission, and persistence in goodness was apt to be met
instead with a certain insolence which all but invited blows. He
requires of them, therefore, an absolute passion for goodness — they are
to be 'zealots for the good'. The phrase is almost an oxymoron, for the
spirit of the zealot did not tend to the kind of goodness which he extols,
the goodness of meekness, patience, and submissiveness. In the pursuit
of such goodness, the Christian is to show the whole-hearted, consuming
eagerness, the single-minded, unwavering concentration which the

zealot displays in seeking to achieve the end to which he has devoted his life.

v. 14. But the thought of 'harm' is capable of being understood in a deeper sense. Men may undergo suffering, and yet not be 'harmed'. In this ultimate sense, the only real 'harm' is that which touches the inner life, attacking the integrity of the personality; and when one's life is devoted to goodness and to God, it does not lie in the power of man so to harm it. Knopf draws attention to the words of Isaiah 50:9 — ἰδοὺ ὁ Κύριος βοηθήσει μοι· τίς κακώσει με; — 'Behold, the Lord will aid me; who will harm me?' The same thought occurs frequently in the Gospels (Lk. 21:16-18; Matt. 10:28; etc.); and there is an excellent parallel in the words of Socrates, reported by Plato in *Apology* 41d — οὐκ ἔστιν ἀνδρὶ ἀγαθῷ κακὸν οὐδὲν οὔτε ζῶντι οὔτε τελευτήσαντι — 'No harm can befall a good man, either in life or after death'.

πάσχω, then, is not used as a mere equivalent for the passive of κακόω. Christians may 'suffer' for righteousness' sake, but in such suffering they will not be harmed, but blessed. Here the writer turns to the words of the beatitude (Matt. 5:10)—μακάριοι οἱ δεδιωγμένοι ἕνεκεν δικαιοσύνης — 'Blessed are they that are persecuted for righteousness' sake'. Yet this still appears to him to be an unlikely contingency. In having recourse to the optative, an obsolete mood which had all but disappeared from the language, he indicates that he is putting before them a future possibility which is far from vivid (cf. also θέλοι, v. 17), as if to strengthen them against an all but unjustified apprehension which they may feel, rather than to prepare them for a danger that is to be seriously anticipated. A person of humane instincts, accustomed to living in a civilized society, finds it all but impossible to believe that human wickedness and depravity can ever go so far as to meet sheer goodness with cruelty. (Our own reluctance to credit the evidence of the sheer viciousness of the Nazi regime is a case in point.) He is capable of imagining the infliction of a punishment out of all proportion to the offence; but the mentality which takes offence at goodness itself, which causes men to suffer for their very righteousness — this passes his powers of imagination. In our passage, it is almost as if he introduced the thought because it belonged to the tradition of Christian teaching, even to the very words of the Lord, rather than because it had any roots in his own experience. He did not yet 'know what was in man', as his Master knew. No other part of the Discourse reflects so clearly the fact that it was composed before the storm of persecution had broken. The time when men would be condemned to torture and death simply 'as Christians' (4:16) had not yet come.

The words which follow are derived from Isaiah 8:12-13—τὸν δὲ φόβον αὐτοῦ οὐ μὴ φοβηθῆτε, οὐδὲ μὴ ταραχθῆτε· Κύριον αὐτὸν ἁγιάσατε, καὶ αὐτὸς ἔσται σου φόβος—'Be not terrified with the fear of him, neither be shaken; sanctify the Lord Himself, and He Himself shall be your dread'. In its original setting, the passage appears to be a warning to the prophet not to be swept away by the feeling of the populace, not to call holy what they call holy, not to fear what they fear; but to call God alone holy, and to fear none but Him. (See the rendering of A. R. Gordon in *The Old Testament: An American Translation*, Chicago, 1939.) The Lxx rendering, however, will hardly bear this interpretation; and it seems that the Greek translators took the words as an exhortation to the people not to fear the king of Assyria or be shaken by the danger threatening them from his power, but to dedicate themselves to God and to fear only Him. In this sense, our writer now applies the words to Christians who may be threatened with persecution for righteousness' sake. φόβον, then, is to be taken here as a cognate accusative with φοβηθῆτε; 'Do not fear their fear', i.e., do not fear them. αὐτῶν is a general reference to any opponents that may present themselves.

v. 15. Κύριος, used in Isaiah for the name of God (יהוה), is here taken as the usual Christian title for Christ — this sense is made explicit by the addition τὸν Χριστόν.

ἁγιάσατε ἐν ταῖς καρδίαις⟩ 'sanctify in your hearts' (the Lord Christ) — i.e., 'venerate and adore Him', thus dispelling all fear of man. ἁγιάζω here, not in the sense of 'make holy', 'purify', 'dedicate', which is the usual range of meaning, but in the sense of 'call holy', 'acknowledge as holy', 'revere' (as in the first petition of the Lord's Prayer — ἁγιασθήτω τὸ ὄνομά σου.) The addition of ἐν ταῖς καρδίαις emphasizes that this must be no formal acknowledgement, no mere outward profession of reverence for Christ, but a true inward dedication to Him, which will lift them above all fear of earthly powers.

ἕτοιμοι ἀεὶ πρὸς ἀπολογίαν⟩ The force of the preceding imperatives is carried over into the adjective, though it is not so much subordinated to them as co-ordinated with them, in a further instruction. The adjective, like the participle, often carries this imperative force in the usage of this writer (cf. πάντες ὁμόφρονες, v. 8); it is a variety of the sentence without the verb εἰμί which is very common in assertions and interrogations in the Greek of all periods (see Paul Regard, *La Phrase Nominale dans La Langue du Nouveau Testament*, Paris, 1919). ἀπολογία — primarily of the argument for the defence in a court of law; cf. Acts 25:16 — 'It is not the custom of the Romans to surrender a man to punishment before the accused meet his accusers face to face and be given opportunity to plead in defence' — πρὶν ἢ . . . τόπον ἀπολογίας λάβοι. This is certainly the force here, for the phrase παντὶ τῷ αἰτοῦντι λόγον can only apply to a judicial interrogation. λόγον αἰτεῖν — 'demand an accounting' — would not be used of an informal inquiry from a private person. It has the force of calling one to answer for the manner in which he has exercised his responsibilities — the converse of λόγον διδόναι, or ἀποδιδόναι — 'to give an accounting' — as in Romans 14:12 — 'Each of us shall give an account — λόγον δώσει — concerning himself to God'. περὶ is regularly used to indicate the matter of the inquiry — περὶ ἑαυτοῦ, in Romans 14:12; περὶ αὐτοῦ (neuter) in Matthew 12:36; etc.). περὶ τῆς ἐν ὑμῖν ἐλπίδος here summarizes the content of the Christian profession as 'hope' (cf. 1:3). This does not suggest that the presiding official will be interested primarily in the future expectations of the accused, for to him the important matter would certainly be the social consequences of the doctrine and discipline. The phrase refers not to the questioner's view of Christianity, but to that which forms the heart of the religion for the Christian. (Cf. Col. 1:27 — 'God willed to make known what is the riches of the glory of this mystery among the Gentiles; which is Christ in you, the hope of glory' — Χριστὸς ἐν ὑμῖν, ἡ ἐλπὶς τῆς δόξης). ἐν ὑμῖν — not collective (in the community), but personal — 'in your hearts'. The hope is not an external expectation, but the very spring of the life within.

v. 16. ἀλλὰ μετὰ πραΰτητος καὶ φόβου, συνείδησιν ἔχοντες ἀγαθήν⟩ of their demeanour in the presence of the investigating authority. Readiness in defence and fearlessness of spirit must not pass over into insolence or defiant challenge. They are not to court martyrdom needlessly; the venom of accusers, and even the hostile attitude of presiding officials must not be met with an answering hostility, but with the gentleness which becomes a Christian in all circumstances. (Cf. 2 Tim. 2:24-25.) μετὰ . . . φόβου — 'with fear' — not of the accuser or of the judge (see v. 14), but as in 2:18 and 3:2, of God. Their conduct is to be determined, not by the behaviour of others, but by their relationship to God. (Cf. Didymus, in Cramer's *Catenae*, Vol. VIII, p. 65 — ὁ γὰρ τὸν περὶ τοῦ θεοῦ λόγον λαλῶν, οὕτως ὀφείλει λαλεῖν ὡς παρόντος τοῦ θεοῦ — 'He that speaks the Word concerning God ought to speak as though God Himself were present'.) ἔχοντες — 'maintaining' (your conscience clear) — still, primarily, of their behaviour before the magistrate. The participle is again used with imperative force, retained from the preceding imperatives, and the adjective is to be taken as a predicate accusative, complementing the noun, not modifying it directly. He is not thinking here of the clearness of conscience that rests upon innocence of life, but of the scrupulous care with which they are to conduct themselves throughout the inquiry into the accusation against them; there must be no word or act that would burden their conscience with the feeling that it was something less than the worthiest. Under the tension inseparable from such a situation, it was no easy thing to show inflexible firmness in the truth, and yet to remain tranquil, showing neither anger nor contempt. In all this, he is setting before them an ideal of true nobility, a restraint, dignity, and self-control that would be the finest fruit of character.

ἵνα ἐν ᾧ καταλαλεῖσθε καταισχυνθῶσιν⟩ 'that they may be put to shame in the very matter wherein you are slandered'. The exhibition of a true Christian demeanour will have the effect of confuting the slanderous accusations of sedition which are laid against them; the accusers will be 'put to shame' in that the falseness of the charges will be patent to all and the accused will be set free. The informer was in any case regarded as despicable, and if his charge were shown to be utterly unfounded, he would indeed be put to shame; the Roman magistrate might even send him away with a tingling ear.

ἐπηρεάζοντες) The word has a distinctly literary flavour; elsewhere in the New Testament it occurs only once, being introduced as a refinement of vocabulary in the Third Gospel (Lk. 6:28 — προσεύχεσθε περὶ τῶν ἐπηρεαζόντων ὑμᾶς), replacing the διώκω of the corresponding Matthaean passage (Matt. 5:44). It is formed upon the noun ἐπήρεια — 'spiteful abuse', and is a more vigorous synonym for καταλαλέω — 'slander'. It suggests that the informers deal in vituperation and vilification, rather in the serious terms which would befit an accusation likely to involve grave consequences for the accused.

τὴν ἀγαθὴν ἐν Χριστῷ ἀναστροφήν) 'the good life which you lead in Christ'. ἀναστροφή again (vv. 1, 2) of the whole tenor of the Christian's life among his neighbours. ἀγαθὴν stands in the closest connection with ἐν Χριστῷ — the quality of the life derives from its dependence upon Christ; it is good because it is rooted and grounded in Him, and lived in communion with Him.

v. 17. κρεῖττον γὰρ, etc.) repeats the thought of 2:20 in a more general context. There, he was speaking of slaves, and of the bearing of punishment inflicted at the whim of an unreasonable master; here he speaks of Christians of any and every condition, and of the penalties that may be imposed upon them by officers of the law. In His wise will, God may decree that they shall suffer at the hands of the governing authority which brings them to trial. Let them only make sure that they commit no offence to justify the penalty, that it may be inflicted not for cause which they have given, but in spite of their manifest goodness.

This return to the thought of ἀγαθοποιοῦντας ... πάσχειν is then related to the sufferings of Christ, and becomes the point of departure for a disquisition on the meaning of His Passion, and of our participation therein through our incorporation into Him by baptism. This theme is developed, with intricate and difficult variations, through the remainder of the chapter and the first six verses of the following chapter.

18 ὅτι καὶ Χριστὸς ἅπαξ περὶ ἁμαρτιῶν ἔπαθεν, δίκαιος ὑπὲρ ἀδίκων, ἵνα ὑμᾶς προσαγάγῃ τῷ θεῷ, θανατωθεὶς μὲν σαρκὶ ζωοποιηθεὶς δὲ πνεύματι.

For Christ also suffered for sins once, the Just for the unjust, that He might bring you into the presence of God; He was put to death in the flesh, but made alive in the spirit.

18 και) om ℵ   αμαρτιων) pr των ℵ : add υπερ υμων A : add υπερ ημων ℵCL 33. boh : ημων (sine υπερ) minusc pauc. vg clem syrP   ἔπαθεν B ς) απεθανεν cett   υμας) om ℵ* : ημας AC ς vg   τω θεω) om B   πνευματι) pr τω 33. ς

If Christians suffer for righteousness' sake (v. 14), for doing good (v. 17), they follow in the footsteps of their Master; He too suffered, not for any wrong that He had done, but as a just man. So far, the sufferings of innocent Christians are analogous to the sufferings of Christ. But the teacher cannot bring forward the thought of the Passion without asking his readers to contemplate its further meaning, as not merely a pattern for Christians, but as vicarious, as expiatory, and as making possible our access to God. He does not thereby imply that the sufferings of Christians have altogether the same significance in the economy of human salvation; that would push the analogy too far. It is simply that once the fact of Christ's sufferings has been mentioned, he seizes the opportunity to stir them by the recollection of all that those sufferings have meant for their life towards God.

ἔπαθεν⟩ This, the reading of B and of ς, seems preferable to ἀπέθανεν, though the decision is difficult; W-H prints ἀπέθανεν in the text, ἔπαθεν in the margin. The weight of textual evidence favours ἀπέθανεν very strongly; the united testimony of the versions, coupled with that of all the Alexandrian witnesses except B, is almost overwhelming; especially as a ready explanation for the substitution of ἔπαθεν is at hand. in the presence of the similar phrase in 2:21. On the other hand, the context requires ἔπαθεν. The theme of the whole passage is suffering, not death; at this point, the possibility of Christians being put to death for their faith is not envisaged. If ἀπέθανεν be read, the connection between verse 18 and the preceding words is abruptly severed; 'Christ too died' — but there has been no word of anyone else dying! But if we read ἔπαθεν — 'Christ too suffered' — then the connection of thought is maintained and the passage allowed to keep its natural unity. These considerations appear to have sufficient force to justify the choice of this reading, even though the mass of textual authority is against it.

ἅπαξ⟩ 'once' (for all) — the Passion of Christ was final and sufficient. He probably has in mind the words of Romans 6:10 — ὃ γὰρ ἀπέθανεν, τῇ ἁμαρτίᾳ ἀπέθανεν ἐφάπαξ· ὃ δὲ ζῇ, ζῇ τῷ θεῷ — 'in that He died, He died unto sin once, but in that He lives, He lives unto God'. The sufferings have an end; the triumph is eternal.

περὶ ἁμαρτιῶν⟩ 'for sins'. Familiar as the phrase sounds, it is used surprisingly seldom by the New Testament writers in reference to the death (or the sufferings) of Christ. The Epistle to the Hebrews speaks nine times of sacrifices and offerings for sins (περὶ, ὑπὲρ τῶν ἁμ.), twice in an O.T. citation (10:6, 8), and only once of Christ's sacrifice of Himself (10:12 — μίαν ὑπὲρ ἁμαρτιῶν προσενέγκας θυσίαν εἰς τὸ διηνεκές — 'Having offered one sacrifice for sins forever'). In the whole body of the Pauline Epistles, there are only two occurrences of the phrase (1 Cor. 15:3 — ὑπέρ — and Gal. 1:4; in the latter, the witnesses are divided between ὑπέρ and περί, but the evidence of P⁴⁶ now inclines the balance in favour of περί). In First John, the phrase ἱλασμὸς περὶ τῶν ἁμαρτιῶν ἡμῶν occurs twice — 'He is the propitiation for our sins, not for ours only, but for the whole world' (2:2); and 'He loved us and sent His Son as a propitiation for our sins' (4:10). (On the meaning of ἱλασμός here, see C. H. Dodd, *The Bible and the Greeks*, London, 1935, pp. 94-5.) In these Johannine passages, it must be observed, the function of Christ as ἱλασμὸς περὶ ἁμαρτιῶν is not connected in thought with His death; He is Himself the 'propitiation' as He is Himself the 'Advocate with the Father' (παράκλητον ἔχομεν πρὸς τὸν Πατέρα, Ἰησοῦν Χριστὸν τὸν δίκαιον· καὶ αὐτὸς ἱλασμός ἐστιν περὶ τῶν ἁμαρτιῶν ἡμῶν).

There are, then, only three passages in the New Testament which afford true parallels to the phrase now before us. 'Christ died for our sins according to the Scriptures' (1 Cor. 15:3); 'He gave Himself for our sins that He might deliver us from this present evil world' (Gal. 1:4); 'He offered one sacrifice for sins forever' (Heb. 10:12). To these we might add the similar phrase (with a different preposition) of Romans 4:25 — 'He was delivered for our offences' — παρεδόθη διὰ τὰ παραπτώματα ἡμῶν. The frequently recurring phrases ὑπὲρ ἡμῶν (ὑμῶν) ἀπέθανεν (ἑαυτὸν παρέδωκεν, etc.), even ὑπὲρ ἀσεβῶν ἀπέθανεν (Rom. 5:6), dwell rather upon the thought of His death as an act of sacrificial love for us as persons, not specifically as an act which deals, in whatever sense, with our sins.

The precise sense in which the sufferings of Christ are sufferings 'for sins' is not greatly clarified by the comparison with these other passages. The author himself, in the phrases which follow, brings out two aspects of the thought which are of the greatest significance for him. Christ's sufferings were vicarious — 'the Just for the unjust'; and they were mediatorial — 'that He might bring you into the presence of God'.

ἵνα ὑμᾶς προσαγάγῃ τῷ θεῷ⟩ The clause is best taken as epexegetic, in close connection with περὶ ἁμαρτιῶν. By suffering 'for sins', Christ breaks down the barriers which sin has established between us and God; He brings forgiveness and reconciliation. προσάγω here is to be interpreted in the light of προσαγωγή — 'access' — as in Eph. 2:18 — δι' αὐτοῦ ἔχομεν τὴν προσαγωγὴν . . . πρὸς τὸν Πατέρα — 'Through Him we have access . . . to the Father' (Cf. Rom. 5:2). The general thought is, then, 'that He might open the way for you, give you access, to God'. But the words depict this function of Christ in a more vivid imagery, which has its counterpart also in the mystery-cults, where the saviour-god who has himself passed through the gates of death and risen to new life takes the initiate by the hand and leads him into the presence of the supreme God. (Egypt and Babylonia offer numerous examples of such scenes in art; see, e.g., H. Gressmann, *Altorientalische Texte und Bilder zum Alten Testament*, Bd. II, Abb. 92, 95.) Similarly, Christ is here conceived as the ψυχαγωγός, the Mediator-Redeemer who leads us into the presence of the Father. (See also Gunkel's excellent note on the passage, and the remarks of Perdelwitz, MR., p. 86.)

θανατωθεὶς μὲν σαρκὶ, ζωοποιηθεὶς δὲ πνεύματι⟩ 'put to death in the flesh, but made alive in the spirit'. This peculiar expression may be of the author's own framing, but it has rather the appearance of a liturgical stock phrase. ζωοποιηθείς — of the Resurrection (Rom. 4:17; 8:11; 1 Cor. 15:22; John 5:21). σαρκὶ, πνεύματι — of the spheres of existence in which He undergoes these experiences. There is, of course, no suggestion of the impossible thought that the spirit of Christ perished along with His body. His death took place in the sphere of 'the flesh', the earthly, temporal existence; His Resurrection took place in the sphere of 'the spirit', the eternal, the indestructible, the heavenly. This does not imply any rejection of the thought of a bodily resurrection, but rather that the body in which He is 'made alive' is itself 'spiritual'.

¹⁹ ἐν ᾧ καὶ τοῖς ἐν φυλακῇ πνεύμασιν πορευθεὶς ἐκήρυξεν, ²⁰ ἀπειθήσασίν ποτε, ὅτε ἀπεξεδέχετο ἡ τοῦ θεοῦ μακροθυμία ἐν ἡμέραις Νῶε κατα- σκευαζομένης κιβωτοῦ, εἰς ἣν ὀλίγοι, τοῦτ᾽ ἔστιν ὀκτὼ ψυχαί, διεσώ- θησαν δι᾽ ὕδατος. ²¹ ᾧ καὶ ὑμᾶς ἀντίτυπον νῦν σώζει βάπτισμα, οὐ σαρκὸς ἀπόθεσις ῥύπου, ἀλλὰ συνειδήσεως ἀγαθῆς ἐπερώτημα εἰς θεόν, δι᾽ ἀναστάσεως Ἰησοῦ Χριστοῦ, ²² ὅς ἐστιν ἐν δεξιᾷ ⟨τοῦ⟩ θεοῦ, πορευθεὶς εἰς οὐρανόν, ὑποταγέντων αὐτῷ ἀγγέλων καὶ ἐξουσιῶν καὶ δυνάμεων.

In the spirit He went and preached also to the spirits in prison, who fell into disobedience of old, when the forbearance of God was waiting out the time, in the days of Noah, while the ark was being constructed, wherein a few persons, eight souls in all, were saved through water. In the counterpart to this, baptism now saves you also — not a washing away of the filth of the flesh, but a petition to God for a good conscience — through the resurrection of Jesus Christ, who is at the right hand of God, ascended into heaven, angels and principalities and powers being made subject to Him.

²⁰ απεξεδεχετο⟩ απαξ εδεχετο 69 : απαξ εξεδεχετο ϛ η⟩ την 𝕹* μακροθυμια⟩– ιαν 𝕹* ολιγοι⟩ ολιγαι C ϛ syrr   ²¹ ω⟩ txt ϛ minusc permult. : om 𝕹* : ο 𝕹ᶜABCKLP 33. 69. υμας⟩ ημας C ϛ   ²² του⟩ B𝕹Ψ 33 om : incl. cett. θεου⟩+deglutiens mortem ut vitae eternae heredes efficeremur vg

The passage is in some degree a digression, moving away from the subject immediately in hand, the exposition of the meaning of undeserved suffering. It may at least be said that the thought is not closely sustained and connected. By a violent *tour de force* the writer seeks to relate the Christian doctrine of suffering to the saving experience of baptism, seeking to exploit the thought (of Romans 6) of baptism as effecting sacramentally our identification with Christ in His death (the consummation of His sufferings), and in His resurrection, whereby we die to the old life of sin and weakness, and rise with Him to the new life of holiness and power. The mighty thoughts of St. Paul are a little too much for him here; he struggles with them, not altogether successfully, yet seeking to make them truly his own and to bring their power to bear upon the minds and lives of his hearers.

v. 19. ἐν ᾧ⟩ the antecedent is πνεύματι, taken by itself, without the participle; it is 'in the spirit', but not as 'made alive in the spirit' (risen from the dead), that He preaches to the 'spirits in prison'. A number of interpreters, ancient and modern (e.g., Augustine, Spitta), take this as meaning an activity of the pre-existent Christ; but it is more natural to take it as referring to His activity in the underworld in the interval between His death and His resurrection. Once He has suffered and died 'for sins', He carries His Gospel of salvation even to that generation of desperate sinners who died unrepentant and were swept away by the Flood.

It has been conjectured that the name of Enoch originally stood in the text at this point (Schultz, R. Harris; followed by Goodspeed, Moffatt, et al.; εν ω και Ενωχ) εν ω και). By postulating a scribal error, easy enough to account for in a mechanical way, it is possible to absolve the author of First Peter of responsibility for the fantastic dream of a descent of Christ into Hades. On the other hand, it is hard to account for the sudden introduction of Enoch into an exposition of the work of Christ. 'Christ was made alive in the spirit; Enoch went in spirit to preach to the spirits in prison'. This is an unimaginable sequence; he is not discussing activities of various personalities 'in the spirit', but the work of Christ, in the spirit as in the flesh. It is impossible to see what relevance Enoch's visit to Hades could have for him in this connection. The conjecture is therefore to be discarded.

In the iconography of the Orthodox Church, the Descent of Christ into the underworld, the abode of the dead, provides the theme under which the Resurrection is represented, and the scene bears the inscription Η ΑΝΑΣΤΑΣΙΣ ('the Resurrection'). It is not a scene of preaching, but of triumphant action. Christ is depicted as the Victor and Deliverer who breaks the gates of Hades, brandishing his cross in his left hand as the weapon of his triumph, while with his outstretched right hand he seizes the hand of Adam to bring him up from the tomb. Behind Adam is seen the figure of Eve, and sometimes that of Abel; and on the opposite side stand David and Solomon, robed and crowned, and with them John the Baptist, the Forerunner (ὁ Πρόδρομος) of Christ, whose coming he has announced in Hades as on earth. Below, beneath the shattered gates of his domain, lies Hades in chains. The clause in the creeds, 'He descended into hell', is understood not as the last extreme of Christ's humiliation, but as the first-fruits of the victory which will culminate in the Ascension into heaven, the Session at the right hand of God, and the subjection of the mighty cosmic spirits ('angels and principalities and powers'—v. 22; cf. Eph. 4:8-10).

The various interpretations which have been proposed for this passage are set forth with great fullness in a long essay appended to the commentary of E. G. Selwyn, 'On I Peter II.18-IV.6' (pp. 314-362). See also the more recent discussions of C. Spicq and K. H. Schelkle in their commentaries (ad loc.).

τοῖς ἐν φυλακῇ πνεύμασιν . . . ἀπειθήσασίν ποτε, . . . ἐν ἡμέραις Νῶε) (He went and preached) 'to the spirits in prison, that fell into disobedience (or, refused to believe) of old, . . . in the days of Noah'. In the speculations of later Judaism, the fate of the generation which perished in the flood attracted much attention, and the strange tale of Genesis 6 and 7 received many accretions, and was made the foundation of much more elaborate accounts and speculative interpretations. These are known to us chiefly through the Book of Enoch, a compilation of works by a number of authors, composed at intervals between 170 B.C. and A.D. 100. It fell into disfavour with the fourth-century church, and was lost from view until it was again discovered in an Ethiopic manuscript, late in the eighteenth century; portions of the Greek version have since come to light in papyri, and some fragments in Hebrew and Aramaic have been found. It was, however, known and honoured in the early church; R. H. Charles lists fifty-eight passages in the New Testament which reflect its influence, and calls these 'a few examples' (*Apocrypha and Pseudepigrapha of the Old Testament*, Vol. II [Oxford, 1913], pp. 180-1). It is undoubtedly the source of the reference to the angels that fell from their first estate and were cast into Tartarus, to be kept in everlasting chains to await the Last Judgment (Jude 6; 2 Peter 2:4; cf. Enoch cc. 6, 10-15). It is not so clear that the words of First Peter have the same origin and significance; they betray nothing more than a general acquaintance with similar speculations, which were doubtless common property. 'The spirits in prison' may indeed mean 'the fallen angels' of whom Enoch tells, the 'sons of God' who were the progenitors of the race of giants (Gen. 6:4), but this is far from self-evident. πνεῦμα, indeed, is commonly used of beings of a higher order than man, of spiritual essences, angels and demons; where it is used of the higher element in man, it implies, as a rule, that this is a divine element (τὸ θεῖον πνεῦμα). But the notion is quite fluid; standing over against the physical part of man (σάρξ, σῶμα, σκῆνος), it represents the intangible, indivisible, indestructible (though not necessarily immaterial) part, and it is capable of being conceived in various ways in accordance with the varying conceptions of the essential nature of man. In our passage, the writer seems to use the word quite loosely, without precision, of the state of those who have perished in the body; in popular language, when life fled from the body, the 'spirit' descended to Hades, or mounted to an aerial paradise. When he describes 'the spirits in prison' as 'those that disobeyed in the days of Noah', he is evidently thinking of the whole generation of mankind that perished in the Flood. If he mentions these only, out of all that died before Christ, it is because they were regarded as the most abandoned of all sinners. For them, Judaism entertained no hope of repentance and restoration,[1] but the Christian teacher holds that none, not even these, are beyond the reach of the saving power of Christ. ἐκήρυξεν—certainly of the preaching of the Gospel of salvation. Christ's Descent into Hades, like His manifestation upon earth, was a phase of His work as the universal Saviour. It is an extension of the thought that is put forward also in Ephesians 4:8-10; descending into the lower parts of the earth, He 'led captivity captive'; the 'spirits in prison' were released. Cf. also John 5:25—'The dead shall hear the voice of the Son of Man, and they that hear shall live'.

On the contemporary usage of πνεῦμα, see Reitzenstein, HMR³, c. xv, 'Die Begriffe Gnosis und Pneuma', from p. 308.

---

[1] Cf. *Mishnah*, 'Sanhedrin', 10.3—'The generation of the flood have no share in the world to come, nor shall they stand in the judgment.'

It is very difficult not to equate the πνεύμασιν . . . ἐκήρυξεν of this passage with the νεκροῖς εὐηγγελίσθη — 'The Gospel was preached to the dead' — of 4:6. In the apocryphal *Gospel of Peter*, there is a story of Christ coming forth from the sepulchre, attended by two angels and followed by a Cross; a voice from heaven asked 'Hast thou preached to them that sleep?' (i.e., of course, to the dead), and the answer from the Cross is 'Yes'. The whole idea is an attempt to give significance to the otherwise meaningless gap between the death on the Cross and the Resurrection; it does not belong to the earliest tradition.

v. 20. ἀπειθήσασιν⟩ 'disobeyed' — the thought is probably that they refused to believe Noah, the 'preacher of righteousness' (2 Pet. 2:5). Unbelief is frequently regarded, in the New Testament writings, as a form of disobedience to God.

ἀπεξεδέχετο⟩ 'waited out the time' — the verb is seldom used absolutely; there is no other instance in N.T. In all the other occurrences, it is used of the attitude of patient expectation in which Christians await the second coming of Christ, and the 'salvation' for which they hope. (Rom. 8:19, 23, 25; Heb. 9:28; etc.) Here the thought is that God waited patiently, delaying the stroke of His judgment on Man's disobedience to afford them time for repentance.

ἡ τοῦ θεοῦ μακροθυμία⟩ 'the forbearance of God', 'God's longsuffering patience' with rebellious men; the mercy which seeks to forgive, and therefore is slow to punish. Cf. Romans 2:4 — 'Despisest thou the riches of His goodness and forbearance and longsuffering (. . . τῆς μακροθυμίας καταφρονεῖς), not knowing that the goodness of God leadeth thee to repentance?'; and 2 Peter 3:9 — 'The Lord is not slack . . . but is longsuffering toward you (μακροθυμεῖ εἰς ὑμᾶς), not desiring that any should perish, but that all should come to repentance'.

κατασκευαζομένης κιβωτοῦ⟩ 'while the ark was being constructed'. The building of the ark was itself a testimony to the imminence of the divine judgment which was to overwhelm the world, and as long as it was in process of construction, there was still time to repent and be saved.

ὀκτὼ ψυχαί⟩ 'eight souls'—the Genesis story gives them as Noah and his wife, and his three sons and their wives. ψυχή here is used in the sense merely of 'living person', not of the essential, inward being, the true life, as elsewhere in the Epistle (1:9, 22; 2:12, etc.). Yet it is probable that he would not have used the word except in collocation with the verb διεσώθησαν — 'were saved'; and that there is an underlying implication that the physical salvation from the Flood was at the same time a moral and spiritual salvation, a salvation from 'the Wrath of God' (cf. Rom. 5:9; 1 Thess. 1:10), resting upon faith in Him.

διεσώθησαν δι' ὕδατος⟩ 'were saved through water'. The ambiguous phrase δι' ὕδατος is chosen to enable him to frame an analogy between the water of the Flood and the water of baptism. We must certainly feel that his language is forced in the extreme, when he asks us to think of the water which overwhelmed the earth with destruction as being in any sense the medium of salvation for the inhabitants of the ark. But the violence of this turn of thought would not be felt by the Christians of the time as it is by us; they were accustomed to an arbitrary treatment of the Old Testament Scriptures. St. Paul does almost equal violence in his treatment of the passage through the Red Sea as a prototype of baptism (1 Cor. 10:1-2 — 'all our fathers . . . passed through the sea; and were all baptized unto Moses . . . in the sea'). For them it was sufficient that water in some form was the important thing in the story, and that the people of God were saved.

Calvin suggests that the real analogy lies between the shutting of Noah in the ark as in a sepulchre, and the 'burial' of the Christian in baptism. 'As Noah won life through death, when he was shut in the ark as it were in a sepulchre, and while the whole world perished, he with his tiny family was saved; so to-day the death which is represented in a figure in baptism, is for us the entrance into life, nor may we hope for salvation unless we be segregated from the world.'

v. 21. ᾧ καὶ ὑμᾶς ἀντίτυπον νῦν σώζει βάπτισμα) 'the antitype whereto now saves you, (even) baptism'. ᾧ is the reading proposed by Erasmus and favoured by Hort, who regarded ὅ as a 'primitive error', though he allowed it to stand in his text. The nominative is the reading of all the uncials (except ℵ*) and many of the good cursives; the dative is found in a large number, probably a majority, of the inferior cursives. In spite of the weakness of attestation, the dative appears to be the true reading; it is impossible to construe ὅ in any reasonable sense. (See also the remarks of Hort, among his *Notes on Select Readings*, p. 102.)

The antecedent of ᾧ is not ὕδατος, but the whole phrase διεσώθησαν δι' ὕδατος. Not the water as such, but the salvation of Noah and his family 'through water' is the type, the prophetic image of the salvation which is brought to Christians 'through water', in baptism. ἀντίτυπον is here used of the substantial reality which is foreshadowed in the type; in Hebrew 9:24 it is used inversely, of the symbol which points to a higher reality. The attitude to O.T. story on which the entire analogy rests is defined in 1 Corinthians 10:6ff.

νῦν) 'now' — may be taken as the correlative of πότε (v. 20) — 'of old'; or more vividly, in reference to the baptism which has just been administered. The latter sense is more in keeping with the object ὑμᾶς, which is far better attested than ἡμᾶς.

σώζει) to be taken in close connexion with δι' ἀναστάσεως Ἰησοῦ Χριστοῦ; cf. 1:3 — ἀναγεννήσας . . . δι' ἀναστάσεως Ἰησοῦ Χριστοῦ ἐκ νεκρῶν. For this writer, as for St. Paul (Rom. 6:4ff; Col. 2:11-12), the saving efficacy of the sacrament lies in that it applies to the baptized the benefits of Christ's death and resurrection; the outward act signifies a spiritual transformation — the end of the old life and the inauguration of the new.

οὐ σαρκὸς ἀπόθεσις ῥύπου⟩ 'not a putting-away of the filth of the flesh' — with the implication, of course, that the baptism was done by immersion; such a phrase would be meaningless in relation to a baptism by sprinkling. (Cf. Heb. 10:22 — λελουσμένοι τὸ σῶμα ὕδατι καθαρῷ — 'having the body washed with clean water'). σάρξ is used here in the literal physical sense. The phrase contrasts the spiritually effective Christian baptism with Jewish ritual ablutions, and with the washings which preceded initiation into the pagan mysteries, which were merely a bodily cleansing. In the Christian rite also, the 'filth of the flesh' was washed away, but this was not the important thing. The writer of Hebrews, in the verse cited above, set first the thought of the cleansing of hearts from an evil conscience — ῥεραντισμένοι τὰς καρδίας ἀπὸ συνειδήσεως πονηρᾶς — and the same thought is in the mind of our writer, but he does not make it explicit.

συνειδήσεως ἀγαθῆς ἐπερώτημα εἰς θεόν⟩ 'a petition to God for a good conscience'. As Windisch suggests (Comm. ad loc.; see also the same writer's Taufe und Sünde, Tübingen, 1908, pp. 231-2), this appears to be a reference to a part of the ritual followed in the administration of the sacrament, a prayer addressed to God by the convert, asking forgiveness and inward cleansing and the power to live in accordance with His will. The 'good conscience' is a conscience liberated from the burden of guilt and dedicated to the fulfilment of His good pleasure. In this he bids them see the true significance of the sacrament (cf. τὰς ψυχὰς ἡγνικότες, 1:22, note).

It is by no means certain that this is the true interpretation. ἐπερώτημα and the corresponding verb ἐπερωτάω are more commonly used in the sense of asking a question than of making a request. However, the verb is found in the latter sense in Matthew 16:1, and in Psalm 136 (137):3 (‭א‬^{c.a} A, et al.), and the simple verb ἐρωτάω is fairly common in this sense. The only other suggested rendering that is at all attractive is that of 'pledge'; this rests upon the occurrence of the word in one or two papyri, in contracts, in the sense of the Latin stipulatio (see M. & M. sub voc., and the new Liddell and Scott, 9th edition). The words would then mean 'a pledge made to God out of a good conscience' (taking συνειδήσεως as subjective),[1] or 'a pledge to maintain a good conscience' (taking the genitive as objective). The latter sense would be illustrated from Pliny's Letter to Trajan concerning the prosecution of Christians, where he reports that, according to the testimony of former adherents, they 'bound themselves by an oath not for any criminal purpose, but that they would commit no theft, brigandage, or adultery, that they would not violate their word, that they would not refuse to return a deposit when called upon to do so'.

σαρκός and συνειδήσεως are made emphatic by their position at the

---

[1] I am now inclined to favour this interpretation; see Selwyn's note, ad loc. (p. 117, sup.), and J. Crehan, op. cit. pp. 10-11.

head of the respective phrases; baptism has to do, not with the outward man, but with the inward, the whole moral personality.

v. 22. With the thought of Christ's Resurrection is now linked the thought of the high glory to which He has been exalted (cf. 1:21). The significance of the Resurrection, as made effectual in the new life of His followers, through baptism, lies in His elevation to the place of supreme authority over the whole of God's universe.

ἐν δεξιᾷ θεοῦ) 'at God's right hand' — i.e., designated as God's vicegerent, as the King unseen, to whom is committed all authority and all power. It scarcely needs to be said that the words are not used in any local sense (*dextra Dei est ubique*). The imagery is derived from the statuary of Oriental temples, especially Egyptian, which frequently represented the King as seated at the right of the god, signifying both his own divinity and his function as bearer of the might and majesty of the divine in relation to the world. It enters into the language of primitive Christianity by way of Psalm 110:1 — 'Sit thou on My right hand, until I make thy foes thy footstool'. (See the remarks of C. H. Dodd, *The Apostolic Preaching*, pp. 23-4.)

The ideas of the Resurrection, the Ascension, and the Session of Christ at God's right hand are always closely linked together in the New Testament; they are, in fact, aspects of a single thought, and there are traces of a stage in Christian thinking in which they were not differentiated. (See the remarks of Amos Wilder in his article 'Variant Traditions of the Resurrection in Acts', *Journal of Biblical Literature*, Vol. LXII, Part IV [December, 1943], p. 307.) The Session is sometimes related particularly to the gift of the Holy Spirit, and the spiritual gifts communicated to the Church (Acts 2:33-35; Eph. 4:7-8); elsewhere, to His office as Intercessor for us (Rom. 8:34; Heb. 9:24), or more generally, to His office as High Priest (Heb. 8:1ff.); but more frequently, the emphasis is upon His power, His dignity, and His victory over the powers of evil (Matt. 26:64 and parallels; Acts 7:55; Phil. 2:9-11; Eph. 1:20-24; Heb. 12:2).

ἀγγέλων καὶ ἐξουσιῶν καὶ δυνάμεων) 'angels and principalities and powers' — under these three heads he embraces all ranks of spiritual beings. These classifications, sometimes much more elaborate, extending to seven classes, are a commonplace of later Judaism; they are mentioned several times in the New Testament with some variations (1 Cor. 15:24; Eph. 1:21; Col. 1:16; 2:15; et al.). The words are perhaps to be taken as meaning both good spirits and evil spirits, the powers of heaven and the powers of hell; but it is more likely that the thought is of the powers of evil that are overthrown by Christ in His victory over death. Cf. 1 Corinthians 15:24 — ὅταν καταργήσῃ πᾶσαν ἀρχὴν καὶ πᾶσαν ἐξουσίαν καὶ δύναμιν, where Christ is to 'put down every dominion and every principality and power', with the clear implication that these are all enemies to be destroyed; and still more clearly,

Colossians 2:15 — ἀπεκδυσάμενος τὰς ἀρχὰς καὶ τὰς ἐξουσίας, ἐδειγ-
μάτισεν ἐν παρρησίᾳ, θριαμβεύσας αὐτοὺς ἐν αὐτῷ — '(God) having
disarmed the dominions and principalities, made an open show of them,
triumphing over them by Him'. The thought will then be that all the
spiritual powers which were arrayed against God have now been overthrown by Christ and made subject to Him, and can therefore have no
more power over His followers.

After *in dextera Dei*, the Vulgate adds *deglutiens mortem ut vitae
aeternae heredes efficeremur* (swallowing up death, that we might be
made heirs of life eternal) — 'apparently from a Greek original which
had the aorist participle καταπιών' (Hort, among his 'Noteworthy Rejected Readings'). The clause was also in the (pre-Vulgate) text used
by St. Augustine. There is some indication of its presence in the
Armenian version also, following οὐρανόν (Tischendorff[8]). Harnack
reconstructs the underlying Greek as καταπιὼν (τὸν) θάνατον, ἵνα ζωῆς
αἰωνίου κληρονόμοι γενηθῶμεν, and argues strongly that it should be
regarded as authentic (*Zur Revision*, pp. 83-6). Certainly, it is no
ordinary gloss. The expression καταπιὼν θάνατον is most unusual;
it derives from the non-Septuagintal version of Isaiah 25:8 which was
known to St. Paul (1 Cor. 15:54 — κατεπόθη ὁ θάνατος εἰς νῖκος —
'Death is swallowed up in victory'; cf. 2 Cor. 5:4). For the ἵνα clause,
cf. Titus 3:7 (where the context again refers to salvation through baptism
vv. 5-6) — ἵνα . . . κληρονόμοι γενηθῶμεν κατ' ἐλπίδα ζωῆς αἰωνίου.

The conjecture that the passages bearing upon the Descent (3:19-21
and 4:6) are glosses, and do not belong to the original text of the
Epistle, hardly deserves serious consideration. Not only is there no
manuscript authority for rejecting them, but there is nothing in the
style or diction to betray the hand of a glossator.

On the whole passage, see the excellent monograph of Bo Reicke, *The
Disobedient Spirits and Christian Baptism: A Study of I Peter iii, 19
and its Context* (Copenhagen: Munksgaard, 1946).

In a recent dissertation presented at the Pontifical Biblical Institute
(*Christ's Proclamation to the Spirits*, Rome, 1965), W. J. Dalton has
advanced a radically different interpretation, which for all its novelty
deserves serious consideration. In his view, there is here no reference to
a Descent; the words πορευθεὶς ἐκήρυξεν speak of the Ascension of
Christ and the submission to him of the cosmic spirits. As in v. 22,
πορευθείς means πορευθεὶς εἰς οὐρανόν (he claims that πορεύομαι is
often used of Christ's 'going to the Father' (John) and never of his
'descending', for which the word is καταβαίνω). ἐκήρυξεν does not
mean 'preached the gospel of salvation', but simply 'made proclamation'
—to the 'spirits in prison'—of their overthrow. The thought is not of
an activity of Christ in the *triduum mortis*, while his body lies in the
tomb, but of the Risen Christ in his glorified body.

4 ¹ Χριστοῦ οὖν παθόντος σαρκὶ καὶ ὑμεῖς τὴν αὐτὴν ἔννοιαν
ὁπλίσασθε, ὅτι ὁ παθὼν σαρκὶ πέπαυται ἁμαρτίας, ² εἰς τὸ μηκέτι
ἀνθρώπων ἐπιθυμίαις ἀλλὰ θελήματι θεοῦ τὸν ἐπίλοιπον ἐν σαρκὶ βιῶσαι
χρόνον. ³ ἀρκετὸς γὰρ ὁ παρεληλυθὼς χρόνος τὸ βούλημα τῶν ἐθνῶν
κατειργάσθαι, πεπορευμένους ἐν ἀσελγείαις, ἐπιθυμίαις, οἰνοφλυγίαις,
κώμοις, πότοις, καὶ ἀθεμίτοις εἰδωλολατρίαις. ⁴ ἐν ᾧ ξενίζονται μὴ
συντρεχόντων ὑμῶν εἰς τὴν αὐτὴν τῆς ἀσωτίας ἀνάχυσιν, βλασφη-
μοῦντες· ⁵ οἳ ἀποδώσουσιν λόγον τῷ ἑτοίμως ἔχοντι κρῖναι ζῶντας
καὶ νεκρούς. ⁶ εἰς τοῦτο γὰρ καὶ νεκροῖς εὐηγγελίσθη, ἵνα κριθῶσι μὲν
κατὰ ἀνθρώπους σαρκί, ζῶσι δὲ κατὰ θεὸν πνεύματι.

*Since Christ, then, suffered in the flesh, do you also arm yourselves
with the same mind — for he that has suffered in the flesh has ceased
from sin — that you may no longer live for the desires of men but for
the will of God, for the remainder of your time in the flesh. For the
bygone time is sufficient to have spent in doing the pleasure of the
Gentiles, to have walked in ways of sensuality, lust, drunkenness,
revelry, drinking-bouts, and the unholy practices of idolatry. Herein
they find it strange that you do not plunge with them into the same
torrent of vice — blasphemers that they are — they shall give account
to Him who stands ready to judge the living and the dead. For it
was to this end that the gospel was preached to the dead also, that
though they were judged according to men in the flesh, they may live
according to God in the spirit.*

¹ παθοντος BC 1739 vg sah)+υπερ υμων ℵ* 69. syrᴾ : +υπερ ημων AKLP
33. ς syrʰˡ boh   σαρκι) pr εν ·Κ 69. ς   αμαρτιας) αμαρτιαις B vg syrᴾ
³ γαρ)+υμιν ℵ. boh : +ημιν CKLP 33. 69. ς   χρονος)+του βιου ς : pr του
βιου 69.   βουλημα) θελημα KLP 69. ς   κατειργασθαι) κατεργασασθαι ς
πεπορευμενους) πορευομενους ℵ 2412. ⁴ βλασφημουντες) και βλασφημουσιν ℵ*
C* syrᴾ (?) ⁵ οι αποδωσουσιν λογον) om ℵ* εχοντι κριναι) κρινοντι B 614.
2412.

v. 1.   Χριστοῦ οὖν παθόντος σαρκί⟩ The thought returns to verse 18
of the preceding chapter, taking up the double thought of περὶ ἁμαρτιῶν
ἔπαθεν and θανατωθεὶς σαρκί. 'Death in the flesh' is the climax and
consummation of the 'suffering for sins'; accordingly, παθόντος here
includes the thought of the death of Christ, or rather, presents that
thought in relation to the general context (suffering for righteousness'
sake).

τὴν αὐτὴν ἔννοιαν ὁπλίσασθε⟩ 'arm yourselves with the same mind' —
i.e., reckon yourselves as having 'suffered in the flesh', as having died
to this present life, as He did. Cf. Romans 6:10-11 — ὃ γὰρ ἀπέθανεν, τῇ
ἁμαρτίᾳ ἀπέθανεν ἐφάπαξ ... οὕτως καὶ ὑμεῖς λογίζεσθε ἑαυτοὺς νεκροὺς
μὲν τῇ ἁμαρτίᾳ, etc. — 'In that He died, He died unto sin once for all . . .;
even so do you also reckon yourselves dead to sin'; also Philippians 3:10

— τοῦ γνῶναι αὐτὸν . . . καὶ κοινωνίαν παθημάτων αὐτοῦ, συμμορ-
φιʒόμενος τῷ θανάτῳ αὐτοῦ — 'that I may know Him . . . and fellowship in His sufferings, being shaped with Him in the pattern of His
death'. This 'death' to the old life is an ἔννοια for the Christian — a
mental concept of himself as 'crucified with Christ' — as having made an
end, in imagination and thought, of the life of the flesh, and having
begun to value the life of the spirit, the new life which is lived in and
with Christ, as the only true life (cf. Gal. 2:20). When the Christian
has learned so to regard himself, he is 'armed' for the struggle, inwardly
fortified against every assault of his spiritual enemies. Accepting for
himself the sentence of death as already executed (cf. 1 Cor. 1:9 and
context), he will not be overcome by the lesser tribulations which he
may have to undergo.

ὅτι ὁ παθὼν σαρκὶ πέπαυται ἁμαρτίας⟩ 'for he that has suffered in
the flesh has ceased from sin' — certainly a proverbial expression, found
in a different wording in Romans 6:7 — ὁ γὰρ ἀποθανὼν δεδικαίωται ἀπὸ
τῆς ἁμαρτίας — 'for he that has died is freed from the claims of sin'.
The proverb, in ordinary usage, may have meant little more than our
'Death pays all debts'; or it may have been a Greek equivalent for the
Latin 'De mortuis nil nisi bonum'. In the form in which it is given
here, it may in some circles have been given an application to martyrdom, in the sense of the doctrine that martyrdom atones for sin and
wins the reward of forgiveness. But in the context, this writer is relating
it to the thought which he is unfolding — that to 'suffer in the flesh' as
Christ 'suffered in the flesh' means for us the ending of the life of sin
and the beginning of the new life of goodness. There is here a double
play upon words; both the participle παθών and the noun σάρξ are
used in two senses — παθών of actual physical suffering, the theme from
which the discussion starts (3:14,17), and also of the moral and spiritual
experience of crucifixion with Christ, the ἔννοια which is to determine
all life for the Christian; σάρξ of the physical body (in which the Lord
suffered), and also of the sinful nature, the Ego, 'our old man' (Rom.
6:6), which must be given over to death with Christ, that the life of the
spirit which we derive from Him may be given full freedom within us.
At this point, the connexion with the theme of 'suffering for righteousness' sake' has become little more than verbal; the writer has become
wholly absorbed in the significance of the moral and spiritual transformation which is figured in baptism.

v. 2. εἰς τὸ . . . βιῶσαι χρόνον⟩ a final clause, dependent upon
ὁπλίσασθε. The unusual phrase βιῶσαι χρόνον is perhaps intended to
suggest the secondary and transitory character of the life still to be lived
on earth; the verb ʒάω being reserved for the higher life, which is not
lived merely for a time (τὸν ἐπίλοιπον χρόνον), nor 'in the flesh'. This
outward life, however, though it be secondary, is none the less to be
governed by the same principles as the inward life; it is not to be at

the mercy of vagrant desires, of mere human passion and impulse, but is to be subject to the will of God.

v. 3. ἀρκετός⟩ 'sufficient'—a *meiosis*; the sense is, of course, 'more than sufficient', 'far too much'. It is not possible to subtract from the time that has already been spent in evil courses, but at least there need be no further waste of life in the pursuit of vanity and vice. ὁ παρεληλυθὼς χρόνος is set over against τὸν ἐπίλοιπον χρόνον; the conversion to Christ divides their past life which has been misdirected and misspent from their remaining days upon earth which are to be dedicated to the only true good. The three perfects — παρεληλυθὼς, κατειργάσθαι, πεπορευμένους — one after another emphasize the thought that this past of theirs is a closed chapter; that part of the story is over and done with. The language here indicates once again that those who are addressed stand precisely at the turning-point of life which is marked by baptism; and also that they were converts from paganism, not from Judaism.

τὸ βούλημα τῶν ἐθνῶν⟩ 'the will of the Gentiles'—as opposed to θέλημα θεοῦ — 'the will of God'. In the old life, their conduct was subject to the mass will, swayed by the ill-directed tyranny of common custom and public opinion, and that, of a society alienated from God.

On the catalogue of vices cf. Romans 13:13-14; Galatians 5:20-21. The plurals are concrete; 'acts of sensuality', etc. ἀθεμίτοις εἰδωλολατρίαις, 'abominable practices of idolatry'—suggests not the mere worshipping of idols, though that in itself is regarded as a moral offence — but rather the dark and shameful practices which too often had a place in the cult. ἀθέμιτος means not so much 'illegal' as 'unholy'—violating the divine ordering of life (contrary not to νόμος, but to the more fundamental θέμις).

v. 4. ἐν ᾧ⟩ The relative is of course in the neuter, and as in 1:6, it attaches rather loosely to the whole thought of the preceding sentence, especially to the sense brought out so strongly in the perfects, that Christians have ceased to comply with the evil customs of paganism — 'In respect of your abandonment of these vicious practices, they find it strange', etc. ξενίζομαι — 'find strange', includes the thought of 'take offence', as ignorant people often feel an unreasonable resentment at anything that does not fit into the pattern of life familiar to them, especially at a conscientious refusal to participate in common diversions. The matter of this resentful astonishment is expressed by the genitive absolute which follows.

συντρεχόντων⟩ literally, 'running with' them; the metaphor suggests the thought of joining in a mad race. τρέχω is used several times in the New Testament of the moral effort of Christians; we are encouraged to 'run the race that is set before us' (Heb. 12:1); so to 'run, that (we) may obtain (the prize)' (1 Cor. 9:24; cf. also Gal. 2:2; 5:7; Phil. 2:16). But in this passage, the thought is of the expenditure of energy on immoral ends, in a 'pouring-out of dissolute living'. ἀσωτία — the noun is formed upon the verbal ἄσωτος from the obsolete σαῶ (σώзω) — 'save', with the negativing particle α; (cf. зῶν ἀσώτως, of the prodigal — 'in riotous living' — Lk. 15:14). The sense is therefore 'that which is ruinous to health', 'dissolute, profligate living'. ἀνάχυσις — literally, 'a pouring forth' — sometimes used in the concrete sense of a lake, an estuary, or a swamp, as of that which is formed by the pouring forth of waters. εἰς τὴν αὐτὴν ἀσωτίας ἀνάχυσιν may then have the sense 'into the same wide-spreading river of dissipation'. It seems better, however, to retain more of the active verbal sense of ἀνάχυσις, and to take ἀσωτίας as an objective genitive — 'outpouring of profligacy'; with the thought of the life of paganism as a feverish pursuit of evil, wherein men vie with one another in pouring forth profligate living.

βλασφημοῦντες⟩ In ordinary Greek usage, the verb is not used exclusively in the sense of speaking evil of sacred things, but of defaming or reviling in any context. It is seldom used absolutely. In Lxx and N.T., likewise, it is sometimes used in the sense of 'revile' or 'taunt', with an object in the accusative (as in Lk. 23:39), or absolutely (as in Lk. 22:65). This general sense may be intended in this passage also. The author has referred several times to the slander and reviling which was directed against Christian believers, and it is possible that here he wishes to say that astonishment at the new standards of conduct which govern the Christian finds expression in bitter and scornful words. But this thought would be more naturally expressed by the co-ordinate καὶ βλασφημοῦσιν (ℵ* C* 1739 et minusc. al. pc.) than by the participle, which has far stronger textual support (A B ℵᶜ C² K L P 69. ç vss.). Adopting the latter reading, it seems better to take the word in the specific sense of 'blaspheming' (as in the accusation laid against Jesus, Matt. 9:3; 16:65), and to treat the participle as a substantive, used as an interjection — 'blasphemers!' The attitude of hostile amazement, the failure to recognize the divine and heavenly quality of the new life is a kind of blasphemy against the God from whom that life proceeds. This thought leads naturally to the minatory declaration which follows.

v. 5. οἱ ἀποδώσουσιν λόγον⟩ 'who shall give account' — i.e., shall be compelled to answer for their blasphemous scorn of the good life of Christian faith. λόγον ἀποδιδόναι is the converse of λόγον αἰτεῖν — 'call to account' (3:15). The Christian may be called to account before an earthly tribunal; his enemies will be called to account before the tribunal of heaven. τῷ ἑτοίμως ἔχοντι κρῖναι — 'to Him that stands ready to judge' (living and dead). The imminence of the great Day is stressed here in relation to its aspect of wrath, as in 1:6 in relation to its aspect of salvation. He who 'stands ready to judge' is Christ; cf. Acts 10: 42 — οὗτός ἐστιν ὁ ὡρισμένος ὑπὸ τοῦ θεοῦ κριτὴς зώντων καὶ νεκρῶν — 'This is He that is ordained by God to be Judge of living and dead'; cf. Acts 17:31; 2 Tim. 4:1 (where Christ's coming in power, and the establishment of His Kingdom are related to His future judging of 'living and dead'); and 2 Clement 1:1. The New Testament writers also speak of

God Himself as the Judge (cf. 1:17; 2:23); but where the Judgment is proclaimed as imminent, it is usually conceived as one phase of 'the revelation of Jesus Christ'; God judges the world by Him. As the 'salvation' which will fulfil the hopes of Christians is 'ready to be revealed', with its attribution of 'praise and honour and glory' to the faithful (1:7, 13), so He to whom their enemies must give account 'stands ready to judge'. His revelation in glory, which brings the fullness of divine grace to His followers, brings at the same time ineluctable condemnation to those that have harassed them.

The alternative reading ἑτοίμως κρίνοντι can hardly commend itself except on an extravagant overvaluation of Codex Vaticanus. The weight of evidence is overwhelmingly against it. It is, of course, capable of interpretation, in the sense that God is always awake to the activities of evil men and is even now judging them; but this is not in keeping with the use of the future in the governing verb.

ζῶντας καὶ νέκρους) The thought that the Judgment involves 'living and dead' is not particularly pertinent to the assurance of the condemnation that awaits the blasphemers, who are not dead but living. It is introduced with the sound of a familiar stock phrase, and the mention of the dead as the objects of judgment facilitates the transition to the thought of the next verse.

v. 6.   εἰς τοῦτο γὰρ καὶ νεκροῖς εὐηγγελίσθη) 'For to this end the gospel was preached to the dead also'. The connection of thought is not entirely clear. νεκροῖς must have the same connotation as the preceding νεκρῶν; i.e., it must mean all the dead from the beginning of time, all that are to stand before the judgment-seat of God. It is quite inadmissible to take it as meaning only those who have lived and died since the coming of Christ, and have heard the Gospel preached in their lifetime. The thought must therefore be associated with Christ's Descent into Hades and his preaching to the 'spirits' (3:19). The γάρ then appears to relate the universality of the Judgment to the universal proclamation of the Gospel; the dead as well as the living will stand before the Judge, because they too have had the Gospel preached to them. Yet the writer appears to move quickly from the menace of the condemnation that awaits blasphemers to the more congenial thought of the life-giving power which attends the Gospel proclamation. The Gospel is preached to the dead 'in order that they may live according to God in the spirit' (John 5:25). κριθῶσι, though co-ordinate with ζῶσι in construction, is best taken as subordinate in thought (almost = κριθέντες), and the difficult phrase κριθῶσι μὲν κατὰ ἀνθρώπους σαρκί seems to mean simply 'though they have died, as all men must die' — death itself being regarded as God's judgment on sin (cf. Rom. 5:12ff.). ζωή — of the true life, the life eternal; it is lived κατὰ θεόν, in the sense that it is not the natural life of man, but depends upon the new relationship to God which is established through the response of faith to the Gospel.

⁷ Πάντων δὲ τὸ τέλος ἤγγικεν. σωφρονήσατε οὖν καὶ νήψατε εἰς προσευχάς. ⁸ πρὸ πάντων τὴν εἰς ἑαυτοὺς ἀγάπην ἐκτενῆ ἔχοντες, ὅτι ἀγάπη καλύπτει πλῆθος ἁμαρτιῶν· ⁹ φιλόξενοι εἰς ἀλλήλους ἄνευ γογγυσμοῦ· ¹⁰ ἕκαστος καθὼς ἔλαβεν χάρισμα, εἰς ἑαυτοὺς αὐτὸ διακονοῦντες ὡς καλοὶ οἰκονόμοι ποικίλης χάριτος θεοῦ. ¹¹ εἴ τις λαλεῖ, ὡς λόγια θεοῦ· εἴ τις διακονεῖ, ὡς ἐξ ἰσχύος ἧς χορηγεῖ ὁ θεός· ἵνα ἐν πᾶσιν δοξάζηται ὁ θεὸς διὰ Ἰησοῦ Χριστοῦ, ᾧ ἐστὶν ἡ δόξα καὶ τὸ κράτος εἰς τοὺς αἰῶνας τῶν αἰώνων. ἀμήν.

The end of all things is at hand; you must therefore cultivate sobriety and alertness of spirit, that you may give yourselves to prayers. Above all, keep your love for one another deep and strong, for love covers a multitude of sins. Be hospitable to one another without complaint. The several gifts that you have received, let each and all spend in mutual service, as good stewards of the manifold grace of God: — if one preaches, let it be as the oracles of God; if one serves, let it be as in the strength that God supplies; — that in all things God may be glorified through Jesus Christ, to whom is glory and dominion for ever and ever. Amen.

⁷ προσευχας) pr τας ς   ⁸ παντων)+δε ς   καλυπτει) καλυψει אLP 69. ς
⁹ γογγυσμου) γογγυσμων KLP 69. ς

This is quite obviously a peroration; apart from the doxology and Amen, the whole tone of the paragraph suggests the conclusion of a discourse, not an intermediate stopping-place. Moreover, it suggests a regular and tranquil communal activity of worship and mutual service, undisturbed by the πύρωσις which sheds its lurid glow over the verses immediately following.

v. 7. 'The end of all things' means, of course, the great consummation for which Christians wait and hope—the end of this present evil age, and the coming of Christ in glory to establish His Kingdom. Cf. the prayer of the *Didache* (X, 6) — 'May grace come, and this world pass away'; and the frequent appeals in the Gospel and in the Pauline Epistles, and indeed in all the literature of the early church, to the imminence of the end. The expectation is held forth in part as a warning against slackness (e.g., Apoc. 2:5; Lk. 12:35-40; and in numerous parables); and in part as a consolation and an encouragement to endure to the end, in times of difficulty (e.g., Apoc. 3:11-12, and indeed the entire book; 1 Thess. 5:4ff.)

One of the ancient Fathers (unnamed), cited in Cramer's *Catenae*, Vol. VIII, pp. 75-6, takes this phrase as the conclusion of the preceding paragraph, and interprets τὸ τέλος personally, of Christ. — ὁ αὐτὸς γὰρ τέλος· ὥστε ἂν τοῦ ζητουμένου τέλους παρ' Ἕλλησιν, ὅτι πότερόν ἐστιν ἡδονή, ἢ ἐπιστήμη, ἢ θεωρία, ἢ ἀρετή, ἢ ἀδιάφορα, ἢ ὁτιδήποτε λέγουσι φιλοσόφων παῖδες, ἡμᾶς εἰπεῖν ὅτι τὸ τέλος ἐστὶν ὁ Χριστός. Perfectly true, but not to be derived from this passage of 1 Peter.

ἤγγικεν⟩ 'has come near', i.e., 'is at hand'; as in the proclamation of Jesus — ἤγγικεν ἡ βασιλεία τοῦ θεοῦ (Mk. 1:15 and parallels).

σωφρονήσατε, νήψατε⟩ The two verbs are closely akin in sense; cf. Hesychius, νήφειν=σωφρονεῖν βίῳ (Knopf). σωφρονεῖν means 'to be sound in mind' (Mk. 5:15); then more precisely, 'to be temperate', 'to be sober-minded' (not puffed up with pride — Rom. 12:3), 'to exercise self-control' (cf. σώφρων καὶ ἐγκρατὴς ἑαυτοῦ — Plato, Gorgias, 491 d). The last of these senses is the best here. On νήφειν, see 1:13, note. Here it combines the thoughts of literal sobriety, abstinence from drunkenness (cf. 1 Thess. 5:7-8), and of clear-headed insight which sees life steadily in the light of eternity and of the impending end of Time. The two verbs together suggest a disciplined life, with all the faculties under control and the energies unimpaired by any kind of excess. εἰς προσευχάς — 'unto prayers' — this discipline of mind and body is not a matter of asceticism for the sake of asceticism; it is enjoined primarily for the sake of the prayers in which the Christian most truly realizes his communion with God and his fellowship with all believers. The mental and moral discipline which is required for the life of prayer is then defined more concretely as the cultivation of mutual love, the maintenance of hospitality, and the exercise of spiritual gifts in the service of the community. ἔχοντες, φιλόξενοι, διακονοῦντες have imperative force; there is a loose subordination to σωφρονήσατε . . . νήψατε, but in effect the relation is rather one of co-ordination.

v. 8. πρὸ πάντων, etc.⟩ The characteristically Christian emphasis on the primacy of love; cf. 1:22. The disciplined life that prepares men for prayer is rooted and grounded in love; the true askesis is the cultivation of a loving heart. Those who are united in their prayers to God must likewise be united one with another in mutual affection. ἐκτενῆ — literally, 'strenuous', 'intense' — a predicate accusative — the mutual love exists; it requires to be maintained strong and constant (Bengel).

ἀγάπη καλύπτει πλῆθος ἁμαρτιῶν⟩ 'Love covers a multitude of sins'. In Didascalia II, 3, this is said to be a saying of Jesus — Et sit misericors et benevolus et caritate plenus, quia dicit Dominus, Caritas operit multitudinem peccatorum. The corresponding Greek text, however, substitutes John 13:35 — 'By this shall all men know that ye are my disciples, if ye love one another'. It is quite possible that the words were included in some early collections of Logia of Jesus; however that may be, it was a well-known Christian proverb. The derivation from Proverbs 10:12 is not established; Lxx renders the verse quite differently — πάντας δὲ τοὺς μὴ φιλονεικοῦντας καλύπτει φιλία — and it is unlikely that another rendering of the Hebrew was current, in the words found here, else this would surely have found its way into some Lxx manuscripts. Like many proverbial expressions, it is employed in different applications. In 1 Clement 49:5 it occurs in a hymn in praise of love, modelled in part upon 1 Corinthians 13, in the sense that 'love leads us to forgive over and over those that offend against us'. This is probably the sense in which it is to be taken here— the love that is strong and constant forgives the offending brother 'unto seventy times seven', and thus the bond of fellowship is kept unbroken. But the words may also be interpreted to mean that the spirit of love is rewarded by God's forgiveness of our transgressions; cf. Luke 7:47 — 'Her sins, which are many, are forgiven, because she loved much' (Tertullian, *Scorp.* 6; Origen, *On Leviticus*, Homily II, 4); and this is the sense in which the proverb is employed by the writer of 2 Clement (16:4). The καλύψει πλῆθος ἁμαρτιῶν of James 5:20 is not spoken of love, but of the man who 'turns a sinner from the error of his way'; here too, the phrase seems to mean 'shall cover a multitude of (his own) sins' — 'shall receive the widest forgiveness of God'. The variant καλύψει in our passage (אLP 69, 1739. ς) is a corruption due to the influence of the future in this phrase of James.

v. 9. φιλόξενοι εἰς ἀλλήλους⟩ cf. Romans 12:13—τὴν φιλοξενίαν διώκοντες. Hospitality was always a sacred duty among the Greeks; Zeus himself, under the title Ζεὺς Ξένιος, guarded the sanctity of the relation between host and guest, and pursued any breach of hospitality with the vengeance of heaven. In early Christian times, the virtue of hospitality was highly prized, partly as a concrete expression of the love which looked upon all the brethren as members of one great family; and partly as the necessary means of providing for the ministry of apostles, prophets, evangelists and teachers as they went from place to place on their mission to the churches (Heb. 13:1-2; 3 John, 5-8).

ἄνευ γογγυσμοῦ⟩ (onomatopoetic)—'without grumbling'—another *litotes*; the sense is positive — 'with gladness'. The plural, which has only late and weak attestation, is probably due to the influence of the phrase χωρὶς γογγυσμῶν in Philippians 2:14.

In practice, the injunctions to hospitality were obeyed with overflowing zeal; the welcome given to travellers was so generous that Christians were often the victims of impostors, and it became necessary to take measures to protect the churches against the impositions of unscrupulous men. (Didache xi-xii; cf. Lucian, *De Morte Peregrini* xvi; and see Harnack, *Mission and Expansion of Christianity* [E. T., London and New York, 1908], pp. 177ff.)

vv. 10-11. On the dedication of individual gifts to mutual service cf. Romans 12:6-8, and the excursus on 'Spiritual Gifts' in the Commentary by Sanday and Headlam (Romans, I.C.C., 1895), p. 358; cf. also 1 Corinthians 12:4ff. The χαρίσματα are the various endowments which God imparts to all the members of the community, not to the leaders alone; natural aptitudes are heightened, and new powers are awakened by His presence with us, that all may be enabled to serve the community in some measure. (1 Cor. 12:7 — ἑκάστῳ δὲ δίδοται ἡ φανέρωσις τοῦ πνεύματος πρὸς τὸ συμφέρον.) St. Paul speaks of a wide diversity of gifts: wisdom, knowledge, faith, healing, miracles, prophecy, discerning of spirits, 'tongues' and interpretation of 'tongues' (ibid. vv. 8-10); in Romans 12:6ff., he mentions further 'ministry' (διακονία), teaching, exhortation, sharing, leadership, works of mercy; the supreme χάρισμα is love (1 Cor. 13). The writer of 1 Peter has already spoken of the primacy of love (v. 8); he now singles out for special mention the gifts of speech and of service, though the employ of every type of gift is a form of service to the community — εἰς ἀλλήλους αὐτὸ διακονοῦντες.

ὡς καλοὶ οἰκονόμοι⟩ 'as good stewards' — emphasizing the thought that the gifts of God are not given to us for our own enjoyment, as a private possession, but are given to us in trust for the community of His people. Cf. Luke 12:42; 1 Cor. 4:1-2. καλοί — of manifest excellence, exhibiting the attractiveness of fidelity and generosity.

ποικίλης χάριτος θεοῦ⟩ The χαρίσματα are concrete manifestations of the χάρις that has been bestowed. This writer makes little use of the Pauline doctrine of the Spirit as the giver of the χαρίσματα; indeed, it is remarkable how little he understands, or at least how little he applies, the doctrine of the Spirit as it had been expounded by St. Paul (E. F. Scott, The Spirit in the New Testament, London, N. D. [1923], pp. 226-7). The adjective ποίκιλος suggests both richness and infinite variety, with an undertone of the harmonious beauty which is exhibited in the union of the different gifts.

'For not only in respect of the possession of money and of outward things generally is he that has more bound to supply the needs of those that are in want; but also in respect of superior natural endowments and the gifts of the Holy Ghost, none would say that aught was the property of him that held it, but that it belonged rather to his neighbour and to him that stood in need and required to share therein.' — οὐ γὰρ μόνον ἐπὶ τῆς τῶν χρημάτων κτήσεως καὶ τῶν ἔξωθεν ὑποχρεώς ἐστιν ὁ πλέον ἔχων τοῖς ἐνδέεσι τὴν χρείαν πληροῦν, ἀλλὰ καὶ ἐπὶ τῶν ἐκ φύσεως πλεονεκτημάτων καὶ τῶν τοῦ Πνεύματος δωρεῶν, οὐκ ἄν τις εἴποι τοῦ ἔχοντος ἴδιον εἶναι τοῦτο, μᾶλλον ἢ τοῦ πλησίου καὶ ἐν ἐνδείᾳ καθεστηκότος καὶ μετέχειν ὀφείλοντος. (Cramer, Catenae, Vol. VIII, p. 77.)

v. 11. λαλεῖ⟩ in the context must be interpreted of the speaking which is charismatic; i.e., the preaching, — = λαλεῖ τὸν λόγον. λόγια cannot reasonably be taken as a nominative (Bigg), but must be an accusative, object of an unexpressed imperative (λαλῶν). The thought is not that the common conversation of Christians should be cast in Scriptural language, as Bigg suggests, but that the preaching should declare the truth that God imparts — the message should be presented as 'God's oracles', the revelation of His will and purpose for man declared through the preacher.

διακονεῖ) likewise of charismatic 'service', the term here embracing all kinds of Christian work except preaching.

ὡς ἐξ ἰσχύος, etc.) of the spirit in which the services to the community are to be performed, without any conceit of one's own powers, but in the full acknowledgment that the strength which enables one to serve is derived from God.

χορηγεῖ) in the literal sense (from χόρος) of 'leading the dance'; also of expense of providing a chorus at the public festivals, such as the Great Dionysia at Athens; then, metaphorically, of providing supply for an army or a fleet; and in a more extended usage, as here, of providing the necessary means for a variety of needs, often with the sense of 'supplying abundantly'. (2 Cor. 9:10 — χορηγήσει καὶ πληθυνεῖ . . . καὶ αὐξήσει.) The verb does not govern a genitive; ἧς is attracted into the case of its antecedent.

ἐν πᾶσιν) a neuter; cf. 1 Corinthians 10:31 — πάντα εἰς δόξαν θεοῦ ποιεῖτε. In the exercise of the gifts with which God has endowed us, we are not to vaunt ourselves, but to glorify Him to whom we owe all that we have. The ἵνα clause, however, does not depend exclusively on the injunctions concerning the use of the χαρίσματα; rather, it sums up the thought of the entire paragraph, and is less a final clause than a new, all-embracing imperative — 'In all things, let God be glorified'.

διὰ Ι.Χ.) God is to be glorified 'through Jesus Christ', because all our relationships with Him are mediated through His Son.

The doxology, which is employed again in much the same form in 5:11 (though the text in the latter passage is uncertain) marks the end of the baptismal discourse.

κράτος) primarily 'power', then 'authority', 'rule', 'dominion' — sometimes also 'victory' — is not found in any of the Pauline doxologies, but occurs in some of the later N.T. writings (Jude 25; 1 Tim. 6:16; Apoc. 1:6, and 5:13). The thought is probably of the victorious power which ensures the ultimate triumph of the divine purpose for the world.

III. THE LETTER PROPER

WITH verse 12, we are immediately conscious of a change in the whole atmosphere. For the first time, we find reflected, indeed vividly portrayed, the living situation of a particular community; the writer no longer deals with the general principles of Christian living in a pagan environment, but with the distress and terror occasioned by an actual persecution.

Some of the earlier commentators perceived clearly enough that the references to persecution in this section are entirely different from those that we have examined in previous passages of the Epistle. (Kuhl — 'hier, anders als 1:6; 3:14, 16, von thatsächlichen Leiden die Rede ist'; B. Weiss — 'Es ist nämlich hier keineswegs von den Leiden die Rede, die einzelne gelegentlich treffen können, sondern von dem, welches die Gemeinde als solche trifft.') The new situation which here emerges is interpreted by these two scholars in the light of their erroneous theory that the Epistle is very early (pre-Pauline) and that it is addressed to Jewish Christians; they think here of a persecution organized by the Jewish authorities, and suggest that the bewildered astonishment of the Asian Christians arises from the fact that this was their first experience of an organized Jewish effort to root out Christianity from the nation, and their first realization that the new faith was forcing upon them a complete and final separation from the national life of Judaism. The historical context which they imagine is quite impossible, but their perception has not been at fault in noting that for the first time in the Epistle the writer is speaking of a persecution which strikes the churches generally, and that the feeling of astonishment (ξενίζεσθε), the sense of something strange (ξένου συμβαίνοντος) is due to the fact that a situation of acute crisis has arisen, for which the ordinary trials of life in a heathen environment, the arbitrary blows of surly masters and even occasional prosecutions before a magistrate, were no preparation.

¹² Ἀγαπητοί, μὴ ξενίζεσθε τῇ ἐν ὑμῖν πυρώσει πρὸς πειρασμὸν ὑμῖν
γινομένῃ, ὡς ξένου ὑμῖν συμβαίνοντος, ¹³ ἀλλὰ καθὸ κοινωνεῖτε τοῖς
τοῦ Χριστοῦ παθήμασιν χαίρετε, ἵνα καὶ ἐν τῇ ἀποκαλύψει τῆς δόξης
αὐτοῦ χαρῆτε ἀγαλλιώμενοι. ¹⁴ εἰ ὀνειδίζεσθε ἐν ὀνόματι Χριστοῦ,
μακάριοι, ὅτι τὸ τῆς δόξης ⟨καὶ δυνάμεως⟩ καὶ τὸ τοῦ θεοῦ πνεῦμα
ἐφ' ὑμᾶς ἀναπαύεται. ¹⁵ μὴ γάρ τις ὑμῶν πασχέτω ὡς φονεὺς ἢ
κλέπτης ἢ κακοποιὸς ἢ ὡς ἀλλοτριεπίσκοπος· ¹⁶ εἰ δὲ ὡς Χριστιανός,
μὴ αἰσχυνέσθω, δοξαζέτω δὲ τὸν θεὸν ἐν τῷ ὀνόματι τούτῳ. ¹⁷ ὅτι ὁ
καιρὸς τοῦ ἄρξασθαι τὸ κρίμα ἀπὸ τοῦ οἴκου τοῦ θεοῦ· εἰ δὲ πρῶτον
ἀφ' ἡμῶν, τί τὸ τέλος τῶν ἀπειθούντων τῷ τοῦ θεοῦ εὐαγγελίῳ;
¹⁸ καὶ εἰ ὁ δίκαιος μόλις σώζεται, ὁ ἀσεβὴς καὶ ἁμαρτωλὸς ποῦ φανεῖται;
¹⁹ ὥστε καὶ οἱ πάσχοντες κατὰ τὸ θέλημα τοῦ θεοῦ πιστῷ κτίστῃ
παρατιθέσθωσαν τὰς ψυχὰς αὐτῶν ἐν ἀγαθοποιΐᾳ.

*Beloved, do not be amazed at the fiery ordeal that is raging among
you, that is befalling you for a testing, as though it were a strange
thing happening to you; but rejoice, in that you are sharing in the
sufferings of Christ, that you may rejoice with jubilation also in the
revelation of His glory. If you are reviled for the name of Christ,
you are blessed, for the spirit of glory and power, even the Spirit of
God rests upon you. For none of you must suffer as a murderer or
thief or malefactor or as an agitator; but if one suffers as a Christian,
let him not be ashamed, but let him glorify God in this name. For it is
the Time of the commencing of the Judgment: it has begun with the
house of God; and if it begins first with us, what shall be the end for
those that reject the Gospel of God? And*

> *'If the righteous man barely finds salvation*
> *Where shall the impious and sinful man appear?'*

*Wherefore let those that are suffering according to the will of God
commit their souls to the faithful Creator, in uprightness.*

¹⁴ om. εν אּ* και δυναμεως) om BKL 69. ϛ vg ᵃᵐⁱᵃᵗ ᵉᵗ ᶜᵒᵈᵈ. ᵃˡ. syrᴾ Tert
Clᵃˡᵉˣ Oec Thphyl : habent אּ (της δυν. αυτου) ACPΨ 33. 1739. 2412.
vg ᶜˡᵉᵐ syrʰˡ sah boh και το) om vg ᵃᵐⁱᵃᵗ syrᴾ αναπαυεται) επαναπαυεται
A 2412. +κατα μεν αυτους βλασφημειται, κατα δε υμας δοξαξεται *fin.* KLP ϛ
vg ᵃᵐⁱᵃᵗ ᵉᵗ ᶜᵒᵈᵈ. ᵃˡ. sah syrᴾ Oec Thphyl   ¹⁵ αλλοτριεπισκοπος) αλλοτριο-
επισκοπος ϛ : αλλοτριος επισκοπος A 69.   ¹⁶ ονοματι) μερει ϛ   ¹⁷ ο) om אּA
ημων) υμων אּ* 69   ¹⁸ ασεβης) pr δε B* syrʰˡ arm   αμαρτωλος) pr ο אּA
¹⁹ πιστω) pr ως KLP 69 ϛ αυτων) om B   αγαθοποιια   אּBKLP 69. 1739.
2412. ϛ sah boh) αγαθοποιιαις AΨ 33 vg syrr

v. 12. μὴ ξενίζεσθε) 'Do not be astonished'. The outbreak of organized
persecution has come as a paralysing shock, and the first effect is a
numb inability to understand why they should become the victims of
such an assault.

τῇ ... πυρώσει) He terms the persecution a 'firing', metaphorically, using the figure of the refiner's fire to which he had previously made allusion in the beginning of the baptismal Discourse (1:7). It is possible, though it cannot be taken for granted, that the metaphor was being given a terrible pointing by actual burnings at the stake. Christians had been burned as living torches in the persecution under Nero (Tacitus, *Annals*, Bk. xv, sec. 44); and the records of persecutions later in the second century speak again of burnings (*Martyrdom of Polycarp; Letter of the Churches of Lyons and Vienne*, etc.). The letter of Pliny, however, does not suggest that such a punishment would be inflicted under his jurisdiction; and Ignatius, also in the time of Trajan, anticipates that he may be cast to the wild beasts in the arena, but not that he may be burned. The choice of the word πύρωσις, therefore, is probably not to be taken as conveying any implication that Christians were being sentenced to the stake; but as interpreting all the sufferings of the persecution as a searching trial of the faith of the persecuted. This sense is defined more precisely in the predicate which follows—πρὸς πειρασμὸν ὑμῖν γινομένῃ.

ξένου) The genitive absolute here sets forth the false (ὡς) ground of their astonishment; they think of the persecution as 'a foreign thing' — something that has no relation to their life in Christ. He now proceeds to remind them that on the contrary such an ordeal is wholly in keeping with their profession of faith in Christ; it admits them to fellowship with Him in His earthly experience of suffering at the hands of the rulers of this world.

v. 13. κοινωνεῖτε) 'you share' — 'you have fellowship' — a new bond of κοινωνία is forged through the endurance of persecution. The power of this thought was realized again and again in the long ordeal through which the Church passed in the ensuing centuries. The Martyr felt that he was truly made one with Christ, when he was called to suffer for His sake. The thought lies implicit in the saying of Jesus that whoever follows Him must 'take up his cross' (Matt. 16:24, etc.), and in the Johannine saying 'If the world hate you, you know that it hated me before it hated you . . . If they persecuted me, they will persecute you also' (John 15:18-20). It was the perpetual comfort of St. Paul in all that he had to endure (e.g. Col. 1:24—ἀνταναπληρῶ τὰ ὑστερήματα τῶν θλίψεων τοῦ Χριστοῦ ἐν τῇ σαρκί μου; Phil. 3:10—τοῦ γνῶναι αὐτὸν καὶ . . . κοινωνίαν παθημάτων αὐτοῦ); and it is brought forward in various ways in many later references to martyrdom.

χαίρετε) 'rejoice' — cf. Acts 5:41 — 'They went out from the presence of the Sanhedrim rejoicing because they had been counted worthy to suffer shame for the Name'. Cf. James 1:2 — 'Count it all joy when you fall into manifold trials' — though this parallel is more verbal than real, since the words do not suggest persecution, but the general hard experiences of life. The ground of rejoicing lies not in the sufferings themselves but in the realization of unity with Christ which they bring.

The final clause does not depend primarily on χαίρετε, but rather on κοινωνεῖτε τοῖς τοῦ Χριστοῦ παθημάτων: the share in the future glory of Christ is the promised counterpart of the sufferings that have been shared. It is not precisely a thought of reward, but rather of an inherent compensation; the same connection of participation in present sufferings as leading to participation in future glory belongs to the common Christian piety, and is frequently adduced by St. Paul also (Rom. 8:17 — εἴπερ συμπάσχομεν ἵνα καὶ συνδοξασθῶμεν — 'if so be that we suffer with Him, that we may also be glorified with Him'; and note in the following verse how he sets 'the sufferings of the present time' over against 'the glory that shall be revealed for us'). In the later N.T. writings, cf. especially 2 Tim. 2:11-12 — 'If we suffer with Him, we shall also live with Him; if we endure, we shall also reign with Him'; and the same thought of a more than compensating weight of glory goes back to Jesus Himself in the saying of Matthew 10:32 — 'Whoever shall confess Me before men, I shall also confess Him in the presence of my Father which is in heaven.' The New Testament knows nothing of a coldly philosophical devotion to virtue for virtue's sake; it sees virtue as consisting ultimately in fidelity to the living God, and rests in the confidence that God will ultimately vindicate the faithful.

ἐν τῇ ἀποκαλύψει τῆς δόξης αὐτοῦ⟩ 'in the revelation of His glory' — again, as in 1:7, 13, of Christ's manifestation upon earth in glory, not of a heavenly vision to be attained by His followers; the thought of this writer still moves in the early atmosphere of vivid expectation of Christ's coming in power.

v. 14. εἰ ὀνειδίζεσθε. . . μακάριοι⟩ clearly appealing to the well-known saying of Jesus in Matthew 5:11; as in 3:14 he had appealed to the saying of Matthew 5:10. These words of our Lord must have been known to the writer in almost the very form in which they have been transmitted to us, and it is not unlikely that our Gospel according to St. Matthew was itself known to him. εἰ is again not truly conditional, but positive (=seeing that); cf. 2:3, note. ὀνειδίζεσθε here must mean something more than the occasional revilings by hostile individuals which are mentioned in 2:12 and 3:16; in this context it suggests rather the shouting fury of the mob that spurs the magistrates to severity.

ἐν ὀνόματι Χριστοῦ⟩ literally 'in the name of Christ' — i.e., 'for, because of' the Name. ἐν is anomalous in the phrase in this hostile sense; everywhere else in N.T. it implies the use of the Name by a follower or friend; here one would expect rather διὰ τὸ ὄνομα (or as in Matt. 5:11 — ἕνεκεν). The proper force of the preposition might be retained by taking ὀνειδίζεσθε not as a passive but as a middle — 'if you undergo reviling in the name of Christ' — taking the prepositional phrase of the attitude of the Christians who are reviled, not of the cause which animates the revilers; but this seems even more strained than the other.

The next clause — ὅτι . . . ἀναπαύεται — is difficult in itself, and the strangeness of the phrasing has led to multiple variations in transmission by which the difficulty is intensified. The writer is here building upon the words of Isaiah 11:2 (Lxx) — καὶ ἀναπαύσεται ἐπ᾽ αὐτόν πνεῦμα τοῦ θεοῦ. The evidence for καὶ (τῆς) δυνάμεως seems too strong and too widely represented for us to reject it; it is equally hard to account for its loss if it be genuine, and for its insertion, if it be false. It is by no means certain that πνεῦμα is to be understood with δόξης καὶ δυνάμεως as well as with θεοῦ; the Clementine text may be truer to the mind of the writer in its vaguer phrasing 'quod est honoris', etc. — 'that whereof the property is glory and power'; but it is perhaps simpler to take it that he is speaking of the Spirit of God as 'the Spirit of glory and power', i.e., the Spirit which sheds a heavenly glory about the life of the persecuted and imparts the power to overcome.

This writer, it must be observed, makes little use of the doctrine of the Spirit; the presence of the Spirit within the believer is not a living idea to him as it is to St. Paul, nor does he ascribe the χαρίσματα to the Spirit. Apart from this verse and the more or less stock phrase of 1:2, he mentions the Spirit only in 1:11-12, where he is speaking of the Old Testament prophets and the preachers of the Christian Gospel. There the thought is of the Spirit accompanying the proclamation of the Word, and only in that context does the idea appear to have substantial meaning for him. In this passage again he seems to think of the presence of the Spirit as an occasional visitation, not as a constant dwelling in the heart of the believer; the Spirit comes upon Christians in the time of their suffering for the Name of Christ, accompanying this testimony of faith as He accompanied the proclamation of the Gospel of salvation by the prophets and the evangelists.

κατὰ μὲν αὐτοὺς βλασφημεῖται, κατὰ δὲ ὑμᾶς δοξάζεται⟩ 'Among them He is blasphemed, but among you He is glorified' — appears to be a gloss, but a very early one, since it is represented in many manuscripts of the Vulgate (not in the Clementine text) and in Cyprian, and also in the Sahidic version, as well as in nearly all the cursives (and P). The subject of the verbs could only be πνεῦμα, and the clause does not fall naturally into the context.

vv. 15-16. These verses make it unmistakably clear that the writer is speaking of governmental action all through this passage; the profession of Christianity is being punished as a crime, like murder and theft. Evidence of loyalty and uprightness of life, which according to 3:16 was to result in the dismissal of the charges and the humiliation of the accusers, is no longer a valid defence; a man is liable to suffer 'as a Christian', i.e., upon conviction on the charge of professing Christianity, in the same sense that he is liable to suffer 'as a murderer or thief'. The Christian's situation in law is no longer the same as that presupposed in 3:15ff., when he was allowed to make a defence 'concerning the Hope'. Now his only defence is repudiation of the Hope and denial of Christ.

But this is precisely the situation created by Pliny in his procedure against the Christians; unable to find evidence of 'the crimes associated with the name (of Christian)', he orders the accused to execution *propter nomen ipsum*. Cf. Introduction, Section IV.

Both κακοποιός and ἀλλοτριεπίσκοπος must refer to acts of criminal activity, in the context. It has been suggested that κακοποιός may be the equivalent of the Latin *maleficus* — 'sorcerer'; but there is no evidence for the use of the word in this sense in Greek legal terminology. More probably, it has a less precise meaning, like 'thug'. ἀλλοτριεπίσκοπος is not found elsewhere, and is probably of the writer's own compounding. It suggests a type of activity alien to the spirit that should animate the Christian; perhaps the best sense that may be given it is that of revolutionary activity (=*cupidus novarum rerum*) — agitation of proletarian revolt for the violent redress of grievances, to which some Christians may well have been tempted. It was easy to strike a spark among the slaves and the very poor from whose ranks the converts were chiefly recruited, and the lesson of patient endurance must have been hard to learn, as indeed it still is.

χριστιανός occurs only twice in N.T., apart from this passage. Both the other instances are found in the book of Acts (11:26; 26:28). In all three places, there is an implication that this was a term applied in the first instance by those outside the fold (the people of Antioch, Agrippa, here the Roman prosecutor). That it was in fact so used by non-Christians is certain, as is shown by the evidence of Tacitus, Suetonius, and Pliny. The Christians themselves on the other hand continued to use the old terms, filled with religious significance — μαθηταί, ἅγιοι, ἀδελφοί — 'disciples, saints, brethren'. The phrase ὡς χριστιανός, then, in this passage almost certainly signifies the literal ground of accusation; it is not simply that the persecuted, though tried on a variety of charges, felt within themselves ('nach ihren eigenen Bewusstsein' — Knopf) that they were suffering 'as Christians'.

μὴ αἰσχυνέσθω⟩ 'let him not be ashamed' — as he would naturally be, at the indignity of arrest, conviction, and sentence on a criminal charge. The natural converse would be — 'let him count it an honour' — but it is turned more forcefully to the thought of the honour that may be done to God in glorifying Him by a steadfast confession.

ἐν τῷ ὀνόματι τούτῳ⟩ 'in this name' — not in this case the name of Christ, but the name 'Christian', which is applied to them in scorn and hatred. By demonstrating under trial the true significance of this name, they will glorify God and teach others to glorify Him. The variant μέρει of the Textus Receptus is too weakly attested to require consideration.

v. 17. ὁ καιρός⟩ the time, the appointed season, the 'Last Time' of 1:6, when the purpose of God is to be brought to consummation. The awaited hour has now struck.

ἄρξασθαι⟩ The aorist is not used lightly; it signifies a definite event in
God's dealing with the world, sustaining the thought that the outbreak
of organized persecution is not a mere intensifying of the normal difficulties which beset the life of Christians in a pagan environment, but is
the first act in the great drama of the Last Judgment. The 'house of
God', i.e., the community of believers, as in 2:5 (cf. Heb. 3:6), is now
standing trial before the Judge to whom all must render account (1:17);
in the last act, not long to be deferred, 'those that disobey the Gospel of
God' must in their turn stand before His throne to face His wrath.

The thought that the Judgment of God begins with punishment of the
derelictions of His own people goes back to the prophets of Israel (Jer.
25:29; Ez. 9:6, etc.), but it is not evident that any O.T. prophecy is laid
directly under contribution here. Rather, the writer is bringing forward
an idea that belongs to the common tradition of Christian teaching and
finds expression in different applications in earlier Christian writings,
especially in the Pauline Epistles, but with a certain basis also in our
Lord's parables of the Judgment, especially those of the Wheat and the
Tares and of the Dragnet (Matt. 13:24-30, 47-50). The thought here,
however, bears less upon the separation of the false from the true within
the community, than upon the testing of those that truly belong to Christ.
It is perhaps permissible to find implicit in the passage something of
the thought suggested by St. Paul in 1 Corinthians 11:31-32, that
Christians who fall short of the scrupulous care of their conduct which
the Gospel demands are visited with the judgments of the Lord in this
life, but that these judgments are salutary and chastening, saving them
from the condemnation that shall befall the world. (εἰ δὲ ἑαυτοὺς διεκ-
ρίνομεν, οὐκ ἂν ἐκρινόμεθα· κρινόμενοι δὲ ὑπὸ τοῦ κυρίου παιδευόμεθα,
ἵνα μὴ σὺν τῷ κόσμῳ κατακριθῶμεν.) Cf. also 1 Corinthians 3:12ff.

τὶ τὸ τέλος, etc.⟩ The ordeal through which the believers are passing
is terrible; the end that awaits unbelievers is beyond imagination. Like
the author of Hebrews, this writer is filled with a profound sense of the
awfulness of Him with whom we have to do; 'our God is a consuming
fire'. But he does not attempt to be specific about the punishment that
is to be meted out to 'them that disobey the Gospel of God'; he permits
himself only to infer that it must far exceed the worst that Christians
are called to endure upon earth. Elsewhere in the New Testament, the
terrors which the Judgment Day holds for unbelievers are vividly
portrayed (2 Thess. 1:8; Apoc. 6:15ff.; etc.). Here, however, the author's
concern is not to warn the disobedient, but to encourage the faithful,
and he goes no farther than to assure them that the sufferings which they
endure in Christ's service, great as they are, still fall far short of what
the enemies of the Gospel must await. In part, his motive is to remind
them that there is no ultimate escape in apostasy; those who might be
tempted to seek an immediate freedom by renouncing Christ are warned
that the imminent menace of far worse punishment hangs over the
disobedient.

v. 18. Cited from Proverbs 11:31 (Lxx) in confirmation of this warning. In the original context, the words have no reference to future judgment, but bear upon the earthly welfare of men; the eschatological application is made, somewhat arbitrarily, by the writer of the Epistle. ποῦ φανεῖται might be taken as implying a doctrine of annihilation; more probably like τί τὸ τέλος above, it suggests the impossibility of imagining the degree of disaster that is to befall 'the impious and sinful man'.

v. 19. ὥστε) 'wherefore'—summing up the thought of the entire paragraph. καὶ ought not to be taken too closely with οἱ πάσχοντες—'even those that are suffering' — since the more appropriate thought would be 'especially those that are suffering' and this sense cannot be attributed to καὶ. It is more naturally taken with ὥστε — 'wherefore also'— serving as connective to the whole sentence.

οἱ πάσχοντες κατὰ τὸ θέλημα τοῦ θεοῦ) Cf. 3:17. The sense in which the sufferings which they endure are inflicted 'in accordance with God's will' is twofold. On the one hand, it is God's judgment that is being executed, to test and to refine the metal of their faith; on the other, the persecutors could have no power over them except it were allowed of God (John 19:10-11; cf. Matt. 26:53-4; John 18:11). The will of God is permissive as related to the persecutors; but in relation to the persecuted it is directive. Like the passion of our Lord, it is 'the cup which the Father hath given'.

πιστῷ κτίστῃ παρατιθέσθωσαν τὰς ψυχὰς αὐτῶν) 'let them commit their souls to a faithful Creator'—as Jesus in the hour of His agony committed His spirit to God (Lk. 23:46 — εἰς χεῖράς σου παρατίθεμαι τὸ πνεῦμά μου). The appeal to confidence in the faithfulness of God as Creator is noteworthy. κτίστης is not found elsewhere in the New Testament; though there are other references to His creation of men and of the universe, the thought is not elsewhere made the ground of confidence in His will and power to save. Windisch remarks acutely, 'Hier bricht eine vom spezifisch christlichen Erlösungsglauben ganz unabhängige Frömmingkeit durch, die durch drei Worte: Schöpfung, Werktätigkeit und Vorsehung bestimmt ist, die reine Religion des ersten Artikels'. It is however grounded in Old Testament piety (Isaiah 64:1-9, etc.).

ψυχή is again used of the 'soul' as the true inward life, the essential being which the death of the body cannot impair, as in Matthew 10:28 and other sayings of Jesus; cf. Ecclesiasticus 3:1ff.

παρατιθέσθωσαν) 'commit', 'entrust for safekeeping'. The verb and the corresponding noun παραθήκη are common in commercial usage, for the deposit of funds or other valuables with a trustworthy person; in the sense of a spiritual commitment it occurs again in 2 Timothy 1:12 — οἶδα γὰρ ᾧ πεπίστευκα, καὶ πέπεισμαι ὅτι δυνατός ἐστιν τὴν παραθήκην μου φυλάξαι.

M*

ἐν ἀγαθοποιΐᾳ) 'in well-doing' — i.e., continuing in a life of active goodness; the place at the end of the sentence and section gives the word great emphasis. The threat of persecution must not drive the Christian to hide his goodness, or to sink into a merely negative abstention from evil; he must continue to love his neighbour and to do him good. Similarly in 3:6 'doing good' is contrasted with that yielding to fright which results in inactivity.

Professor W. C. van Unnik has devoted a long article to 'The Teaching of Good Works in I Peter' (*New Testament Studies*, Vol. 1, No. 2, Nov. 1954, pp. 92-110). He recognizes that of three possible interpretations of 'good works' — Greek, Jewish, and Christian — the conception in I Peter 'is closely alike to the first one but for its foundation' (p. 108). It would seem to follow that we have here further evidence for the generally Hellenistic, rather than Jewish, background of the author of the Epistle — certainly this investigation lends no support to its attribution to Peter or even to Silvanus, the trusted representative of James and the Jewish-Christian church of Jerusalem (Acts 15:22). Naturally the writer, though he employs the language and thought-forms of Hellenistic ethics, brings his words into a Christian frame of reference; nobody will pretend that the 'foundation' of the teaching of I Peter is Greek! Van Unnik seems to think, however, that he has found in this usage some support for the Petrine authorship of the epistle: he finds 'no cogent arguments which prevent us from seeing in Peter the mind which directed the hand of Silvanus'. There appears to be more sound reasoning in the contention of W. Grundmann (Kittel's *Theol. Wörterbuch zum N.T.*, s.v. καλός [Bd. III, Stuttgart, 1938]) that here as in the Pastorals, the conception of 'good works' points to a post-apostolic situation (die Stellung der Christengemeinde der zweiten Generation). Cf. the remark in Van Unnik's second article on the same theme: 'It seems evident to me that the terminology of I Peter is here derived from Greek sources and should be interpreted accordingly. . . . It shows once more that Peter, as was set out in my previous paper, was moving, with this terminology about "good works", in the Greek sphere' ('A Classical Parallel to I Peter ii, 14 and 20' in *New Testament Studies*, Vol. 2, No. 3, February 1956, pp. 198-202). Peter?

5 ¹ Πρεσβυτέρους οὖν ἐν ὑμῖν παρακαλῶ ὁ συμπρεσβύτερος καὶ μάρτυς τῶν τοῦ Χριστοῦ παθημάτων, ὁ καὶ τῆς μελλούσης ἀποκαλύπτεσθαι δόξης κοινωνός· ² ποιμάνατε τὸ ἐν ὑμῖν ποίμνιον τοῦ θεοῦ, μὴ ἀναγκαστῶς ἀλλὰ ἑκουσίως κατὰ θεόν, μηδὲ αἰσχροκερδῶς ἀλλὰ προθύμως, ³ μηδ' ὡς κατακυριεύοντες τῶν κλήρων ἀλλὰ τύποι γινόμενοι τοῦ ποιμνίου· ⁴ καὶ φανερωθέντος τοῦ ἀρχιποίμενος κομιεῖσθε τὸν ἀμαράντινον τῆς δόξης στέφανον. ⁵ Ὁμοίως νεώτεροι, ὑποτάγητε πρεσβυτέροις· πάντες δὲ ἀλλήλοις τὴν ταπεινοφροσύνην ἐγκομβώσασθε, ὅτι ὁ θεὸς ὑπερηφάνοις ἀντιτάσσεται, ταπεινοῖς δὲ δίδωσιν χάριν.

The elders among you I exhort, therefore, as your fellow-elder, and a witness to the sufferings of Christ, who am to be a sharer also in the glory that shall be revealed: — shepherd the flock of God which is in your keeping; not under compulsion, but willingly, in accordance with God; not for base greed of gain, but with eager zeal; not as playing the master over the congregations, but by making yourselves examples to the flock; and when the Chief Shepherd shall be manifested, you shall receive the unfading crown of glory. Likewise, you that are younger, be subject to the elders; and, all for one another, clothe yourselves in the vesture of humility, for

> 'God resists the proud,
> But to the humble He gives grace'.

¹ ουν) τους KLP ς boh syrʰˡ : +τους ℵ vg αποκαλυπτεσθαι δοξης) transp. A ² εν υμιν) om A μη) pr επισκοπουντες Aℵᶜ 69. ς vg boh syrr : txt Bℵ* 33 sah κατα θεον) om BKLP ς syrᵖ : post προθυμως 2412 μηδε) μη AL lat vet syrʰˡ ³ om. versum B add. μακροθυμως fin. 69. (ex animo —vg) ⁵ ομοιως)+δε ℵ* 33. syrʰˡ : +δε και οι 2412 πρεσβυτεροις) pr τοις ℵ αλληλοις)+υποτασσομενοι KLP 69. ς syrʰˡ : +υποταγωμεν 2412 ο) om B

v. I. Πρεσβυτέρους) for the noun without the article in addressing the entire group, cf. 3:1 — γυναῖκες. The 'elders' are here the local leaders, as in Acts, and the admonition has striking similarities to St. Paul's address to the elders of the Ephesian church, as reported in Acts 20:17ff. Though the word clearly denotes an office, with definite functions of administration and pastoral care (ποιμάνατε), it still retains an element of the original sense of age; the leaders are not neophytes, but older members of the community.

οὖν) 'therefore' — refers back particularly to ἀγαθοποιΐα, moving to specific indications of the kind of 'well-doing' that is required of elders, under these dangerous circumstances.

The variant τούς which is substituted for οὖν in many manuscripts (with the conflate reading οὖν τούς-ℵ) is the result of an attempt to reduce to the commonplace level a phrase which as it stands has individuality and character.

συμπρεσβύτερος, μάρτυς, κοινωνός〉 The only attempt in the body of the letter to bring forward the personal status of Peter. The words are, of course, part of the apparatus of pseudepigraphy. The mock-modesty which first sets the Apostle on a level with the elders, only to emphasize in the next breath his unique experience and peculiar privilege would ill become Peter himself, but is perfectly natural in the language of another man writing in his name. Peter, he would say, was likewise an 'elder', commissioned to feed the flock of Christ (John 21: 15ff.); but more than that, he bore testimony as an eye-witness to the sufferings of Christ and he now shares Christ's glory which is shortly to be revealed. His example should be an inspiration and an encouragement to hope that the elders who bear the same faithful testimony will also share that glory. Peter is represented as addressing them from that eminence which he has already attained, to which they too may aspire.

Canon Streeter (*The Primitive Church*, pp. 136ff.) felt that there was a distinct incongruity in calling Peter an 'elder'. The office of Apostle, he held, was quite different from that of elder. This consideration, more than any other, led him to view with favour the theory of Harnack that the address and the closing greetings, which alone convey unmistakable references to Peter, were subsequent additions to the book. Accordingly, he sought for a possible leader of the Asian church who might conceivably describe himself by the threefold designation of this verse, and he thought he had found a likely person in Aristion of Smyrna. But it is not at all evident that the functions of elder and Apostle were conceived to be so utterly distinct as all that; rather, as the First Epistle of Clement clearly shows, there was in this later generation a prevailing theory that the Apostles had appointed the elders to succeed them, and to fulfil all the necessary duties for the churches in their place. Even if 'the apostles' were clearly distinguished from 'the elders' in the Apostolic Age — and this is by no means certain — it would still not follow that the ecclesiastical theory of the following age would preserve the same distinction.

μάρτυς τῶν παθημάτων τοῦ Χριστοῦ〉 'a witness of the sufferings of Christ'. Strictly speaking, μάρτυς does not mean 'eye-witness' but 'one who testifies'—not necessarily to what he has seen, but more generally, to what he holds to be the truth. The secondary sense which has survived in our word 'martyr' had also already become attached to the word — in death, the 'martyr' bore the supreme and unanswerable testimony. Since Peter was already honoured in the churches as one of the most glorious in the noble army of martyrs, the word can hardly fail to carry at least an undertone of this sense here. Cf. First Clement, 5:4—λάβωμεν πρὸ ὀφθαλμῶν Πέτρον, ὃς . . . οὐχ ἕνα οὐδὲ δύο ἀλλὰ πλείονας ὑπήνεγκεν πόνους καὶ οὕτω μαρτύρησας ἐπορεύθη εἰς τὸν ὀφειλόμενον τόπον τῆς δόξης.

κοινωνός〉 a 'sharer' — with Christ, not with his fellow-elders; the latter association would almost require συγκοινωνός, in keeping with συμπρεσβύτερος. The thought is both present and future; Peter now shares the glory of Christ in heaven; he is likewise to share in the imminent 'revelation'.

τῆς μελλούσης ἀποκαλύπτεσθαι δόξης⟩ 'the glory that shall be revealed'. This glory has already been given to Christ (1:21; 3:22), in His Resurrection, Ascension, and Session at the right hand of God; it is to be 'revealed', in that He will be manifested in His glory to the world which He once visited in humiliation. The thought that His followers will have part in that manifestation is frequently expressed, both in the teachings of Jesus (Matt. 19:27-29, etc.), and in the Pauline Epistles (1 Thess. 4:14ff., etc).

* v. 2. ποιμάνατε, etc.⟩ 'Shepherd' the flock—the thought bears especially on the hazardous duties of leadership, as is shown by the warning against the temptation to assert domination (v.3). More widely, the picture of the 'good shepherd' as drawn in John 10:11ff. (cf. Psalm 23) may be suggested — the shepherd may be called to 'lay down his life for the sheep', to bring others into the fold, to see that the flock is provided with spiritual nourishment even in the presence of its enemies (cf. Acts 20:28-31). The aorist may be taken as ingressive — 'take up the task of shepherding'. The itinerant ministry of apostles, prophets, teachers, and evangelists would be hampered by the activity of the persecutors, with the consequence that wider responsibilities would fall upon the local officials.

τὸ ἐν ὑμῖν ποίμνιον⟩ 'the flock that is committed to your charge'. ἐν ὑμῖν can hardly mean 'among you', as in v.1; the flock cannot be said to be 'among' the shepherds. This must be taken as a pregnant use of the preposition.

The spirit in which the task is to be undertaken and executed is indicated in the threefold antithesis which follows — 'not under compulsion, but willingly; not for greed of gain, but with zeal; not as seeking to dominate, but leading by personal example'.

μὴ ἀναγκαστῶς⟩ 'not under compulsion'—not as reluctantly yielding to the insistence of the Church. In all ages, many devoted servants of Christ have accepted the responsibilities of office only when their people refused to allow them to escape. This shrinking was never looked upon as a fault; on the contrary, it often revealed a true apprehension of the magnitude of the service to which they were called, and a modest sense of personal limitations. In times of stress, however, persistence in seeking to remain in the ranks, yielding only reluctantly and in an unwilling spirit to the pressure of the Church's demands, might reflect primarily the desire to evade a clear and imperative duty. The refusal which might be respected when it sprang merely from disinterested humility became a reproach when it arose from the hope of escaping a prominence that might prove dangerous.

* For additional note to v. 2, see p. 202.

κατὰ θεόν must be taken closely with ἑκουσίως. The willing spirit, which accepts the dangerous responsibility without reluctance, is 'in accordance with God' (cf. 1:15), who is the model set before us for our imitation.

μὴ αἰσχροκερδῶς⟩ 'not for base greed of gain' — appears to imply that some who were capable of giving the needed leadership could be induced to accept office by the promise of pay, when the love of Christ and of their brethren did not suffice to persuade them. It seems strange that such a thing should be, but the writer must have had experience to justify his implication. Similar warnings against the spirit of greed in office-bearers are given in the Pastoral Epistles (1 Tim. 3:3; and especially Tit. 1:7 — ⟨δεῖ οὖν τὸν ἐπίσκοπον ... εἶναι⟩ ἀφιλάργυρον; ... μὴ αἰσχροκερδῆ).

προθυμῶς⟩ 'zealously' — a stronger word than ἑκουσίως — not merely 'willingly', but 'with eagerness'.

v. 3. μηδ' ὡς κατακυριεύοντες, etc.⟩ 'not as lording it, not as playing the master' (cf. Mk. 10:42-45) — a more subtle temptation than greed. The exercise of authority, acquired by consent, easily prompts in men a desire to dominate, a haughty demand for compliance.

τῶν κλήρων⟩ An unusual expression: its precise sense is difficult to determine. O. Holtzmann has sought to explain it with reference to the use of κλῆρος in Acts 1:17,26 — 'had obtained the *lot* of this ministry'; 'the *lot* fell to Matthias'. He suggests, on the strength of these verses, that in some areas men were chosen for leadership in the Church by lot, and that the κλῆροι are the offices which have been obtained by lot, specifically, the bishoprics; he then interprets the verse as a warning to the presbyters not to seek to hold the bishops under their authority! Such an explanation betrays a pathetic faith in the concordance! The κλῆροι must certainly mean the local communities, almost 'the parishes' — though of course it would be a glaring anachronism to think of any formal parish system as in operation at this early period. The plural certainly suggests the thought of a divided responsibility, in contrast with the singular ποίμνιον, which embraces the whole body of the faithful; presbyters would have charge of the believers of a particular locality or of a limited area.

τύποι, etc.⟩ The shepherding is to be done by force of example, not by the pressure of formal authority. The leaders must themselves know how to suffer for the good cause if they would encourage the flock to endure. Like St. Paul, they must seek 'not (their) own advantage, but the good of the many'; and they may become examples only as they pattern themselves after the example of Christ. (Cf. 1 Cor. 10:32-33; and for a parallel antithesis, see 2 Thess. 3:9 — οὐχ ὅτι οὐκ ἔχομεν ἐξουσίαν, ἀλλ' ἵνα ἑαυτοὺς τύπον δῶμεν ὑμῖν εἰς τὸ μιμεῖσθαι ὑμᾶς — 'Not that we have no authority, but that we make ourselves an example to you for you to follow.')

v. 4. ἀρχιποίμην⟩ Once a *hapax legomenon* and therefore thought to be of the writer's own coining, this word has now been found in Egyptian documents (papyri and mummy-tablets) in the sense of 'master-shepherd'. Christ Himself, called in **2**:25 'the shepherd and bishop of souls', is now presented as the master-shepherd under whom the presbyters care for the flock, each in his own measure. The flock itself is God's.

φανερόω⟩ Used in 1:20 of the past manifestation of Christ, but here of His coming in power to judge the earth, as also in Colossians 3:4. 'When Christ, who is your life, shall be manifested, then shall you also be manifested with Him in glory.'

στέφανον⟩ The 'crown' was the prized recognition of the Greek cities, given to athletes who were victorious in the great games and to citizens who distinguished themselves in the public service. Paul is thinking of the games when he writes 'Everyone who enters a contest practises self-control in all things — they, that they may obtain a corruptible crown; but we, for an incorruptible' (1 Cor. 9:25). Here the thought is rather of the reward of public service. It is a crown 'of glory', i.e., of heavenly, not of earthly, honour; cf. the imagery of Revelation 4:4, where the presbyters are seen seated on thrones, clothed in white robes and wearing on their heads golden crowns. The golden crown, however, derives from a different motif, from the nimbus which the Oriental painter set about the heads of the gods of light. Knopf is in error in importing the notion into this passage: 'Strahlenkrone und Strahlen-kranz sind Beigaben der Lichtgötter, und in den Kreis der Lichtgötter sind die Seligen und Verklärten eingerückt, deshalb erhalten sie auch deren Abzeichen.' This writer has no thought of the rayed circle of light to which Knopf refers; he remains in the framework of Greek practice. Only, in place of the (fading) bay or ivy or wild olive which composed the Greek crown, he suggests amaranth, the unfading flower, as the symbol of immortality. Note that ἀμάραντος (1:4) is the verbal of μαραίνω (plus α privative), while ἀμαράντινος is a denominative adjective formed from ἀμάραντος in its substantival use as the name of the flower.

The thought of a 'crown' to be awarded to the faithful by Christ at His coming now belonged to the common imagination of Christians; cf. 2 Tim. 4:8; Apoc. 2:10, 3:11, etc.

v. 5. νεώτεροι⟩ If the 'younger' are now addressed, following the word to the 'elders', it is clear that the sense of age as well as of office or function still attaches strongly to the latter word. There is no question of taking the νεώτεροι to be a kind of office-bearer (=διάκονοι) as was done by some of the earlier commentators and has lately been proposed again by James Moffatt and O. Holtzmann (on the basis of Acts 5:6).

ὑποταγῆτε⟩ The spirit of submission needs to be inculcated, for there was a tendency, to which First Clement bears witness, to grow dissatisfied with the existing leadership, perhaps from the feeling that it was not sufficiently vigorous in its reaction to the crisis. This writer is convinced that in patient submission, not in impetuous vigour, lies the true path of Christian conduct.

Polycarp likewise enjoins the νεώτεροι to be submissive — ὑποτασσομένους τοῖς πρεσβυτέροις καὶ διακόνοις ὡς θεῷ καὶ Χριστῷ (5:3). (Knopf observes that here the νεώτεροι are clearly distinguished from the διάκονοι.) ἀλλήλοις should be taken closely with πάντες rather than with the verb. Set thus in juxtaposition at the beginning of the clause, the two words have the effect of a motto which is to guide all their conduct. 'All for one another' is to be the watchword; 'all for each and each for all'. Note how the writer returns again and again to the thought of the *mutual* responsibilities of Christians.

εγκομβώσασθε) ἐγκομβόω is used of fastening on a garment with a knot or bow. Pollux (*Onomasticon* IV, 119) tells us that the ἐγκόμβωμα is an apron which the slave tied over his undergarment, the sleeveless ἐξωμίς; this has led commentators to interpret the phrase as suggesting that Christians should display towards one another the humility of the slave — wearing humility as the slave's apron. Hesychius, however, gives στολίσασθαι as a synonym; this would suggest rather the donning of beautiful apparel — 'robe yourselves in humility'. In any case, there is no thought that the humility should be merely put on as an external show; it is donned as the garb of the spirit. (Cf. Col. 3:12 — ἐνδύσασθε . . . ταπεινοφροσύνην.)

The Scripture cited in support of the injunction is taken from Proverbs 3:34 (Lxx), which however reads κύριος instead of ὁ θεός. In James 4:6 the same verse is cited again in the Petrine form, and is followed by the injunction 'Submit, then, to God' (ὑποτάγητε οὖν τῷ θεῷ). In most of the passages which show literary relationship between these two epistles, the question of priority is difficult to settle, but here the connection of thought is so much more natural in First Peter as to suggest strongly that it is James which is secondary.

Additional Note on the text of v. 2. *p.* 199.

The participle ἐπισκοποῦντες 'exercising oversight' should probably be retained in the text. Besides the witnesses cited in the apparatus, it is supported by the Latin versions, both the Old Latin (*curae habentes*—S; *perspicientes*—T) and the Vulgate (*providentes*). It now has also the support of 𝔓72. The formidable combination of B and Aleph for the omission, with the far from negligible support of the great cursive 33 and the Sahidic version, is bound to make us hesitate; but on the other hand, it is almost impossible to account for a late insertion of the verb cognate with *episcopos* into a passage addressed to *presbyters*, while it would not be at all unnatural for a scribe of a later date to excise the participle, in the conviction that St. Peter could never have charged presbyters to exercise the office of bishops.

⁶ Ταπεινώθητε οὖν ὑπὸ τὴν κραταιὰν χεῖρα τοῦ θεοῦ, ἵνα ὑμᾶς ὑψώσῃ ἐν καιρῷ, ⁷ πᾶσαν τὴν μέριμναν ὑμῶν ἐπιρίψαντες ἐπ' αὐτόν, ὅτι αὐτῷ μέλει περὶ ὑμῶν. ⁸ Νήψατε, γρηγορήσατε. ὁ ἀντίδικος ὑμῶν διάβολος ὡς λέων ὠρυόμενος περιπατεῖ ζητῶν καταπιεῖν· ⁹ ᾧ ἀντίστητε στερεοὶ τῇ πίστει, εἰδότες τὰ αὐτὰ τῶν παθημάτων τῇ ἐν τῷ κόσμῳ ὑμῶν ἀδελφότητι ἐπιτελεῖσθαι. ¹⁰ Ὁ δὲ θεὸς πάσης χάριτος, ὁ καλέσας ὑμᾶς εἰς τὴν αἰώνιον αὐτοῦ δόξαν ἐν Χριστῷ, ὀλίγον παθόντας αὐτὸς καταρτίσει, στηρίξει, σθενώσει, θεμελιώσει. ¹¹ αὐτῷ τὸ κράτος εἰς τοὺς αἰῶνας τῶν αἰώνων. ἀμήν.

Humble yourselves, therefore, under the mighty hand of God, that He may exalt you at the Time appointed. Cast all your anxiety upon Him, for He cares for you. Be sober! Be vigilant! Your Adversary the Devil as a roaring lion walks about seeking victims to devour. Resist Him, firm in the faith, showing yourselves able to fulfil the same meed of sufferings as your brotherhood in the world. And the God of all grace, who called you to His eternal glory in Christ, after you have suffered for a little shall Himself renew you, make you firm, strengthen and establish you. To Him be dominion for ever. Amen.

⁶ χειρα) χειραν Α𝕏 καιρω)+επισκοπης ΑΡ 33. vg syrʰˡ boh (sah -εν παντι καιρω, ut vid)   ⁷ υμων) ημων 𝕏* 33   ⁸ ο) pr οτι 𝕏°L 33. 69. vg syrr sah boh καταπιειν) καταπιη Α (33) ς vg syrr : pr τινα Α𝕏KLP 33. 69. 1739. 2412. ς vg syrr: om τινα Β   ⁹ τω) om ΑKLP 33. 69. ς   ¹⁰ υμας) ημας Κ vg syrᴾ Χριστω) pr τω Β:+Ιησου Α ς καταρτισει) καταρτισαι υμας ς στηριξει) στηριξαι ς (simil. σθενωσαι, θεμελιωσαι). θεμελιωσει) om ΒΑ vg ¹¹ αυτω)+η δοξα και test. omn. exc. ΒΑ vg των αιωνων) om Β boh

v. 6. ταπεινωθῆτε⟩ The citation which was introduced to confirm the preceding exhortation now becomes the starting-point for a new group of injunctions. As humility is to mark their attitude towards one another, all the more must it mark their attitude towards God as they make proof of His will in the trials which beset them, and acknowledge it to be 'good and acceptable and perfect' (Rom. 12:2).

κραταῖαν χεῖρα⟩ The 'mighty hand' of God is a simple anthropomorphism, frequently found in Lxx as the literal rendering of a common Hebrew phrase. It usually conveys the thought of God's power exhibited in action in the experience of men, whether for deliverance or for chastisement. Here the writer employs it to keep before the minds of his readers the assurance that God has not forsaken them in their tribulation or left them unprotected in the hands of their enemies. His 'mighty hand' is over them — for judgment, but also for their protection; they are still 'guarded by God's power through faith unto salvation' (1:5).

ἵνα ὑμᾶς ὑψώσῃ⟩ As in 4:13, the hope of the compensating future glory is brought forward as a powerful motive for accepting the hardships of the present without complaint; humble acceptance of that which God now causes them to endure is the title to ultimate exaltation. ὑψόω in this sense, of God 'exalting' those that put their trust in Him, is Septuagintal; see especially Psalm 9:13 — ὁ ὑψῶν με ἐκ τῶν πυλῶν τοῦ θανάτου, and Psalm 149:4 — ὑψώσει πραεῖς ἐν σωτηρίᾳ. More directly, the promise of future exaltation as the counterpart of the present humbling of self finds expression in the saying of Jesus '(Everyone that exalted himself shall be abased, and) everyone that humbleth himself shall be exalted' — πᾶς ὁ ταπεινῶν ἑαυτὸν ὑψωθήσεται (Matt. 14:11).

ἐν καιρῷ⟩ Not merely 'bye and bye', in some indefinite future; but 'at the appointed time' (=ἐν ἐσχάτῳ καιρῷ, 1:5). The addition ἐπισκοπῆς (A et al.) is an intrusion from 2:12.

v. 7. The verse is framed about a reminiscence of Psalm 54(55):23 (Lxx) — ἐπίριψον ἐπὶ Κύριον τὴν μέριμνάν σου. The subordination of the participle to ταπεινωθῆτε suggests that true humility before God expresses itself above all in unwavering trust in Him and confidence in His unfailing love. To be overwhelmed with anxiety is to be concerned with self rather than with Him. Jesus likewise had based the injunction 'Be not anxious' — μὴ μεριμνᾶτε, upon firm confidence in the providence of God (Matt. 6:25-34).

ὅτι αὐτῷ μέλει περὶ ὑμῶν⟩ He 'cares' for you; or more literally, 'is concerned' for you; He is not indifferent to your sufferings. The conception of God as concerned with the afflictions of man is the peculiar treasure of Judaic and Christian faith; Greek philosophy at its highest could formulate a doctrine of His perfect goodness, but could not even imagine in Him an active concern for mankind.

v. 8. νήψατε, γρηγορήσατε⟩ The aorists ring sharply: 'Be alert! Be awake!' Confidence in God must not lead to slackness; the spiritual warfare which they wage demands vigilance.

ὁ ἀντίδικος ὑμῶν διάβολος⟩ Behind the persecuting power stands the spirit of evil, and it is this spiritual adversary that they must at all costs resist. They have been taught to 'submit to every human institution' (2:13), accepting unjust punishment without being provoked to rebellion or to any kind of retaliation, for in this patient endurance they will receive no harm, but blessing. To submit to the spiritual adversary, however, would be to succumb to the ultimate danger — to fall away from the faith. Therefore they must 'resist him, steadfast in the faith'. This conception of 'the devil' as the 'adversary' of the people of God, who seeks to turn them from their allegiance to Him, is a late development in Judaism; in the canonical books of the Old Testament scarcely a trace of the notion is to be found. Even in the book of Job, Satan appears in the role of an emissary of God, who inflicts calamities upon Job to test the disinterested purity of his faith. (See the article διαβάλλω, διάβολος in Theologisches Wörterbuch zum Neuen Testament, edited by G.

Kittel [Stuttgart: Kohlhammer, 1935 f.] Vol. 2, pp. 69-88.) The later doctrine, which is presupposed in the New Testament, was developed under the influence of Persian (Zoroastrian) dualism; the 'prince of the power of the air, the spirit that now works in the sons of disobedience' (Eph. 2:3) is none other than the Angra Mainyu of Persian mythology, who opposes Ahura Mazda, the 'Wise Lord', in all his works, and seeks to seduce the Mazdaeans from the loyal service to which they are pledged. To the New Testament writers, and indeed to all the members of the early church, 'the devil' was a personal spirit, the embodiment of all the evil forces in the universe, and the moving power behind all human opposition to the Gospel. This dualistic conception exercised great power over the Christian imagination until recent times without being seriously questioned. Much recent German theology, faced with the incredible concentration of evil which manifested itself most openly in Hitlerism but certainly also in the general trend of modern civilization towards a godless materialism, has sought to revive this ancient doctrine, not as a mythological concept, but in the literal sense in which it was held in the earliest times. There is, however, an air of artificiality about the language which they use; and one may be permitted to question whether any good purpose is served by the effort to return to a view of evil so naive. The evil in the world, even when it is marshalled so formidably as we have seen it in our time, has its roots in the unregenerate heart of man, and is not made more awful by the attempt to cast it back upon a personal devil. The truth behind the doctrine remains as valid as ever: that the evil which we have to fear is that which assails us in the spiritual realm, the evil that means the death not of the body but of the soul, the evil of renouncing the highest good that God has revealed to us — ultimately, the denial of God Himself.

The figurative description of the devil as a 'roaring lion', who 'walks about seeking victims to devour', may be suggested in part by the presence of the lion in Oriental representations of the mother-goddesses (Cybele, Atargatis). It is not necessary, however, to look so far; the lion, for the ancients, is thought of not as the splendid 'King of beasts', but as the typical beast of prey. Some Old Testament passages contribute to the figure; especially Psalm 22:14 (Lxx) — ἤνοιξαν ἐπ' ἐμὲ τὸ στόμα αὐτῶν ὡς λεὼν ὁ ἁρπάζων καὶ ὠρυόμενος — 'They opened their mouths against me as a lion that preys and roars', and Job 1:7.

ζητῶν ⟨τινα⟩ καταπιεῖν⟩ τίνα with the infinitive is certainly erroneous; if the interrogative is kept, we must also read καταπιῇ with A. But the indefinite is somewhat feeble — 'seeking someone to devour'; and it is likely that ζητῶν καταπιεῖν is the true reading, and that all the variants are merely attempts to remove the difficulty of the absolute καταπιεῖν. The idea of 'devouring' belongs, of course, to the figure of the lion. Men are 'devoured' (or 'swallowed up') by Satan, when under the pressure of persecution they apostatize.

v. 9. εἰδότες . . . ἐπιτελεῖσθαι⟩ This clause is full of difficulties; almost every word offers a problem. οἶδα followed by the infinitive cannot mean 'know that', but 'know how to', 'be schooled to', 'be able to'. ἐπιτελεῖσθαι therefore must be taken as middle, not passive; and τὰ αὐτά is not the subject of the infinitive, but its object. The general force of ἐπιτελέω is 'bring to an end, complete, accomplish fully'. Its use here has been explained by reference to the phrase of Xenophon (*Memorab.* iv. 8.8) τὰ τοῦ γήρως ἐπιτελεῖσθαι 'to pay the tax of old age', i.e., to suffer from the disabilities of old age. This is not really a very satisfactory parallel. A better approach to the interpretation is offered if we take the middle of ἐπιτελέω in a sense which is well established for the active in the classical writers, of 'fulfil a religious duty', 'perform the obligations of piety'. This would give point to the phrasing τὰ αὐτὰ τῶν παθημάτων in place of the simpler τὰ αὐτὰ παθήματα; τὰ αὐτά will be a cognate accusative with ἐπιτελεῖσθαι 'to make the same fulfilment (of duty towards God)', and τῶν παθημάτων will be a genitive of definition. The dative ἀδελφότητι is unusual, standing in direct dependence on αὐτά. The word, peculiar in the New Testament to First Peter, expresses the solidarity of the community in the face of persecution, and emphasizes the thought that this is not an ordeal of individual Christians but of the 'house of God' (4:17).

ἐν τῷ κόσμῳ) suggesting not so much that the persecution is world-wide, as that the 'meed of suffering' is inseparable from the experience of Christians so long as they are 'in the world'. Cf. John 16:33 — ἐν τῷ κόσμῳ θλῖψιν ἔχετε — 'In the world, ye have tribulation'; and John 13:1 — ἀγαπήσας τοὺς ἰδίους τοὺς ἐν τῷ κόσμῳ.

v. 10. A final assurance of the providence of God, who will in the end make them fit for the glorious destiny to which He has called them in Christ.

πάσης χάριτος) God is 'the God of all grace' in that grace governs all His dealings with His people, and in that from Him all grace proceeds. His grace has already been manifested to them in the call to have part in His eternal glory; and will be manifested further in the future, when He will heal and strengthen them. On the 'call' of God, the thought of the Divine initiative to which they have responded, cf. 1:15; and the frequent expression in the Pauline Epistles, e.g., 2 Thessalonians 2:13-14 εἵλατο ὑμᾶς ἀπ' ἀρχῆς εἰς σωτηρίαν . . . εἰς ὃ καὶ ἐκάλεσεν ὑμᾶς διὰ τοῦ εὐαγγελίου ἡμῶν, εἰς περιποίησιν δόξης τοῦ Κυρίου ἡμῶν Ἰησοῦ Χριστοῦ.

ὀλίγον παθόντας) 'after ye have suffered for a little' — not minimizing the severity of their sufferings, but reminding them of the limited time for which they must endure in contrast to the 'eternal' glory that is set before them. Cf. ὀλίγον ἄρτι . . . λυπηθέντες (1:6).

αὐτός) The pronoun is emphatic, linking the promised future blessings of God to the call that has already brought them into His fold. Cf. Philippians 1:6 — ὁ ἐναρξάμενος ἐν ὑμῖν ἔργον ἀγαθὸν ἐπιτελέσει ἄχρι ἡμέρας Ἰησοῦ Χριστοῦ — 'He that has begun a good work in you will bring it to completion, until the day of Christ Jesus'; and I Thess. 5:24 — πιστὸς ὁ καλῶν ὑμᾶς ὃς καὶ ποιήσει.

καταρτίσει, etc.⟩ The best witnesses are united in reading the future in all four verbs; the aorist optative is found only in late and inferior manuscripts; and is probably influenced by the καταρτίσαι ὑμᾶς in Hebrews 13:21; cf. the optatives of I Thess. 5:23.

θεμελιώσει, omitted in B, A, a handful of cursives, and the Vulgate, is rejected by Hort. It is, however, difficult to account for the intrusion of such an unusual verb, whereas it could easily fall out through homoioteleuton.

καταρτίζω is used of repairing and refitting a damaged vessel. Something of this thought attaches to the word here. God will repair the ravages of persecution and make them fit for perfect service to Him. This general assurance is set forth more particularly in the three following verbs. The persecuted Christians must not be discouraged by moments of wavering; God will give them firmness (στηρίξει). If they display a passing weakness, let them be assured that He will give them strength (σθενώσει). Finally, if the ground on which they stand seems to tremble, let them know that He will set them on a firm foundation; their faith will pass into perfect knowledge.

v. 11. On the form of the doxology, see 4:11, *note*. ἡ δόξα καὶ in this passage is an intrusion from the former doxology; it is not found in any good witnesses except ℵ and 33.

¹² Διὰ Σιλουανοῦ ὑμῖν τοῦ πιστοῦ ἀδελφοῦ, ὡς λογίζομαι, δι' ὀλίγων ἔγραψα, παρακαλῶν καὶ ἐπιμαρτυρῶν, ταύτην εἶναι ἀληθῆ χάριν τοῦ θεοῦ· εἰς ἣν στῆτε. ¹³ Ἀσπάζεται ὑμᾶς ἡ ἐν Βαβυλῶνι συνεκλεκτὴ καὶ Μᾶρκος ὁ υἱός μου. ¹⁴ Ἀσπάσασθε ἀλλήλους ἐν φιλήματι ἀγάπης. Εἰρήνη ὑμῖν πᾶσιν τοῖς ἐν Χριστῷ.

IV. THE CLOSING GREETINGS

By the hand of Silvanus, the faithful brother, as I count him, I have written to you briefly, exhorting you and confirming the testimony that this is the true grace of God: in it, stand firm.

Your sister-church in Babylon sends you greetings, as does Marcus my son. Greet one another with a kiss of love.

Peace be with all you that are in Christ.

¹² στητε) εστηκατε ϛ   ¹³ συνεκλεκτη)+εκκλησια ℵ vg syrᵖ   ¹⁴ αγαπης) αγιω minusc. pauc.   Χριστω)+Ιησου αμην ℵ ϛ (vg) syrᵖ boh

The personal allusions in this subscription will be interpreted quite differently, according to our judgment of the authenticity of the letter. For those who regard it as the work of Peter, Silvanus is the amanuensis and interpreter, to whom Peter has entrusted the task of presenting his message in smooth-flowing Greek; the suggestion is sometimes added that Peter wrote these last sentences in his own hand. Kühl, however, takes it that Silvanus is merely the messenger who is to carry the letter through the provinces. The commendation of Silvanus as a faithful brother in Peter's estimation is intended, some commentators think, to counteract a possible distrust of him in some parts of Asia Minor. The συνεκλεκτή is generally taken to signify the church (at Rome); but it is thought necessary to discuss the conjecture that Peter here refers to his wife. 'Babylon' is variously interpreted — (1) of the Roman garrison-city on the Nile, just above the present Cairo; (2) of the ancient Mesopotamian capital; and (3) of Rome. Mark is called Peter's 'son' in affectionate recognition of close spiritual relationship, as Paul calls Timothy his 'beloved child' (1 Corinthians 4:17).

To those who reject the attribution of the letter to Peter, whether of his own composition or in collaboration with Silvanus, the personal allusions offer no obstacle. The men who are here mentioned are prominent figures of the Apostolic Age, their names familiar to all Christians; it required no great effort of the

imagination to place Marcus and Silvanus in the entourage of
Peter at Rome. In an authentic letter, on the other hand, it would
be somewhat surprising to find that there was not a single Asian
Christian in Rome who would desire Peter to send his greetings
to his persecuted countrymen; cf. the long list of those who send
greetings to Colossae by Paul (Col. 4:10-14).

v. 12. διὰ Σ. ἔγραψα⟩ cannot in any case mean that Silvanus is merely
the bearer of the letter. It is simply fatuous to think of a single courier
conveying such a letter to all parts of the four provinces mentioned in
the Address; it would take him months, or even years to accomplish
such a task. Silvanus is mentioned as the amanuensis, nothing less, but
also nothing more. The employment of 'ghosts' is not likely to have
occurred to the Apostles, and the attempt to get around the linguistic
impossibility of ascribing the letter to Peter by making Silvanus responsible for the good Greek is a device of desperation.[1] Paul made no
difficulty about naming his younger colleagues as co-authors with
himself (Sosthenes in 1 Cor.; Timothy in 2 Cor., Phil., Col.; Silvanus
and Timothy in 1 and 2 Thess.); and if Silvanus had had the large part
in the framing of this letter that these theories of 'ghost-writing' are
compelled to allow, we might reasonably count on him being named
with Peter in the salutation.

δι' ὀλίγων⟩ 'briefly'. As letters go, First Peter cannot be called 'brief';
the phrase is, however, less exaggerated than the διὰ βράχεων of Hebrews
13:22. In both cases the writer is thinking of the magnitude of his
theme, and the multitude of thoughts bearing upon it which remain
unexpressed in his mind.

ἔγραψα is the epistolary aorist—'I am writing'. παρακαλῶν is used
absolutely; the accusative and infinitive clause depends on the second
participle alone. ἐπιμαρτυρῶν—'confirming the testimony'. The preposition has the force of 'adding' to the testimony that had previously
been given. They had been instructed in the meaning of the Gospel
and its expression in life, in earlier days; they might now, in the
bewilderment caused by the persecution, begin to wonder whether they
were indeed pleasing God, or whether they had brought the vengeance
of heaven upon themselves by abandoning their ancient religion to
embrace the faith of Christ. The letter confirms the earlier testimony.
'This is the true grace of God.' Persecution and suffering belong to it,
and do not bring its truth into question.

v. 13. ἐν βαβυλῶνι⟩ 'Babylon' is undoubtedly a cryptic reference to
Rome; there is nothing to connect the memory of Peter with either
Egypt or Mesopotamia. The use of the symbolical designation is
another — though not in itself decisive — indication of pseudepigraphy;
such a letter is much more likely to have been written by an Asian leader
in Asia than by someone in distant Rome.

[1] See the further discussion of the Silvanus hypothesis in the essay on 'First
Peter in Recent Criticism' (1946-1969)', pp. 212ff.

συνεκλεκτή⟩ The addition ἐκκλησία, found in ℵ and a few cursives, and represented in the Vulgate and the Peshitto, is interpretative; the interpretation is certainly correct. This word again suggests an Asian origin; cf. 2 John 1, 13, where 'the elect lady' and 'thy elect sister' clearly refer to churches.

Μάρκος ὁ υἱός μου⟩ Mark was the nephew of Barnabas, who accompanied Paul and Barnabas on part of their 'First Missionary Journey', and is later found with Paul at Rome. According to later tradition, he accompanied Peter as his interpreter, and received from him the reminiscences of Jesus which he gathered together and published in the Gospel that bears his name.

v. 14. The exchange of the kiss in the early Christian meetings is mentioned also in several of the Pauline letters; Paul uses the phrase ἐν φιλήματι ἁγίῳ, and this reading has been introduced into some manuscripts of First Peter in this passage. In the middle of the second century, Justin Martyr again refers to the custom; later, it fell into disuse.

The closing benediction is unique; the Pauline and deutero-Pauline letters invariably speak of 'grace', usually of 'the grace of the Lord Jesus Christ'. The words used here may reflect a form of benediction which was spoken at the close of sermons.

SUPPLEMENT

FIRST PETER IN RECENT CRITICISM (1946-1969).

I.   DEFENCE OF THE AUTHENTICITY OF THE EPISTLE: THE SILVANUS HYPOTHESIS.

A few months before my own commentary was to appear, Dean Selwyn's massive work was published. It offered a strong defence of the Petrine authorship of the Epistle, not indeed in the sense that the Apostle actually composed the letter, but that he employed the services of Silvanus as a secretary to whom he accorded the widest freedom in the task of putting his teachings and exhortations into good literary shape.

This was not, indeed, a new hypothesis; in one form or another, it had been put forward by a considerable number of nineteenth century critics (Weisse, Ewald, Gardthausen, Spitta, Usteri, and others). Some of them went further still. Recognizing that the historical situation envisaged in the Epistle made it impossible to accept it as a document written during the lifetime of St. Peter, they raised the possibility that it had been composed by Silvanus himself, perhaps with some assistance from Mark, a generation after the death of the Apostle, in his name and spirit (von Soden, Seuffert). Von Soden thus asks: 'Why should it be impossible that twenty-five years after Peter's death his faithful helpers, Silvanus in company with Mark, on the occasion of a wave of persecution which had broken over all Asia Minor, should allow the Apostle, who had once laboured there and was now in glory, to send his counsel of courage and steadfastness?' (Commentary, ad 5:12-13). This suggestion was further elaborated nearly thirty years later by W. Bornemann in an article in the *Zeitschrift für die neutestamentliche Wissenschaft* 19 (1919-20), under the title 'Der erste Petrusbrief-eine Taufrede des Sylvanus?' He revived Harnack's hypothesis that the document was not an epistle at all, that it was sent out in the first instance without the address or the concluding greetings (apart from the one phrase διὰ Σιλουανοῦ), and that 1:1-2 and 5:12-14 were added subsequently, when the origin of the work had been forgotten and it was necessary to give an apostolic name to a treasured possession of the Asian churches. He imagines a gathering of Christian leaders from all the provinces of Asia Minor about A.D. 90. The aged Silvanus was present and was invited to address the gathering; he delivered a sermon on Psalm 34, to the admiration of all. Nothing would content them but that he should revise it for publication, and this he did, giving it the form which it now has in I Peter 1:3-5:11; and it was copied and circulated in the churches of the region, with the appended note διὰ Σιλουανοῦ. This fascinating but wholly fanciful reconstruction has been all but matched, as we shall see, in Dr. Selwyn's romantic portrait of Silvanus.

Dean Selwyn was far from thinking of Silvanus as composing the letter independently, long after the Apostle's death. He represented the letter as the fruit of a close collaboration between congenial associates; long nights under the stars in his fishing-boat on the lake of Galilee will have developed in St. Peter a strain of poetry, which 'would not give him the style of I Peter, but . . . would give him the qualities of mind which would have made him see in the cultured Silvanus a kindred soul after his own heart' (p. 27). We shall return to this 'cultured' Silvanus conjured up by Dr. Selwyn's imagination. The new element which he contributes to the development of the hypothesis does not lie in such fanciful delineations of a character which is in fact virtually unknown, but in the attempt to show (1) that I Peter has close links with the epistles of St. Paul to the Thessalonians, in which Silvanus is named as joint author; and (2) that Silvanus may be supposed to have done a good deal of the actual work of composition of those letters for St. Paul, as here for St. Peter. Unfortunately, there is not the slightest resemblance in style between the Thessalonian epistles and I Peter. As W. L. Knox remarked in his review of Selwyn (*Theology* XLIX, No. 317, November, 1946, pp. 342-44), 'I and II Thessalonians are, next to Galatians, the low-water mark of Pauline style.' If Silvanus helped with their composition, he failed signally to communicate anything of 'the magic of Greek style' which Selwyn finds throughout I Peter (p. 27); and the apocalyptic revelations of the Pauline epistles have been quite abandoned. Moreover, it would be hard to find a writing in the New Testament more different in its underlying tone from I Peter, than II Thessalonians; directed as it is to a situation of acute persecution, it is penetrated with a sombre menace that is far removed from the warmth and inextinguishable joy of I Peter. It may be remarked that the latest editor of the Thessalonian epistles, Father B. Rigaux, rejects flatly the hypothesis that Silvanus had a hand in their composition. 'Le recours à Silvain est inutile,' he tells us, 'et contredit par ce que nous savons avec certitude des méthodes pauliniennes dans la rédaction des lettres Même en supposant Silvain secrétaire, les mots, la grammaire, les phrases et les pensées sont de Paul' (*Saint Paul: Les Épitres aux Thessaloniciens* [Gembloux: Duculot; and Paris: Gabalda, 1956] 'Etudes Bibliques,' p. 107; and see the whole acute criticism of Selwyn's position, pp. 105-111). The relationship between I Peter and the Thessalonian epistles is most naturally understood (it must be said that Rigaux does not agree) as one of direct literary dependence.

The fact is that Silvanus, for what little we know of him, is no more likely to have been capable of writing such a work as I Peter than the Apostle himself. They came from the same background—the primitive church in Jerusalem. To quote Selwyn's own words: 'It is evident that both (Judas Barsabbas and Silas-Silvanus) were men of recognized standing in the Church at Jerusalem, such as would hardly have been conceded to any but members of the original circle of Christians there' (p. 11). There is no indication that he belonged to the Hellenist group associated with Stephen and Philip. Nor is there anything whatsoever in the narrative of Acts to give substance to the fanciful picture of him which Selwyn draws—the 'charm and polish' which 'the leading society women' of Thessalonica and Philippi found 'more attractive perhaps than the ruggedness of St. Paul' (p. 13). The fact is that unless it be first conceded that Silvanus is responsible for the Greek of I Peter, with its wealth of classical allusions (see Selwyn's Index II, giving references to no less than forty-four Greek writers), there is nothing to lead us to imagine that he was likely to be capable of writing it. To quote again from the review of W. L. Knox: 'The primary problem of authorship is the question—Who in the early Church could produce this admirable essay in rhythmical prose of the Attic type? . . . The argument that Silvanus in 5:12 may have been the draftsman, not merely the messenger, that he may be Paul's companion Silas, that he may have been the draftsman of the Thessalonian letters, fails to meet the point.' This 'essay in the adaptation of Christianity to Hellenism', as Knox terms it, is hardly likely to have been composed before the second or third generation. It may be observed that the essential Hellenism of the ethical teaching of I Peter is fully recognized by Van Unnik, though he does not find in this any ground for denying the Petrine authorship, mediated through Silvanus (see page 170, *supra*).[1]

It is clear that the part of St. Peter in the writing of the Epistle is greatly reduced in this form of the Silvanus hypothesis—to the point, indeed, that one wonders what can be allotted to the Apostle's responsibility at all. Selwyn tells us (1) that he lent the epistle the weight of Apostolic authority which the churches needed in their time of trial (this, be it remarked, might be offered as a good reason for the unknown author to issue his homily under an apostolic name); and (2) that 'an

---

[1] The Hellenic character of the vocabulary is fully recognized by Selwyn also, though it does not lead him to draw the (to me) natural consequences. 'It is not without significance,' he writes, 'that Liddell and Scott's *Greek Lexicon* throws far more light on this Epistle than Moulton and Milligan's *Vocabulary of the Greek Testament*: its affinities, that is to say, are far less with the vernacular of the papyri and the *ostraka* than with literary Greek' (pp. 26–7). I might add that there is perhaps no book in the New Testament which has less light shed upon it from Billerbeck's *Kommentar zum N.T. aus Talmud und Midrasch*; and despite the best will in the world, I have not been able to fall in with the current vogue of the Dead Sea Scrolls by finding anything in them that would have any particular bearing upon the interpretation of the epistle. See, however, the article of K. G. Kuhn, 'Πειρασμός, ἁμαρτία, σάρξ' im N.T. und die damit zusammenhängenden Vorstellungen', in *Zeitschrift für Theologie und Kirche* 49 (1952), pp. 204–208; and Nauck's comments ('Freude im Leiden', pp. 77–79: these associated ideas have their roots in the Maccabaean troubles and the literature to which they gave rise).

impression of eye-witness runs through the Epistle, and gives it a distinctive character' (p. 28). I find these traces of eye-witness singularly unconvincing. The argument, as Selwyn presents it, involves a succession of critical assumptions that are questionable, to say the least. Is 'the substance of the risen Lord's teaching on the way to Emmaus' (p. 29) really to be taken as the report of an actual conversation? Are the words attributed to St. James at the Council of Jerusalem to be taken for anything resembling a stenographic report, or even for something remotely resembling what was then said (the whole point of the citation depends upon the error in the LXX text of Amos); or are they a relatively free composition of the author of Acts? And if the second clause in 5:1 'referred, and would have been accepted as referring, to the Transfiguration and to St. Peter's part in it ' (pp. 30-31), does this not involve a somewhat literal acceptance of the Transfiguration (which in St. Matthew is called a 'vision')? If the story is not wholly legendary, as many reputable scholars would take it to be, would St. Peter himself have described his drowsy part in it as a participation in the glory to be revealed? Can we take Christ's charge to St. Peter in John 21:15-17 as any more likely to be a report of words spoken by the risen Christ than are the discourses of the body of the Gospel to be taken as the report of words spoken by the historical Jesus? Can we then say that 'the command to tend (ποιμάνατε) the flock of God in their midst would come with special force from one who had received Christ's last charge to do this very thing?' (p. 31). If John 21 comes into the matter at all, I should take it rather as evidence that the Epistle was later than the Fourth Gospel (i.e., *post* A.D. 100). And was Peter, in the Gospel story, 'a witness of the sufferings of Christ', (if we are talking about eyewitness)? According to Mark 14:50, when Jesus was arrested, 'they all forsook him and fled.' Finally, and above all, the appeal to the Passion in 2:21-25, far from affording evidence that the writer was an eye-witness, suggests rather one whose knowledge of the Passion is literary and theological (apart, that is, from its *religious* power), since it is framed wholly in phrases of the Second Isaiah and the Apostle Paul; there is not a shred of personal reminiscence.

Selwyn's defence of the Petrine authorship, in this sense of a Petrine collaboration with Silvanus, was accepted widely by British scholars, though not so unanimously as would appear from the publications. It was warmly supported by Bishop Headlam in a lengthy review (*CQR* 142. No. 283, April-June, 1946, pp. 98-118) and is adopted in the brief commentaries of Cranfield and Hunter (without serious discussion). Archbishop Carrington defended it, with an attempt at refutation of my arguments, in his essay in *The Joy of Study*. It was rejected by Professor D. E. Nineham (*Central Society of Sacred Study*: Leaflet No. 189, April 1947), and by nearly all American scholars known to me. M. S. Enslin, for instance, reviewing Selwyn in *The Jewish Quarterly Review* (N.S. 37, 1946-47, pp. 295-299). remarks that 'his evidence is of a nature to strengthen my long-held conviction that the author was a Paulinist who drew very heavily upon several at least of the Pauline letters and that the reference to Silvanus is a pure literary fiction, a manifest reflection of Paul's similar references to Timothy'. Recent Continental writers, except for the Roman Catholics, seldom take the argument for authenticity—with or without the collaboration of Silvanus —at all seriously. Lohse, while giving high praise to Selwyn's work generally, as must all who appreciate careful and thorough scholarship, remarks that 'with secretary-hypotheses one could attempt to prove the authenticity of any letter. One unknown is replaced by another. And what have we won with all this? Can Silvanus, a member of the primitive Church, really have composed our letter? If so, why not Peter himself? Such hypotheses are of no great help to the exegesis.'

2. THE QUEST FOR SOURCE MATERIALS OR FORMS PROVIDED BY THE COMMON TRADITION OF THE CHURCH.

The claim that 'the facts of literary relationship between First Peter and several of the Pauline Epistles are patent' still seems to me to be perfectly valid, but it is certainly not unchallenged; nor can it any longer be said with even a semblance of justice that 'all critics are now agreed that the dependence is on the side of First Peter' (p. 9, *supra*). It is now held by a number of scholars that these relationships reflect not literary dependence, whether of I Peter on Paul or of Paul on I Peter; but the independent use by both writers of liturgical and cate-chetical forms already created, perhaps even circulating in written manuals, for the use of Christian teachers and preachers. This approach, which is one of the distinctive features of Dean Selwyn's commentary, has been followed and its conclusions further developed in the important articles of Lohse and Nauck, though without any thought of bringing its results forward as evidence of authenticity in any sense.[1]

Selwyn distinguishes 'four main types of material current in the Church in the middle of the first century . . . which are we entitled to describe as 'sources' (p. 17). As his fourth type is *verba Christi*, the use of which is not denied by anyone, we may confine our discussion to the first three, viz.:

(i) Liturgical—hymns and primitive credal forms. To take one example, the passage περιέχει ἐν γραφῇ (2:6) is rendered 'it says in the hymn'; and thus interpreted it is said to *prove* 'that St. Peter was here quoting from a documentary source other than the text of Scripture

---

[1] Lohse in particular explicitly dissociates the investigation of common sources from the question of authenticity, and deplores their linking in Selwyn's work. ' Selwyns gründliche Untersuchungen, die in der Tat neue Wege für das Verständnis des I Ptr weisen, sind jedoch leider durch zwei Gesichtspunkte belastet, die die sorgfältigen Einzeldarlegungen nicht zu einem richtigen Gesamt-bild zusammenzufügen vermögen: einmal wird die formgeschichtliche Arbeit unglücklich mit der Echtheitsfrage verknüpft . . .' ('Paränese und Kerygma,' p. 71).

itself' (p. 163). In an Additional Note ('E. Critical Problems of ii. 4-8'; pp. 268-277) it is pointed out that the first problem here is 'to account for the combinations of O.T. citations common to I Peter ii.4 ff. and Rom. ix, 32 ff., *and their common deviations from the Lxx* (italics mine); 'which attract attention,' he tells us later in the Note, 'because there is no doubt that both normally quote from the Lxx and not from the Hebrew'. Selwyn thinks it improbable that this came from a collection of Messianic proof-texts such as may have been compiled fairly early; he proposes that we think rather 'of a hymn already known to the recipients of the Epistle', which might underlie both I Pet. ii, 6-8 and Rom. ix, 33'. This, in his view, 'appears to account better than any other theory for their similarities and also for their deviations both from the Lxx and from one another'. I should have to agree with Father Rigaux (*op. cit.*, p. 107) that this construction is 'mounted on pins'. The hypothesis of a direct literary dependence of I Peter on Romans is far simpler and more natural.

I Pet. iii. 18-22, the Dean thinks, 'rests in all probability on the credal hymn quoted in 1 Tim. iii, 16' (pp. 17f.). But it is now all but universally agreed that I Timothy dates from no earlier than the last decade of the first century; many good scholars would bring it down to the time of Marcion; and it would be hard to prove that the 'credal hymn' in it was composed forty or more years earlier. If such a relationship between the two epistles is admitted, this points again to a date of ±A.D. 100 for I Peter.

(ii) A Persecution Fragment. It is suggested that the parallels between the Thessalonian epistles and I Peter are most easily explained by postulating the use of 'a homiletic and hortatory document' compiled 'for use by evangelists and teachers in their work of strengthening the faith of the infant Christian communities' (p. 18; and cf. Essay II, Part III, 'Teaching Called out by Crisis: Traces of a Persecution-Form (P)', pp. 439-458).

This part of the discussion is strongly developed by E. Lohse ('Paränese und Kerygma'). He discounts any direct connection of the Epistle with baptism, such as is involved in the hypothesis that it is in the main a baptismal-discourse, taking the baptismal references to be merely incidental to the main theme, which is the conduct of Christians under unmerited affliction of every kind, and especially under persecution. The author pursues his aim of comforting and strengthening Christians in distress by exploiting 'paraenetical' materials which are supplied to him by the tradition. Lohse, however, thinks primarily in terms of forms of *oral* instruction rather than written manuals. So in comparing Romans 13:1-7 with I Peter 2:13 ff., he traces the numerous parallelisms in thought and expression, but holds that they do not lead to the conclusion that the one letter stands to the other in a relation of literary dependence, but that both, independently of one another, go back to material transmitted in the tradition, probably by word of mouth ('beide gehen unabhängig voneinander auf [wahrscheinlich mündlich] überliefertes Traditionsmaterial zurück', pp. 73-4). Now it would be generally admitted, I think, that St. Paul, in Romans 13, is not introducing a new doctrine of 'Church and State', but stands in the established Christian tradition of 'Render unto Caesar the things that are Caesar's'; but I find it hard to believe that he is simply rehearsing, with minor variants, the words of a current catechetical form, written or oral. If such instruction were contained in handbooks already in general circulation, or if the Apostle can take it for granted that the unknown founders of the Roman church have given substantially the same instruction to their converts in much the same words, why does he waste half a sheet of papyrus? I see not the slightest reason to doubt that St. Paul is framing his exhortation in his own words as he goes along; they have his characteristic forthrightness and vigour; and if this be granted, then I Peter unquestionably makes use of the Pauline passage, and not of some imagined oral or written source which St. Paul happened to have at his disposal some years previously.

Nauck's article, 'Freude im Leiden,' follows Lohse and Selwyn in a critical analysis of passages which he selects from 'an abundance of examples' for the *topos* 'Persecution a Ground of Rejoicing'. His investigation has a particular interest and value in that it goes beyond the limits of Selwyn's study by making use of 'religionsgeschichtlich' material. He rejects the division of the epistle, and specifically the distinction between persecution envisaged as a possibility for which one must be prepared, and persecution as a horror which is actually being experienced, chiefly on the ground that such a distinction does not fit into the pattern of persecution-teaching, inherited from the Jewish and primitive-Christian tradition, by which he holds I Peter to be bound. This appears to me to be much too Procrustean altogether; it subordinates the data of the text before us to an overriding theory of what it ought to contain, if it is to fall into the common pattern which it is alleged to be employing. It allows no weight at all to the hypothetical εἰ δέον of 1:6, or to the naive confidence of 3:13 that if Christians will only show themselves eager for the good, no harm will come to them; together with the optatives of vv. 14 and 17, which can hardly be interpreted at all except in the sense that the writer is speaking of eventualities which are somewhat remote.

(iii) Catechetical. Here Dr. Selwyn builds upon the work of Archbishop Carrington (*The Primitive Christian Catechism:* Cambridge, C.U.P., 1940), and refers to the work done along similar lines by Professor A. M. Hunter (*Paul and his Predecessors:* London, SCM, 1940), and the much older work of A. Seeberg (*Der Katechismus der Urchristenheit* (Leipzig, 1903); there is further relevant discussion in M. Dibelius' *Brief des Jakobus* (Meyer-Kommentar 15, 8th ed., Göttingen: Vandenhoeck und Ruprecht, 1956), in the first section of his Introduction, 'Die literarische Gattung des Jakobusbriefes', pp. 1-10; and in the same scholar's *Geschichte der urchristlichen Literatur* II (Sammlung Göschen, Bd. 935:1926, pp. 65-76).

Selwyn's essay 'On the Inter-Relation of I Peter and the other N.T. Epistles' is almost a book in itself, occupying as it does 102 pages of text, with a large number of tables in which the parallel passages are set forth, and a great deal of closely-argued discussion of particular sections. It would clearly be impossible to summarize such a mass of material in a few paragraphs, or to debate the issues in any adequate way without a comparably long and involved treatment. I shall therefore content myself with saying that the evidence here presented still seems to me to point to quite different conclusions from those drawn by the Dean of Winchester. It seems to me to establish more clearly than ever the literary dependence of I Peter upon several, if not all, of the epistles of the Pauline corpus, and upon a number of other N.T. writings as well. This would indicate that it was not composed until after the Pauline letters had been collected, which can hardly be earlier than the last decade of the century. For Ephesians, the case for literary dependence would seem to have been demonstrated beyond dispute by Professor C. L. Mitton, especially in his later essay, 'The Relationship of I Peter and Ephesians' (*JTS*, n.s. I. 1, 1950), which takes direct account of Selwyn's massive argument. He examines with great care the passages in which Ephesians is 'not only closely related to I Peter, but still more closely related to Colossians' (p. 68), and finds them to be 'of decisive importance in forming a judgement on the relationship between I Peter and Ephesians' (p. 73). His final conclusion, which appears to be irresistible, is that no explanation will satisfy the facts except that 'the author of I Peter was closely enough acquainted with Ephesians for its phrasing and thought to be from time to time reproduced in his own epistle' (p. 73). This accords with a remark of Professor Goodspeed (in a personal letter dated February 16th, 1949): 'As for the haustafeln idea, we at Chicago were never able to find any such "haustafeln" as it is claimed anciently existed. Most scholars simply accept Weidinger's say-so, but the natural explanation seems to be a germ in Col., expanding in Eph., and then in I Peter'. I entirely agree. But as the deutero-Pauline character of Ephesians has been amply demonstrated by Goodspeed[1] and Mitton,[2] to say nothing of my colleague Professor George Johnston,[3] the late W. L. Knox,[4] and myself,[5] the demonstration of its use by I Peter at the

[1] Most recently, *The Key to Ephesians* (Chicago: Univ. of Chicago Press, 1956).
[2] *The Epistle to the Ephesians* (Oxford: Clarendon Press, 1951).
[3] *The Doctrine of the Church in the New Testament* (Cambridge C.U.P., 1943). Detached Note A. 'The Authenticity of "Ephesians",' pp. 136–140.
[4] *St. Paul and the Church of the Gentiles*, c. IX, 'The Ephesian Continuator' (Cambridge: C.U.P., 1939).
[5] 'The Epistle to the Ephesians: Introduction and Exegesis', in *The Interpreter's Bible*, Vol. X, (New York and Nashville: Abingdon Press, 1953), pp. 597 ff.

same time rules out all possibility of Petrine authorship, mediated or not through Silvanus. St. Peter was certainly dead before Ephesians was written.[1]

The application of form-critical methods to the analysis has yielded and will yield valuable results. But it is well to keep in mind that even in the study of the Gospels, the use of the techniques of form-criticism does not obliterate the facts of *literary* dependence; the most ardent form critic will be the first to admit the literary dependence of Matthew and Luke on Mark, if not also on the hypothetical 'Q'. Even if the existence of catechetical and liturgical forms in the first century could be much more amply demonstrated, this would not rule out the facts of literary dependence, as of Ephesians on Colossians, and of I Peter on Ephesians.

3. THE NATURE AND PURPOSE OF THE EPISTLE.

The view that I Peter is in the main a baptismal discourse is now widely shared, but a number of scholars (Selwyn, Lohse, Moule, Bieder and others) are inclined to regard the references to baptism as more or less incidental. Professor Moule, who 'whole-heartedly agrees that I Peter is connected with baptism', discounts the effect of this admission by continuing: 'But this much is true, of course, of many other parts of the New Testament . . .; and in itself, it proves no more than that the early Church writers continually had the 'pattern' of baptism in mind." Lohse also doubts whether baptism is really the central theme of the body of the letter. In his view, the real theme is found in the encouragement of suffering Christians. Preisker, on the other hand, in his supplement to Windisch's commentary, treats the epistle as the transcript of a baptismal service (ein urchristlicher Gottesdienst einer Taufgemeinde), which from 4:12 merges into the conclusion of a general service (Schlussgottesdienst der Gesamtgemeinde); thus we have before us 'das älteste Dokument eines urchristlichen Gottesdienstes' (p. 157). Professor Cross, concurring in the main with Preisker's analysis, is able to point to a remarkable series of parallelisms with the Paschal rites of the *Apostolic Tradition* of Hippolytus (Baptism and Confirmation followed by Eucharist); and he ventures to suggest that I Peter is less a homily than a liturgy (he notes that the distinction is not sharply drawn in early times), and that it is nothing else than ' the Celebrant's part for the Paschal Vigil, for which, as the most solemn occasion in the Church's year, the Baptismal-Eucharistic text must have been very carefully prepared' (p. 31). Cross is rather at a loss to fit the latter

[1] The Abbot of Downside (*Dominican Studies*, July, 1948, pp. 266-270), thinks ' that to attribute Ephesians to a later "Paulinist" and not to St. Paul himself, seems to me comparable to affirming that Shakespeare had a disciple capable of writing *The Tempest*'. Yet he will remember that Socrates had a disciple capable of writing the *Republic*, and Plato had a disciple capable of writing the *Nicomachean Ethics*. Such a succession of genius is not *utterly* inconceivable in first century Christianity.

part of the Epistle (4:12 ff.) into his theory; but with respect to the former part of it, he stresses the almost artificial, certainly thematic, character of the references to suffering (pp. 19-20), and suggests that the writer is playing variations on the theme πάσχα-πάσχω,[1] as later Greek theologians were wont to do (Melito, Hippolytus, Cyril of Alexandria, and others). We find ourselves faced, accordingly, with two diametrically opposite interpretations: (1) that the Epistle is essentially a persecution-document, making incidental references to baptism, and (2) that the Epistle is essentially a baptismal or baptismal-eucharistic document, which makes incidental references to persecution as an aspect of the life which is entered upon at Baptism.

Opinions are again sharply divided over the question of whether there is a significant break after 4:11. Those who view the epistle as a persecution-document hold as a rule that there is no break in the thought here (Selwyn, Lohse, Nauck). Nauck, for instance, convinced that the author of I Peter leans more heavily upon the established tradition than any other writer in the New Testament, insists that in both parts of the epistle the references to the suffering of Christians must be traced back to their roots in Jewish and primitive Christian *Verfolgungstradition*, and that within the framework of this tradition 'it is no more possible to speak hypothetically of joy, conflict, and persecution than to speak hypothetically of faith' ('Freude und Leiden', p. 80). The references to persecution before 4:11 must therefore be just as concrete as those of the later verses. Moule, on the other hand, is sufficiently impressed by the more concrete character of the references after 4:11 to propose that 'the writer sent two forms of epistle, one for those not yet under actual duress (i. 1-iv. 11 and v. 12-14), and the other—terser and swifter—for those who were in the refining fire (i. 1-ii. 10, iv. 12-v. 14)'. A similar suggestion was made long ago by J. H. A. Hart in *Expositor's Greek Testament*,[2] but Moule supports it with new arguments, which are somewhat less than convincing. Those who take the epistle to be a baptismal document are unanimous in perceiving a significant break after the doxology of 4:11.

Preisker's analysis of the structure of the epistle is grounded in the first instance on considerations of style. He holds that the following problems remain to be solved. It may be remarked that he is clearly not acquainted with my commentary, which meets most of his questions; but Hauck has already gone a long way to answer them.

(1) Before 4:11, sufferings of Christians are spoken of only as a possibility (nur gleichsam konditional, hypothetisch); after 4:11 concrete sufferings under persecution are envisaged. Granted.

---

[1] It is worth noting that Cross (quite rightly) takes the use of the word-play πάσχα-πάσχω as sufficient in itself to prove that Melito's *Homily on the Passion* was composed in Greek, not Syriac (n. 6, p. 45); the play on the words would be impossible in the Semitic tongue. (Would it then occur to St. Peter?)

[2] Vol. V. London: Hodder and Stoughton, 1910.

(2) No satisfactory explanation has been offered of how and why this particular exhortation (Mahnschreiben) of 4:12 ff. has been attached to the baptismal discourse. If it is an actual outbreak of persecution that has occasioned the addition, why was not the whole of the discourse adapted to the new situation?—a simple thing to do. A good enough question, but preachers have been known, like other people, to leave undone the things which they ought to have done. He probably saw no necessity to revise his sermon.

(3) The change of tenses with 1:22 is not sufficiently explained. In the preceding verses, we have *injunctions* to holiness; from v. 22, we have *affirmations* that they have sanctified their souls; they are 'newborn infants'. Yet surely the contrast is overstated. In v. 3 their regeneration is mentioned as an accomplished fact: God is blessed as 'He who has begotten (ἀναγεννήσας) us'; surely the speaker is not excluding from the ranks of the newborn the people to whom he is speaking; here at least he is not speaking of this 'als von einem Imperativ und zukünftigen Akt'.

(4) The document consists of separate, self-contained sections, laid side by side without transitions, each with its own stylistic peculiarities.

These observations lead to the proposal to treat the work as neither epistolary nor homiletic, but liturgical in character: 'the earliest documentation of an early Christian service of worship'. Failure to mention the action of baptism is ascribed to *Arkandisziplin*. The writing is then analyzed as follows, with particular attention to the variations in style as we move from section to section.

1:3-12. A 'Prayer-psalm' (Gebetspsalm), with a strong eschatological flavour. There is a distinct weakness in the interpretation of the present participle φρουρουμένους as anticipating the *future* privilege of the baptizands who are addressed. It seems quite arbitrary to neglect the aorist ἀναγεννήσας and to treat the present participle as a future. The plain sense of the text is that God *has* regenerated them, and they *are being guarded* by his power. What justification is there for saying that this really means that they *will* be reborn and *will* come under the protection of God's power after they have been baptized?

1:13-21. A 'Teaching Discourse' (belehrende Rede — διδαχή), employing liturgical formulas which point to the approaching baptism, with a lavish use of O.T. themes (holiness in conformity with God's holiness, fear of God, redemption through sacrifice).

It is postulated that the candidates to whom the foregoing words have been addressed are actually baptized at this point.

1:22-25. A short 'Baptismal Dedication' (Taufvotum—ἐπευχή). Let us remark, however, that the centre of this paragraph is still imperative—ἀλλήλους ἀγαπήσατε ἐκτενῶς, 'love one another earnestly'. Preisker is so fully persuaded that the writer is greatly concerned to dampen 'enthusiasm', the wildness to which eschatological expectations could give rise, that he makes the absence of an 'enthusiastic' hymn the

chief feature of this section: 'Bezeichnend ist, dass sich an den Ein-
weihungsakt nicht ein enthusiasticher Hymnus anschliesst'. Is this
really of such significance? Was there an imminent danger that the
newly-baptized would forthwith break out into Montanist or Millerite
extravagances?

2:1-10. A 'Festal Song' in three strophes, which is ascribed to a
Spirit-filled individual (Pneumatiker).

2:11-3:12. An 'Exhortation' (Paränese), which is attributed to 'a
new preacher' who stands up in the meeting. In the midst of his
sermon, the congregation bursts in with a 'Christ-hymn' (Christuslied,
Ψαλμός—2:21-24). Here Preisker appears to adopt Bultmann's thesis
('Bekenntniss- und Liedfragmente'). Must we really take this hyper-
imaginative reconstruction seriously?

3:13-4:7a. An Apocalypse, apparently conceived as contributed by
still another participant in the service—'ein Apokalyptiker'. A singularly gifted group of collaborators, almost certainly imported from I
Corinthians 14, as if that gave a standing pattern of Christian public
worship. The 'potential optatives' of 3:14 and 17 are taken as 'stylistic
peculiarities'; they are, however, easily enough explained on other
grounds (see my notes, *ad loc.*).

4:7b-11. An 'epistolary substitute' (briefgemässe Ersatz) for the
Closing Prayer (the prayer is reshaped into an exhortation!)

At this point the baptismal service is over; the remainder of the
epistle is a Closing Service (Schlussgottesdienst) for the whole congregation. This is the reason why persecution is now spoken of as a fact of
experience, no longer as a mere possibility which must be envisaged.

4:12-19. Another 'Apocalypse'.

5:1-9. A 'Hortatory Discourse' (Mahnrede) to the presbyters, the
youth, and finally the whole assembly; we are now being edified again
by the same preacher as in 2:11-3:12; he likes the imperatival participle,
the particle ὁμοίως, and the verb ὑποτάσσω.

5:10 The closing Blessing, pronounced by a presbyter, who has
presumably been sitting quietly in a corner until this time.

5:11. The Doxology, in which the whole congregation joins.

The opening and closing formulas have only to be added, and the
'epistle' is ready to be sent on its way. The Roman church, the heir of
St. Peter, writes in his name to the Asian churches and communicates
to them the order of divine service for the administration of baptism,
conceived in the spirit of the martyred Apostle. It is committed to writing
by the scribe Silvanus, a Christian of the second or third generation.

Lohse ('Paränese und Kerygma') accepts the distinctions of style
which Preisker has alleged, but holds that he has taken the wrong way
of accounting for them. He is not prepared to grant that there is any
evidence to support the theory that the individual prophets would have
prepared a written version of what they had offered to the church in the
way of exhortations and revelations, or that there was this varying

succession of psalm, teaching discourse, hymn, exhortation and apocalypse in the service of worship. One would indeed be inclined to
feel that the free participation of a number of gifted members in the
service would not be likely to be accompanied by the reduction of these
inspired outbursts to writing. It is doubtful if the charismatics of
Corinth, who appear to be in the back of Preisker's mind, would ever
have been capable of producing a written record of their 'hymns,
lessons, revelations, tongues and interpretations' (I Cor. 14:26 ff.).
Lohse would take the stylistic differences as evidence of provenance
from different sources.[1] Here he links hands with Selwyn, though with
much less confidence that the sources employed by the writer were
available to him in writing, and he deprecates any attempt to reconstruct
such sources.[2] He finds that the first main section of the letter (1:3-2:10)
introduced by a 'prayer-psalm' (Preisker's term) which differs markedly
in style from all the rest of the book, takes as its main theme the holy
People of God; and he claims that this governing thought 'reminds us
in astonishing fashion of the Palestine texts and the Damascus-docu-
ment' (p. 78). It is a question, however, if anything is gained by fishing
in the Dead Sea Scrolls for the background of phrases like ἔθνος
ἅγιον (p. 79), which come directly out of LXX. And I must confess
that I am not in the least inclined to agree that the features which
Preisker and Lohse regard as stylistic pecularities indicating a change
of speaker or of underlying source material are in fact anything more
than the variations of a good prose stylist. All through the epistle, we
have a rhythmical prose of exceptional attractiveness and a quiet
warmth of feeling, such as is hardly conceivable in a patchwork such as
Preisker and Lohse, in their different ways, propose to us.

Professor Cross also regards the epistle as liturgical, but in a different
sense. He relates it specifically to the rites described in the *Apostolic
Tradition* of Hippolytus, which 'gives us a detailed account of the
Paschal Baptism and Confirmation Rite, followed by the Eucharist'
(p. 9). But far from thinking of it as the transcript of a series of charismatic outbursts by a succession of participants, he sees in it the carefully prepared text of ' the Celebrant's part for the Paschal Vigil . . . the
most solemn occasion of the Church's year' (p. 37). In his analysis,
which closely follows that of Preisker, he refers to the Celebrant—
'without prejudice'—as the 'Bishop'. He is sure that Preisker is right in
holding that 'the body of the "Epistle" is a liturgical text, the successive
sections of which are a series of formularies for use in the Baptismal
Rite' (p. 38). His own analysis runs as follows:

---

[1] Die Stilunterschiede . . . erklären sich nicht durch die Abfolge eines Gottesdienstes, in dem mehrere Prediger zu Worte kommen, sondern müssen aus der
verschiedenen Herkunft des Traditionsgutes hergeleitet werden (p. 72).

[2] Gegen ein solches konstruktives Verfahren werden immer gewichtige Ein-
wendungen zu erheben sein, weil man sich dabei zu leicht auf das Gebiet von
nicht beweisbaren Hypothesen begibt (p. 72).

1:3-12   Opening Prayer.
1:13-21   Formal Charge to the Candidates;
          at its conclusion, the actual Baptism.
1:22-25   Welcome of the Newly Baptized into the Redeemed Com-
          munity.
2:1-10   Address on the Fundamentals of the Sacramental Life;
          at its conclusion, the Eucharistic Consecration and the
          Communion of the Newly Baptized.
2:11-4:6 Address on the Duties of Christian Discipleship.
4:7-11   Final Admonitions and Doxology.
The remainder may be an address to the whole congregation, gathered
with the newly baptized.[1]

In a chapter on 'The Baptismal Setting of I Peter' (pp. 28-35),
Cross strengthens immeasurably the case for regarding the rites of
Baptism as the *leitmotif* of the Epistle. The argument for an 'Easter
setting' is perhaps less convincing,[2] though not in the least implausible;
the case here rests upon the play on the words πάσχα-πάσχω, with
the parallel usage in early Paschal orations.

But the most striking feature of this contribution offered by the great
Patristics scholar is the manner in which he relates the epistle to the
Apostolic Tradition. Unfortunately, he does not himself undertake the
exhaustive examination of the texts which would be necessary for the
demonstration of his point. But I do not see how anyone who makes
the comparison for himself can fail to see that there is a certain, even a
marked degree of formal relationship between the two documents.
As we cannot possibly date I Peter *later* than Trajan, this comparison
would appear to lead to the conclusion that Hippolytus actually does
preserve ancient material, which if not strictly 'Apostolic' does reflect
forms which were in use in the Roman church at least a century before
Hippolytus wrote his treatise. Incidentally, this leads me to abandon
the view that I Peter was produced within the region to which it is
addressed (p. 31, *supra*); a Roman origin now seems unquestionable
(see below, section 5).

The Dominican scholar M.-E. Boismard, in his two articles in the
Revue Biblique, adopts the view that I Peter is based on a baptismal
liturgy, and seeks to investigate the influence of the same liturgical
form upon Titus, I John, Colossians, and James. While so many
Anglican and Protestant scholars are still concerned to defend the
authenticity of the epistle, it is startling to find a Roman Catholic

[1] W. Nauck points out that the *Apostolic Tradition* shows unmistakeable
parallelisms also with the charge to the presbyters in c. 5 ('Probleme des frühchristlichen Amtsverständnisses,' p. 206).
[2] W. Nauck's article 'Freude im Leiden' shows quite convincingly that the
'coexistence of joy and suffering' is not merely 'the dominant note in the ethos
of Easter', but is firmly grounded in the pattern of teaching inherited from
Judaism: 'dass hier eine gemeinsame spätjüdisch-urchristliche Tradition über die
Freude angesichts des Leidens vorliegt' (p. 76).

venturing to speak of the 'redactor' of the work, and otherwise paying
no heed to the question of authorship. His analysis of the epistle seeks
to distinguish between elements borrowed from a baptismal liturgy,
and additions made by the redactor. The parts attributed to the liturgy
are the following:

1:3-5	Baptismal Hymn.
1:6-9	Fragment on Suffering and Future Glory.
1:13-21	Homily, preparatory to baptism.
1:22-2:10	Homily, following baptism.
2:11-3.7	and 5:1-5 Charge to the newly baptized, on the ideal of Christian living.
5:5-9	Baptismal Hymn, 'reprise assez librement'.
3:8-12	and 4:7-11 Concluding general charge, and doxology.

Boismard suggests that 3:13-4:6 did not form part of the primitive
baptismal liturgy, but is a composition of the redactor framed in the
same spirit. The address and the final greetings both echo the theme of
the 'exile'— the Christian sojourner in an alien land. Even 'Babylon'
is the counterpiece to 'Diaspora', and need not mean Rome. 'Je
songerais plutôt à une désignation plus générale de notre lieu d'exil,
par opposition à la patrie céleste vers laquelle nous cheminons' (II, p.
181, n. 2).

Rather than the direct use of fragments of a liturgy, the evidence
seems to me to indicate a sermon developed along lines suggested by the
structure of the liturgy, perhaps with an occasional outright quotation
of familiar credal formulas, but as a rule freely expressed in the writer's
own words and style. He quotes directly from the Greek Old Testament, though even then he feels free to adapt the words to the context
(See notes, p. 135). His use of Pauline language is not by direct
quotation, but rather by way of half-unconscious reminiscence of phrases
and thoughts which by long acquaintance have become part of him.

4. THE PLACE OF WRITING.

The mention of 'Babylon' in 5:13 has long seemed to most commentators to imply that the letter was written from Rome; and as long
as the Petrine authorship was admitted, there was every reason to
suppose that the Apostle had sent it from the capital city of the Empire
not long before his death. Once the evidences of pseudonymity were
accepted, there seemed to be good grounds for doubting that the
indication of a Roman origin was anything more than a part of the
apparatus of pseudonymity, almost a matter of course at a time when
Rome and Peter had become linked together in Christian thought. The
chief difficulty in the way of admitting that the epistle originated in
Rome lay in the lack of evidence for its use in the West in the second
century (silence of the Muratorian canon; earliest Western use in the
works of the Asian Irenaeus, etc.). This absence of Western testimony
however, can hardly be allowed to determine the issue in the face of
(a) the evident relationship between the pattern of the baptismal rite

which has left its mark on the structure of I Peter, and the old Roman
rite which is described by Hippolytus and assumed by him to be based
on ancient use; and (*b*) the relationships between I Peter and I Clement,
which seem to indicate a common background for the two letters.

The influences of a baptismal liturgy on the structure of I Peter
have been clearly enough demonstrated, especially by Cross and
Boismard; and Cross has pointed to the resemblances between it and
the liturgy of Hippolytus.[1] The points of contact between I Clement
and I Peter have been most completely drawn out by Lohse (*op. cit.*, pp.
83-85), with the conclusion that the relationships do not indicate that I
Clement has cited I Peter, but that both epistles draw upon like *Traditions-
gut* and probably had their origin in the Roman church. This solution
of the relationship between the two epistles had long since been
proposed by Goodspeed,[2] who brought his observations into the
service of his general theory that Hebrews was a challenge to the Roman
church to assume the task of teaching others (Hebrews 5:12); and that
I Clement and I Peter were written in response to this challenge, I
Peter specifically to counteract the fiery hostility to the State and the
Emperor which had recently been expressed in the Apocalypse of John.

Boismard has suggested that the epistle may have been written from
Antioch (*op. cit.*, II, p. p. 181, n. 2). From the interesting suggestion
that 'Babylon' may not after all be a cryptogram for Rome, but a more
general symbol for the land of the Christian's exile, he offers two
considerations which tell, he thinks, in favour of Antioch. First, the
doctrine of the Descent into Hell is established in the Syrian churches
very early: it appears in official *Acta* for the first time at the Council of
Sirmium in 359, under the influence of a Syrian father; its Syrian
origin is hardly open to question, 'c'est en effet un "syriacisme" pour
mentionner l'ensevelissement'. And secondly, the name 'Christian'
occurs in the New Testament in only two other places, viz., Acts
11:26—'the disciples were called Christians first in Antioch'; and Acts
28:28—the words of Agrippa to St. Paul at Caesarea; both in a Syrian
setting. The resemblances to the pattern of the Hippolytean liturgy
would not tell against this hypothesis, for there appear to be grounds
for holding that the *Apostolic Tradition* has a Syrian background. It
must be said, however, that it would become extremely difficult to
account for the absence of all trace of the Epistle in the letters of the
martyr bishop of Antioch, Ignatius; and equally, to account for the
resemblances with I Clement.

[1] An interesting bit of collateral support for Cross is contributed incidentally
by W. Nauck, who has pointed out parallelisms between the *Apostolic Tradition*
and the charge to the elders in 5:2 f. (*ZNTW* 48 [1957], p. 206: 'Die Parallelität
der beiden Texte ist nicht zu erkennen ' (p. 206).

[2] *A History of Early Christian Literature* (Chicago: Univ. of Chicago Press,
1942), p. 14. 'The resemblances of the *Letter of Clement* to I Peter are generally
taken to show his use of that letter but are probably due to the fact that both
letters emanated from the church at Rome at about the same time and probably
under the same impulse.'

ADDITIONAL NOTE

ON THE LITERATURE ATTRIBUTED TO PETER IN THE ANCIENT CHURCH

The ancient church was acquainted with at least six documents which were attributed to St. Peter, and with a book of Acts of Peter which was chiefly concerned with him. Besides the two epistles which attained canonical recognition, there was a Gospel according to Peter, an Apocalypse of Peter (second in importance only to the Apocalypse of John among the Christian apocalyptic writings), a letter of Peter to James, and an apologetic writing known as the Preaching of Peter (Κήρυγμα Πέτρου). All except the First Epistle are unquestionably works of the 2nd century, composed long after the death of the Apostle. Even the Second Epistle, despite its established place in the canon, no longer finds any serious defenders of its authenticity—it is generally dated about the middle of the 2nd century or even later.[1] Its right to a place among the scriptures was not generally acknowledged until late in the 4th century in the Greek and Latin churches, and it was never admitted by the Syrian churches except those of the Monophysites.[2] The Apocalypse enjoyed a measure of canonical recognition for a time. It is mentioned in the Muratorian fragment (a more or less official Roman list of acknowledged books, dating from the late 2nd century), along with the Apocalypse of John, but with the note that 'we accept it, but some of our people do not wish it to be read in church'. The important 4th-century lists do not mention it, though we are told by Sozomen that in his time (early 5th century) it was read on Good Friday in Palestinian churches. The Greek original has not survived, except in a few citations from Clement of Alexandria and in some fragments which were discovered at Akhmîm in 1887; its text in its entirety is known only in Ethiopic and Arabic translations. The Gospel of Peter was accepted for a time in some sections of the church in Syria, but as soon as its docetic character was recognized it was rejected by Serapion,

---

[1] A. C. McNeile speaks of 'the decisive indications that the epistle was written at a date in the second century, eighty years or more after St. Peter's death' (*Introduction to the Study of the New Testament*, 2nd edition revised by C. S. C. Williams [Oxford: Clarendon Press, 1953], p. 247. See also Feine-Behm-Kümmel, *Introduction*, §30. K. H. Schelkle suggests a date around the turn of the 1st century as possible: 'Gemäss alledem mag Ende des 1. Jahrhundert oder noch Anfang des 2. Jh. eine mögliche Datierung von 2 Petr sein', but he has no qualms about asserting its pseudonymity: '2 Petr muss offenbar als pseudepigraphische Schrift beurteilt werden'. Schelkle also offers a sagacious excursus on 'Biblische Pseudepigraphie' (*Die Petrusbriefe, der Judasbrief*, in *Herders Theologischer Kommentar zum Neuen Testament*, Bd. XIII, 2, pp. 179, 181, 245ff.).

[2] See my article, 'Canon of the New Testament' in *Interpreter's Dictionary of the Bible*, Vol. I, pp. 520-532, especially Section E., 'The Growth of the Canon in the Syrian Church'.

bishop of Antioch (from 199 to 211) with the comment: 'We receive both Peter and the other apostles as Christ, but we reject the writings falsely attributed to them' (Eusebius, *Hist. Eccl.* vi.12.31). The letter to James (attached to the Clementine Homilies), and the Preaching of Peter belong to the literature of Jewish Christianity.

The First Epistle of Peter is in a far stronger position historically than any of these, and still finds defenders of its authenticity. Its canonical attestation is relatively good. Though it is not listed in the Muratorian fragment on the canon and is not found in Syriac until the making of the Peshitta (5th century), it is ranked among the acknowledged scriptures by Origen (early 3rd century) and by Eusebius (early 4th century), and it appears in all the canonical lists from that time on. None the less, there are solid reasons for doubting that it can be an authentic work of the Prince of the Apostles. Even the defenders of its authenticity are reduced to the claim that it was actually composed by Silvanus (I Pet. 5:11)—not at the dictation of St. Peter, but as a free composition based upon some kind of general directions provided by the apostle.[1] It has been argued in this commentary that no defence will hold, and that First Peter, like the rest of the Petrine literature, is a pseudonymous work of the 2nd century.

[1] The position expressed by Johannes Schneider in his recent commentary is typical of many. 'Dass Petrus selbst den Brief verfasst hat, muss . . . als ausgeschlossen gelten. Das eigentliche Verfasser des Briefes ist Silvanus, aber der Brief ist von Petrus autorisiert und inspiriert worden. Er ist dann unter seinem Namen ausgegangen' (*Die Kirchenbriefe*, in Das NT Deutsch 10, 9th edition [1st edition of new series], p. 41). But why would Silvanus, the trusted representative of the Jerusalem Church from early days (Acts 15:22, 25-27), and the associate of St. Paul at Antioch and in South Galatia and in his first mission to Macedonia and Achaea (Acts 15:40-18:5), require an authorization from St. Peter to write a letter to the churches of Asia Minor? Are we to suppose that the Papacy is casting its shadows before, and that a Christian leader of the stature of Silvanus could not publish in his own name or without an *Imprimatur*? I must confess also that I find it impossible to think of this beautiful little epistle, or sermon, as 'inspired' by anyone except the man who composed it (apart, of course, from the inspiration of the Spirit which we attribute to all the sacred scriptures).

INDEXES

I. SCRIPTURE REFERENCES

A. Old Testament, with Apocrypha (and later Jewish writings).

II. EARLY CHRISTIAN WRITINGS

III. Classical and Post-Classical Literature

IV. Names, Places and Subjects